D1567558

The GOOD SEX *Book*

THE NEW ILLUSTRATED GUIDE

PAUL BROWN, Ph.D & CHRISTINE KELL

Illustrated by John Raynes

AN IMPRINT OF RUNNING PRESS
PHILADELPHIA • LONDON

TO A.N.K. AND J.O.C.B.

CLB 4020

Created by CLB International, Godalming, Surrey, England.

9 8 7 6 5 4 3 2 1
Digit on the right indicates the number of this printing.

Library of Congress Cataloging-in-Publication Number 96-71602

ISBN: 0-7624-0006-4

CREDITS

Editor
Philip de Ste. Croix

Designed by
THE BRIDGEWATER BOOK COMPANY

Color artwork
John Raynes
Mike Courtney

Reference photography
Peter Pugh-Cook

Index
Richard O'Neill

Production
Ruth Arthur
Neil Randles
Karen Staff

Color reproduction
Advance Laser Graphic Arts, Hong Kong

Printed and bound in Italy by New Interlitho Italia S.P.A.

Published by Courage Books, an imprint of
Running Press Book Publishers
125 South Twenty-second Street
Philadelphia, Pennsylvania 19103-4399

ACKNOWLEDGMENTS

The publisher would like to thank Allyn & Bacon, the publisher of *Human Sexuality in a World of Diversity*, Third Edition, by S.A. Rathus, J.S. Nevid and L. Fichner-Rathus (© 1997 by Allyn & Bacon) for permission to use certain illustrations in this title as reference for the diagrams which appear on pages 16, 17, 22, 23, 24, 25, 26, 27, 117, 119, 120, 128, 129, 130, 131 and 133 of this book. These diagrams are adapted by permission.

Contents

The Authors

DR. PAUL BROWN

Dr. Paul Brown is a consulting clinical and occupational psychologist. Educated at Kingswood School, Bath, England, long before girls were admitted, alas, he read psychology at Durham University and then trained clinically at the Institute of Psychiatry, University of London.

In the days before the 1967 Homosexual Law Reform Act in Britain he became especially interested in the plight of men who appeared before the courts for wanting relationships which are now widely accepted; and established National Health Service clinics for treating sexual difficulties of all kinds.

This was in the days before the early 1970s' revolution in knowledge about how the body works sexually which was brought about through the research efforts of Masters and Johnson in the United States. Shortly after their work was published he set up clinics in Warwickshire and Coventry especially for the treatment of couples who were having sexual difficulties. This led to him being invited to establish a training program for the National Marriage Guidance Council (now called Relate), to bring the new knowledge about treating sexual difficulties into mainstream counseling work.

This training and research program was funded by the British Government. At the end of three years, in 1976, the training program that had been developed was widely dispersed throughout the Marriage Guidance Councils of the country, and he was awarded a PhD from the University of Leicester for the research. The training program also resulted in a best-seller self-help book, *Treat Yourself to Sex* (with Carolyn Faulder), which Penguin Books have had continuously in print for twenty years.

Since 1974 Paul Brown has been in private practice in London. His increasing interest over that time in relationships within organizations has led to him working in Hong Kong, America, France, and Spain whilst still maintaining a busy clinical practice. He spent three years (1976-9) as managing director of a career counseling consultancy in London and Paris, and has worked extensively on the development of individuals within organizations through mentoring programs; the management of conflict in private company boardrooms; and the commercial leisure side of landed Estates.

A training program for one organization created a second book (with Fiona Hackett) on managing meetings, which he wanted to call *Must We Go On Meeting Like This*, but the publisher insisted on just *Managing Meetings* (1990). His clinical interests also extend to forensic work in the assessment of individuals after head injury prior to returning to work or whilst seeking compensation.

Over the years Paul Brown has held honorary academic appointments at the Universities of Birmingham and London; has contributed some thirty papers to learned journals and a dozen chapters to other people's books; was the founding Chairman of the British Association of Sexual and Marital Therapists and the founding editor of its scientific journal; and has been the Honorary Secretary of the Clinical Division of the British Psychological Society and a member of the Council of that Chartered body.

He is a Fellow of the British Psychological Society; a Corresponding Associate of the Royal College of Psychiatrists; a Justice of the Peace for North Westminster; an aspiring fly fisherman; and has a passing interest in heraldry.

CHRIS KELL

In 1948 Alfred Kinsey published his major survey into the *Sexual Behavior of the Human Male.* This was also the year that Chris Kell was born into a family where sex was never talked about. She writes, "I was still unaware of the 'facts of life' by the time I sat in a biology lesson at the age of 15 and learnt about the reproductive system in rabbits.

"At 16 I entered co-education, and tried to catch up with my peer group. With a girls' boarding school behind me and the immaturity of my own sexual development, I only succeeded in breaking my heart. It took until I entered the world of work before I began to have any sexual confidence and any sexual experience. By that time, the Women's Movement had started and a sexual revolution was taking place. I was happy to join both. In 1970 I read Germaine Greer's influential book *The Female Eunuch* and ditched being a young lady to become a woman.

"Many of us living through the same decades, and the subsequent two, will have our own stories of sexual liberation and the struggle to find how men and women can relate. I was fortunate to be able to combine my own personal journey with a professional one, starting in 1968 with an assignment to work as a 'temp' for the Albany Trust in London (the social work branch of the Homosexual Law Reform Society). After a year of learning how to spell transsexualism and transvestism, and discovering that sexuality is far wider than marriage and children, I left to train as a social worker, join a consciousness-raising group, live in a commune, and ultimately to become a Community Worker.

"In 1980 my daughter was born and I stayed at home to look after her, before retraining in Sex Therapy. I began to give talks, workshops and courses on sexuality and joined the Family Planning Association in 1982 as a Trainer in Sex and Personal Relationships. I qualified as a Counsellor in 1986, and now use my knowledge of sexuality in my work with individuals and couples who come to see me for counseling.

At present I live in an all-female household with my daughter. This happy arrangement will reach its natural conclusion when her own sexuality takes her off elsewhere. I myself look forward to the variety of intimacy that is possible as middle-age moves into aging."

Loving Sex

Sex is perfectly natural, but it's not always naturally perfect. Adults are driven by a complex interaction of body chemistry and a human history based upon at least half a million years of evolution. Extraordinary creatures that we are, each person's life is a private journey of discovery usually made by people forming sexual relationships with one another based upon psychological, economic and social needs, as well as their capacity to reproduce.

That's not all there is to the human experience, of course. Art, literature, architecture, quantum mechanics, building sand castles and making bows and arrows are but a few of the achievements of the human race which have developed over the past five thousand years. But whatever the state of social evolution that the human race has reached, it could not have achieved it without being reproductive.

The sexual act is central to the human experience. In the twentieth century, the quality of human relationships and individual experience have come to the foreground. These relationships are a major preoccupation of our times, and sex is at the center of this preoccupation. For the first time in the history of the world reproduction and the sexual act have been separated through the availability of reliable birth control. The result is that men and women are free to explore the nature of the purely sexual aspect of their relationships, untroubled by its possible reproductive consequences.

In the early days of the contraceptive pill, the possibility of relatively free sexual relationships became a goal for many. New forms of marriage were proposed – often referred to as open marriage – which made space for there to be sexual relationships with more than one partner.

Such experiments as did take place created as much confusion as found answers. Within twenty years not only had the pandemic spread of HIV and AIDS appeared to haunt sexually liberated or tolerant societies, but prior to that it had become apparent that the nature of personal commitment to a partner and families was too closely bound up with the sexual act to permit simple new forms of sexual encounter to flourish. Added to this, over the same period, was the emergence of feminism and the world-wide spread of telecommunications, which could impact cultures in ways never before experienced. The period since the pill has therefore been one of unprecedented social change. In some ways sex has been one of the few constants.

Over the last twenty-five years a great deal more knowledge about the physical aspects of sexual function has become available, thanks to the pioneering work of William Masters and Virginia Johnson who made the medical and psychological study of sexual behavior respectable areas of academic activity. People with more leisure, greater knowledge, yet more confusion and less certainty than ever before find themselves struggling with something that is eternally constant and yet for which the context is dramatically changed. It is still the case that we each have to find our own way into the mysteries of the sexual encounter with another person. No one can do that for us or act as a surrogate.

Fortunately for our society the days when sex was a forbidden subject are gone. For better or worse sex now seems to be more easily thought of as a social skill. Yet it is a skill which can be so affected by brain chemistry that people can act in an insane manner when they fall in love. Rational thought processes can leave a person entirely and people may become obsessed with sex or with another person.

Yet the human experience tells that if knowledge and skill are brought to bear upon a subject, illumination of all kinds gradually makes for easier control of situations that previously were difficult.

The intention of this book is to stress one particular aspect of the sexual encounter which, we believe, might be of real benefit to couples struggling to establish the meaning and purpose of sex within their own lives in the social maelstrom in which we presently find ourselves.

The matter that we want to address concerns the differences between men and women. This might in some ways seem an extraordinary objective when, to most people's immediate observation, men and women are obviously very different indeed. Anatomically this is so. Evolution has designed them for quite different functions in the world. Psychologically it is so too, though much less is understood about that.

What we are concerned about is that, in the arguments for equality between men and women, whose intention we totally endorse, the simple enjoyment of the *differences* between the genders is at risk of getting lost. We want to draw attention to the pleasure inherent in recognizing the differences, especially in their sexual aspect, so that being male and being female can both be equally appreciated.

It is our view that real loving comes from appreciating and enjoying the differences between men and women, from loving the differences, and from learning to enjoy them at their best. To this end we have written from a male and female perspective in the main sections of the book, in the hope that men can learn from women and women from men.

PAUL BROWN

We thought that the reader might be interested to know how this book was put together. The first and last sections were written by Paul Brown. The middle section was written by both of us separately – not referring to one another. We wanted to test our own hypothesis through the writing process – that men and women focus differently on the same sexual experience – so we took each set of drawings that you will find in Section Two and wrote from our different gender perspectives "blind."

Inevitably, we found that there are similarities and differences. Some differences are quite marked; others more subtle. Interestingly, there is a male-female difference in the two styles of writing: one written objectively and the other subjectively. Although we both bring our personal and professional experiences to bear when we write about the genders, we do not of course pretend to write for all men and all women. We hope that we have said enough that is generalizable, while leaving room for the unique sexual experience of each individual.

Men and women are desperate to be good lovers. Relying on innate, intuitive skills and hoping that strength of feeling will see us through, we approach each sexual encounter wanting to please the other and wanting to be pleased in return. Sadly, faced with someone of the other gender, we cannot possibly get it right without understanding our differences. Our bodies, emotional needs and social conditioning are all different. Men and women can communicate about sex with love and honesty, but it is often embarrassing and difficult. One of the aims of this book is to help the communication process, so that some of the talking can take place out of the bedroom.

In trying to be as explicit as possible, we have had to think about the language we use in the book. We were tempted to use the language of the bedroom but recognize that, in print, the effect of the vernacular is to diminish rather than enhance the level of a reader's comfort. We therefore use medical terms – penis, vagina, testes, clitoris, vulva, etc. – rather than colloquial or vernacular words which might be erotic in one context but are alienating in another.

This is an obviously heterosexual book but – we hope – not heterosexist. We have been greatly encouraged to see that there are now sex books specifically for lesbian and gay lovers. It can only be a matter of time before the first sex book addresses all the different sexual orientations.

Finally, this book would not have been possible without the help of the models portrayed in the pictures. The artist, John Raynes, has sensitively captured the feelings that they display to complement the text, which, in the central part of the book, has been written in parallel from the perspective of both a woman and a man. We hope that the combination of text and illustrations convincingly captures the atmosphere and sensations of sex.

CHRIS KELL

SECTION ONE

Myself As I Was

Unless we are identical twins, we each have inside us a unique genetic make-up that is traceable to our parents. Similarly we each have a unique psychological make-up, traceable to the circumstances of our life, and to how we ourselves experienced and responded to these circumstances and made sense of what was happening to us.

Thus our genetic *individuality is paralleled by, and interacts with, and in part shapes, what has been called our* memetic *individuality,* memes *being the name that Professor Richard Dawkins has proposed for describing the encoded experience upon which we rely for aspects of our behavior.*

Within these life-producing processes of genes and memes in combination, a self is fashioned. That self is massively circumscribed by what gender we happen to be – whether we are male or female. Not only does society see us differently, whether we are boys or girls, but we ourselves see things differently because we are *boys or girls. Built into us – what these days is called "the hard wiring," rather like the circuit boards of a computer – is a vast array of body chemistry which is hugely different between men and women. It can be different between men and men, and women and women too. There is a great deal of variability within each sex. But not nearly so much as* between *the sexes.*

Nowhere is the difference more vividly apparent to everyday observation than in the differences between male and female body shapes and functions. We have similar vital organs that ensure our survival – hearts, lungs, stomachs, kidneys, and so on; but we are completely different in our reproductive functions.

A man's rather simple contribution to the continuation of life is to insert his penis into a partner's vagina and ejaculate. Happily for a man he is likely to have an orgasm in this process. The organ of procreation is also his main center of sexual excitement, so that the pursuit of sexual excitement and the mechanics of procreation are entirely linked together if he is heterosexual. Even more happily, if he feels loved in doing it, he will feel more complete.

A woman's contribution to the continuation of life is much more complex. As the person accepting the male's intrusion into her body she may or may not have

a climax. The creation of life does not require that she should. For her the organ of sexual excitement, the clitoris, is quite separate from the vagina where the man's sperm might be lodged on its way to fusing with an egg in one of her fallopian tubes. If life is created, she will bear that child for nine months inside her body in preparing it for birth, and will almost certainly be very involved for many years afterwards in sustaining and nurturing that life into independent adulthood. So for her the sexual act of procreation reaches forwards certainly for nine months and probably for many years. For the man it may last no longer than a single occasion bounded by the few seconds of an ejaculation. But as for the man, if the woman feels loved in the process of procreation she will also feel more complete.

Each of us began in these circumstances, loved into existence or not as the case might have been. Each of us is then destined to become one or other of the people capable of re-enacting the eternal drama of the creation of life.

It is, however, not just a physical drama but a psychological one too. The child who is given life will spend that life engaged with the experience of becoming and being a person. A major part of this process comes about through interaction with other people. A most significant part of being involved with other people is being engaged with the opposite sex – the relatively unknown half of the world. In the normal course of life none of us can ever know what it is to be another person, but we may get a glimpse through getting close to the mysteries of another's body and another's heart. The closer we get, and the more we value what we understand, the happier life is likely to be: for the sexual act contains within it the possibilities of the greatest happiness to which humans might aspire.

In the pages which follow you will become re-acquainted with how it all began, bearing in mind both the simplicity and complexity of it all. The goal of loving sex is to love the experience of it and to give love through it. We think that requires some measure of knowledge as well as experience, so it is to the knowledge that we first turn our attention.

In The Beginning

NEW LIFE – conception – is created when a single male sperm unites with a single female egg within a woman's body. Like so much in reproduction throughout nature, it seems a miracle that they do.

A woman carries within her several hundred eggs in her ovaries. Throughout her mature sexual years – from the beginning of menstruation to the end of menopause, perhaps forty years in all – eggs ripen on a monthly basis. Usually just one travels down from one ovary to the uterus or womb through one of the fallopian tubes. Conception occurs when this egg meets just one of the *several hundred million* sperms that have been ejaculated into the vagina by a man during sexual intercourse and have survived the journey from the vagina, through the cervix into the womb, and into a fallopian tube. The sperm move by thrashing their whip-like tails to propel them along.

The woman's egg carries twenty-three X chromosomes. The man's sperm carries twenty-three chromosomes that are either X or Y. A girl is conceived if an X-bearing sperm fertilizes the egg, making a combination of twenty-three XX chromosomes; and a boy if it is a Y-bearing chromosome, making twenty-three XY chromosomes. A girl will always in the future have just XX chromosomes, and a boy will have X Y.

X-bearing sperm swim more strongly than Y, and so more male than female fertilizations take place. But X-fertilized eggs fail to implant themselves into the lining of the womb more frequently than Y-fertilized eggs; and because of this, the eventual ratio of girls to boys born and surviving is almost equal.

Once safely implanted into the wall of the uterus, the combined sperm and egg, now called a zygote, which is less than 1/100th of an inch (0.25mm) in size begins to establish itself as an embryo by dint of its cells dividing in half, time and time again. In this miniscule zygote all the genetically coded information that will determine the characteristics of the mature adult is already in place. But at this early stage all embryos appear similar, and essentially female. It is not until around the seventh week after fertilization that the XX or XY sex chromosome begins to assert itself, so that separate development of male and female sexual structures can take place. Thus all humans are essentially female at conception. The Y element in the sex chromosome subsequently causes some to deviate from female into becoming male.

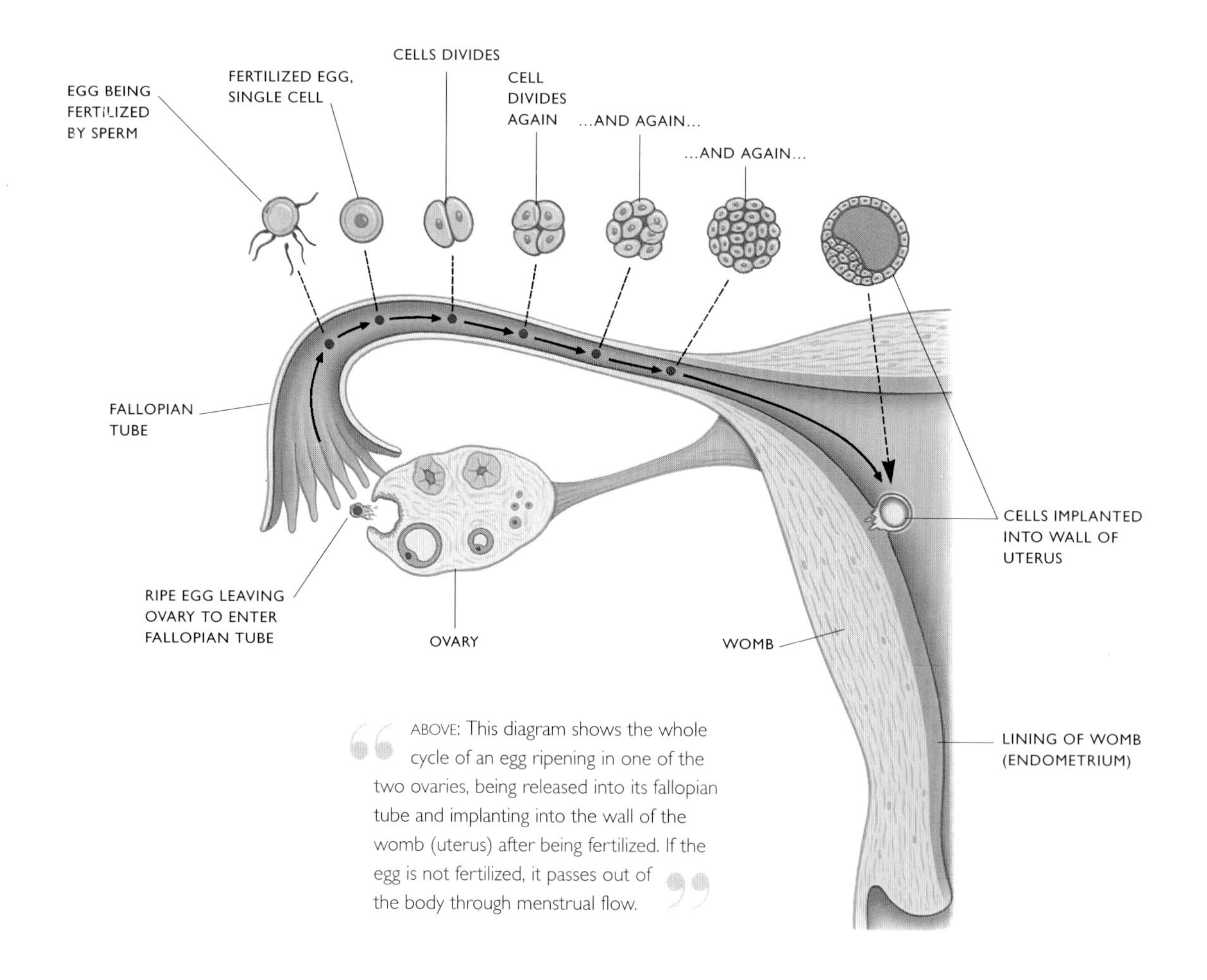

ABOVE: This diagram shows the whole cycle of an egg ripening in one of the two ovaries, being released into its fallopian tube and implanting into the wall of the womb (uterus) after being fertilized. If the egg is not fertilized, it passes out of the body through menstrual flow.

By about the fourth month male and female sex characteristics are firmly established. Male sex hormones – the chemical messengers of the body that circulate through the bloodstream – have turned the embryonic female into a male.

Thus our gender – male or female – is established in the first third of embryonic life. Barring very rare abnormalities, our XX or XY status will be with us for ever. The rest of our lives will revolve around that fact as we form an identity based on gender.

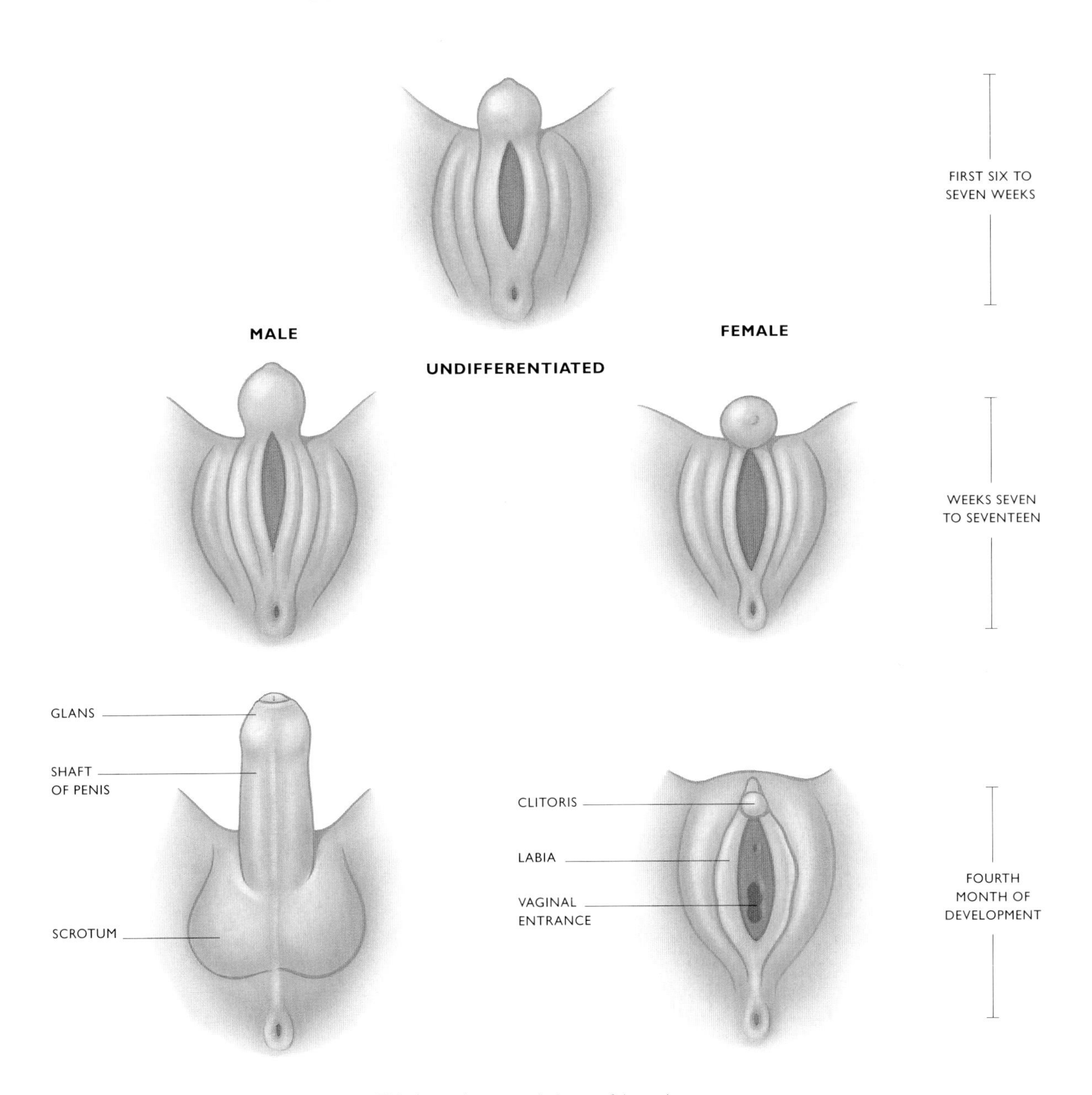

ABOVE: This shows the anatomical part of the embryo which becomes the sex organs. In the first six to seven weeks of life all embryos have an undifferentiated female appearance. Over the next nine or ten weeks the anatomy becomes recognizably male or female under the influences of hormones circulating in the embryo's bloodstream.

Infant Sexuality

NOT ONLY ARE the physical and sexual structures of male and female bodies different; aspects of the brain are too. Different sensitivities to various hormones develop in the embryo, which then act as controllers of sexual and reproductive systems throughout life. They are probably also reponsible for the different ways in which male and female brains function, which result in the differences between how men and women see the world.

There is, therefore, a very powerful interaction between what our body is genetically programmed to do, how that affects our growing understanding of ourselves (being male or female), and how that understanding shapes the way we think about our bodies and ourselves.

It is clear that from the very earliest attempts at sucking, infants have a real sense of sensual pleasure. Some little boys are born with penises already erect. Erections have been observed in ultrasound scans of male fetuses, and most baby boys will have spontaneous erections of their small penises. Signs of arousal in the sexual organs of little girls are less easy to detect, though evidence of genital swelling has been reported. The act of touching an infant's sexual organs during bathing or applying talcum powder also seems to generate excited pleasure responses.

These reflex responses in infants should not be taken to mean that they are experiencing sexual feelings in the sense that adults understand that word. Infants do not give meaning to the great variety of physical sensations that they experience in all the years before they can put words or concepts to what is happening to their bodies. Nevertheless, as early as five months in boys and four months in girls, behaviors have been observed which look very like orgasms in adults. There is of course no ejaculation from little boys, as that appears only at puberty. But something that looks like the tension of arousal followed by the relief of climax is by no means unknown in infants.

This kind of pleasure tension in sexual organs is often accompanied by spontaneous rubbing of the sexual areas, either through pelvic contact with a soft object, such as a cuddly toy; or through

RIGHT: Being attached to a nursing breast is the most profound of human experiences. It forms the basis of all the feelings of belonging that human beings experience throughout the whole of their lives. Being held – closely, tenderly, and warmly – is as crucial to good sex as it is to good mothering.

finger contact with genitals. Masturbation to a state that looks like orgasm is relatively rare until the second year of life, when in both little boys and little girls it is quite common.

Children are also naturally quite curious about each other's sexual anatomy. While little boys' sexual aspects are physically quite obvious, those of little girls are not. In consequence there are a large number of words which both little boys and little girls learn to use to decribe the penis and, to a lesser extent, the scrotum, but very few to describe female genitals. There has also been a longer history in many cultures of inhibiting open discussion of female sexuality. Many girls grow up having no clear idea at all of the genital structure between their legs, and refer to genitals, urethral opening and anus in an undifferentiated way as being "down there" or as their "bottom." This can have adverse effects for girls in growing up, if their adult sexuality is dependent upon very vague notions of their sexual anatomy. It does not help to make much sense of things for men either. If girls have not sorted out an understanding of the sexual aspects of their bodies by the time they become women, how are men to develop any better understanding?

It is not surprising that, as part of our genetic design, the infant develops immature activity sexually just as he or she does with regard to every other aspect of human behavior. So much depends for the human race on each generation reproducing itself that it would be strange if early signs of sexual behavior were not built into the infant's behavioral repertoire.

RIGHT: Children can delight in each other's bodies with a healthy curiosity in which there is no sense of shame or disgust – just surprise and delight. Alas, it is all too easy for little girls to become conscious of *not* having a penis, as if that defined them, before having the chance to become aware of the miraculous powers of their own bodies as young women. Wise parents make sure the positive is affirmed for children growing up.

Growing Up Sexually

WHETHER WE ARE destined to be a boy or girl, man or woman, will have been decided in the first three months of life in the womb. After that our anatomy, and perhaps more of the hard-wiring of our nervous system than we presently understand, firmly differentiates little boys and little girls. Excluding the exceptional case of transsexualism, that's how it is for the rest of life.

Up to the age of puberty, though, all children are really adults in waiting. Though the late 20th century has seen a huge increase in child-focused societies from a social perspective, biologically and sexually children are fundamentally the carriers of the next generation's genes. It is principally because of maturing sexual development that children's bodies begin to change during puberty as they develop towards the quite different appearances of the adult male and female shapes.

Boys are designed to become the men that have a sperm-delivery system. Girls are designed for the much more complex task of not only receiving that sperm but nurturing new lives within their own bodies once the process of conception has taken place. Biology will not let us escape these facts. Were it to do so, we could not, as a human race, survive.

From a sexual perspective, childhood is about letting the complex programming of growth and development towards sexual maturity take place. We know that it is happening when the developmental sexual characteristics of puberty begin to appear. The beginning to the end of puberty takes about three years for girls and four for boys.

Light-colored strands of pubic hair are usually the first visible signs that puberty is starting in both boys and girls. The hairs grow darker and thicker as puberty advances, and take on the typical triangular spread across the lower abdomen of pubic hair.

In girls, menstruation is the most obvious sign of puberty. The age at which this begins has steadily dropped in western countries over the past 150 years. In the mid-19th century the average age was around seventeen. Now it is between twelve and thirteen. Better diet and body-weight/fat ratios are probably responsible for this.

Between the ages of nine and fifteen breasts begin to develop, preceded by an enlargement of the dark area around the nipple (the areola). Underarm hair appears, and sex organs both internally and externally develop. The vagina becomes longer and the labia become more pronounced.

Breasts will have achieved their full adult shape by the time the girl reaches the age of nineteen. Pubic hair will fully cover the mons (a fleshy pad which covers the underlying pubic bone), and may spread to the inner thighs. The voice may deepen a little, though not nearly so much as in boys, and the menstrual cycle should have settled into a regular pattern by the end of the second decade of life.

Throughout all this, psychological development has been taking place too. *Becoming* a man or a woman, and having a comfortable identity as one or the other, is a very complex business indeed. It is all shaped around the self – something which has no anatomy but which is the powerhouse of all action.

RIGHT: Puberty is the time of change from the physical immaturity of childhood to becoming capable of sexual reproduction. Body mass and shape change towards being recognizably adult. Sexual organs become fully formed. Boys get anxious about comparing their sexual organs with those of other boys, and worry about whose is biggest. No-one tells them that there is very little similarity between the size of a limp penis and its size when fully erect – small penises can become very large at erection, and large ones hardly change size at all.

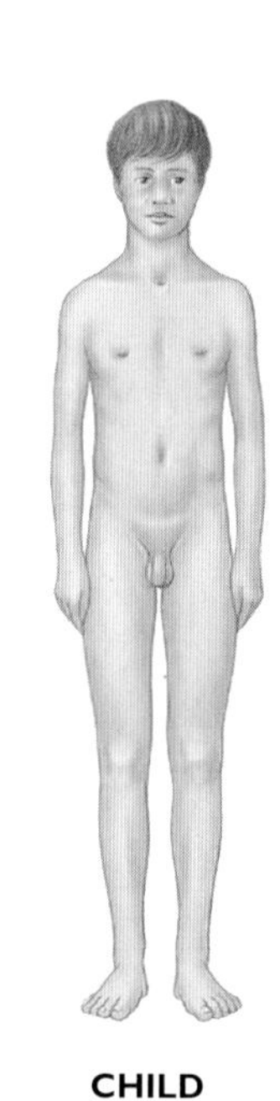
CHILD

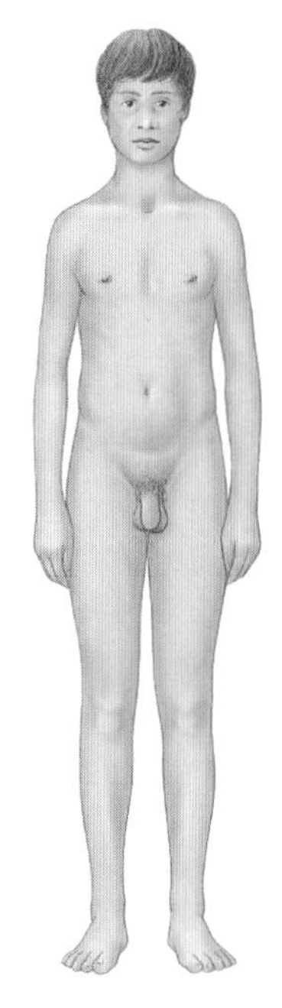
ADOLESCENT

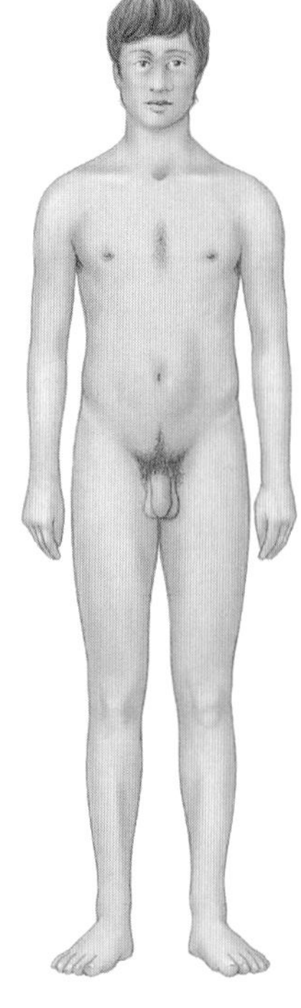
ADULT

Evidence is increasing that the "self" is a complex neuro-chemical structure centred in a part of the brain called the amygdala. It is fashioned through communication with the external world from – and perhaps before – the first day of life.

In boys, the early signs of sexual maturation beginning are a few pubic hairs appearing at the base of the penis; the testicles enlarge; muscle mass develops; and, as with girls, the area surrounding the nipple becomes darker. Then the penis begins to grow, as do the testicles and scrotum; shoulders broaden and hips narrow; and as the larynx enlarges, so the voice deepens. Sparse facial and underarm hair appears.

And so matters go on. By the age of eighteen facial hair will have developed, first ejaculations will have occurred, and increased skin oils may have produced the dreaded blight of facial acne. Pubic hair may spread upwards to the stomach and downwards to the inner thighs. It may be not until the early twenties that full muscular development has finally taken place.

These then are the physical processes that make sure the human race will perpetuate itself. By the time of full sexual maturity, boys are clearly men and girls have become women.

How boys and girls learn to use their sexual maturity as they develop into men and women is immensely conditioned by the culture in which they find themselves. Arguably nothing has been of greater cultural significance in recent years than the availability and acceptance of reliable methods of contraception.

Before the widespread dissemination of Hollywood films in the 1930s, sex was generally seen as, first and foremost, important for procreation. This had been the case for centuries.

The romanticism of films began to change people's attitudes in the 1930s, '40s and '50s. Although sex was not very explicitly depicted in films of the period, it became possible for millions of people to see scenes of intimacy that they had almost certainly never witnessed before. Sex began to have a more explicit cultural presence, and a general awareness developed that sex was somehow important in forging and maintaining relationships. More importantly, perhaps, moral standards other than those the viewers would encounter in their immediate family or social circle were portrayed. Sex moved from being a procreational matter to a relational one.

Then, with the advent of the contraceptive pill in the 1950s, sex started to become a recreational matter. The creation of life and the act of sex started to diverge. It was no longer possible to resist sex because of a fear of pregnancy if contraception was available. Often, of course, it was not – but the social climate encouraged sex anyway. Now, a generation on from the introduction of the pill, most of the taboos about having children outside marriage have completely disappeared, and couples living together without being married are widely accepted. The social stigma of such a domestic arrangement has largely disappeared.

These are extraordinary shifts in social attitudes and customs in a very short space of time. We are now able to write explicitly about what is good, enjoyable, healthy and life-affirming sex in a way that would have been impossible a generation ago.

Becoming sexually mature lets life-giving and life-affirming sex become a source of life-long pleasure for both men and women. This book is about that process.

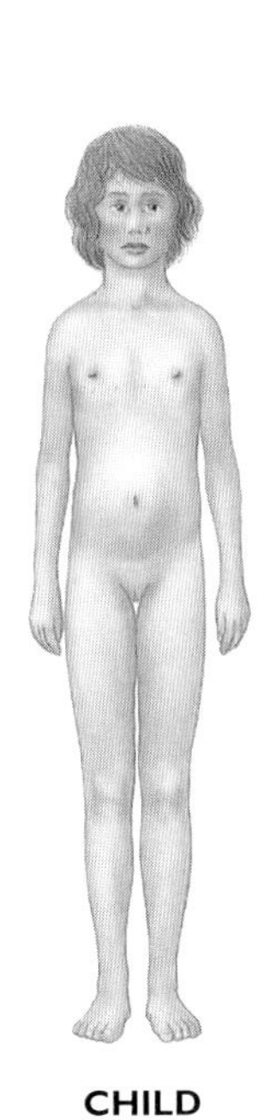

CHILD

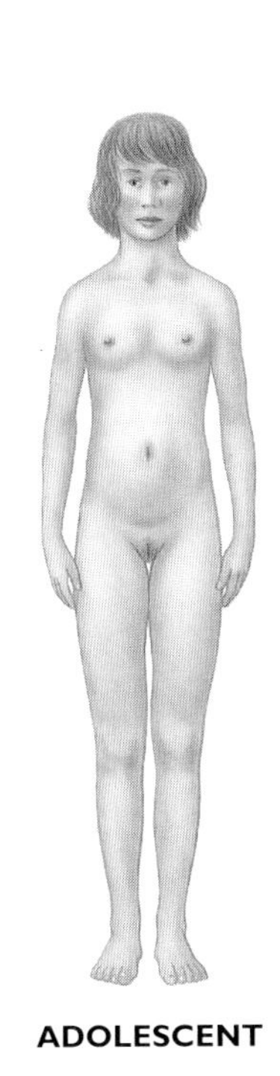

ADOLESCENT

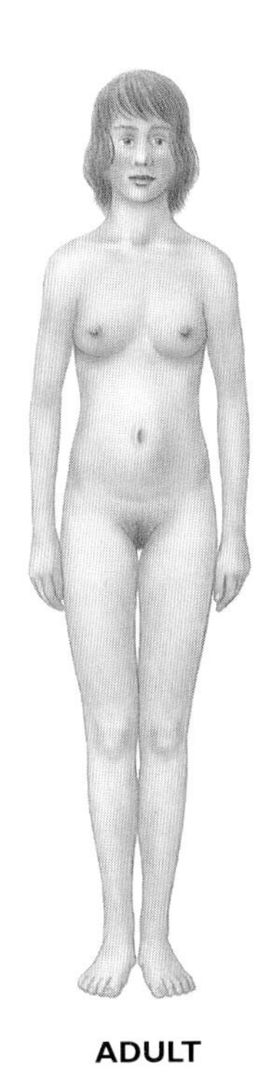

ADULT

LEFT: At puberty bodily changes prepare a girl for being both sexual and capable of carrying, delivering and nursing a child. Puberty is much more complex, both physically and psychologically, for girls than for boys. Unlike boys, girls have little chance of directly comparing their sexual anatomy with other girls', and often worry about their bodies for lack of proper information. Boys are generally not a good source of reassurance either!

When The Hormones Hit

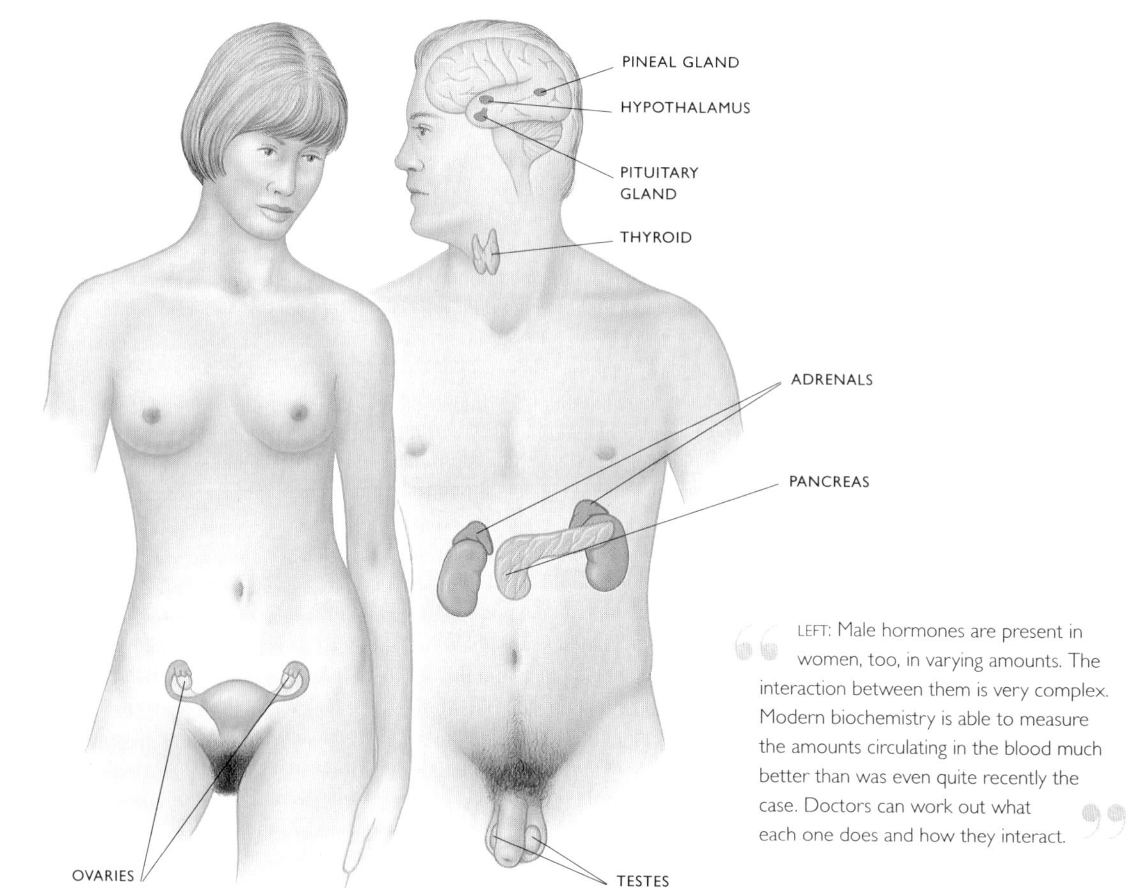

RIGHT: Chemical messengers – hormones – are released by special glands (shown here) and carried by the blood stream to control all our bodily functions. Like so many things we take for granted, we really only notice them when they fail to function properly or create moods we do not want.

LEFT: Male hormones are present in women, too, in varying amounts. The interaction between them is very complex. Modern biochemistry is able to measure the amounts circulating in the blood much better than was even quite recently the case. Doctors can work out what each one does and how they interact.

HORMONES ARE chemicals which regulate bodily functions. They are released directly into the blood stream through ductless glands, called endocrine glands, and other organs, including the kidneys.

It is quite difficult for most of us to imagine all the hidden bits of our bodies working to keep us functioning. Chemical messengers are perhaps the most difficult to imagine, yet without them none of the growth that propels us to maturity would happen; none of our sexual development would take place; and we would not be able to reproduce at all. Clearly they're vital to the whole of our well-being.

Female sex hormones are called *estrogens*. The "*...gens*" means "becoming" or "starting," and the "*estro...*" comes from "estrus" and refers to the stage of coming into egg-bearing. In other words being reproductive, starting the menstrual cycle and being sexually responsive.

Male sex hormones are called *androgens*. "*Andro...*" comes from the Greek meaning a man. Even in the origins of these basic terms, it is interesting to reflect that the word applied to women refers to their sexual state, while the word relating to men is more connected to their gender identity.

There are two female sex hormones produced by the ovaries. These are *estrogen* and *progesterone*. Estrogen is really a mixture of separate hormones. It controls and creates the changes in puberty and regulates the menstrual cycle.

Progesterone also influences the menstrual cycle, but has the special job of preparing the uterus for pregnancy by stimulating the development of the lining of the womb (endometrium) each month so that, if an egg is fertilized, it will have the right environment in which to begin to grow.

Men tend to take most direct notice of women's hormones, alas, when women are not behaving as men think they should. Women suffer a good deal from men believing that their moods are more dependent on their hormones than men's are.

It is true that many women do experience mood changes around their menstrual cycle. In general, however, the hormonal changes at this period tend to magnify the mood that is already there, which is much more likely to reflect day-to-day life – and especially person-to-person experiences – than hormones alone. Thus a man can have a very direct effect upon a woman's mood – through appreciating that pre-menstrual mood may be only an exaggerated expression of the background mood that he is partly responsible for creating.

Among the androgens, testosterone is the most important

ingredient in male sexual development. It triggers the differentiation of male sexual organs in the embryo; controls sperm production; and stimulates the secondary sexual characteristics, such as deepening of the voice, beard growth and muscular development.

Testosterone can have such a powerful effect on the developing child at puberty that adolescent boys have been referred to as testosterone on two legs. The amount of androgens circulating in the adolescent boy's bloodstream is closely linked with his level of interest in sex, though the precise relationship that exists between male sex hormones and sexual behavior is not fully understood and is certainly not simple.

The evolutionary intent of the hormonal processes in adolescent boys is to change them from being group-based to becoming individually assertive. In consequence the actual changes in their behaviour can be readily observed. Estrogens in an adolescent girl, on the other hand, create much more widespread changes in preparing her body to be reproductive than is the case in boys. She has to learn about her menstrual cycle and become involved with her bodily functions in a way that is completely alien – and often quite frightening – to growing boys.

When hormones hit at puberty, boys and girls start becoming men and women. That's the way they will be for the rest of their lives. Each will be one half of the male/female divide. Though we take it totally for granted, life is always seen through eyes that are defined by being male or being female. Life is also made much richer by trying to look at the world through the other's eyes, and by learning how to value the part of the world that is otherwise hidden from us.

ABOVE: Hormone balances can have a very direct effect on mood, especially in exaggerating a background mood already established. Hormones can brew powerful mood cocktails, which may affect women particularly around the time of their menstrual cycle.

The Menstrual Cycle

At the end of each menstrual cycle – around 28 days – a woman's body needs to get rid of any unfertilized egg and the lining of the womb (endometrium) that might otherwise have nurtured a fertilized egg. The monthly period flow of blood is the evidence of this happening.

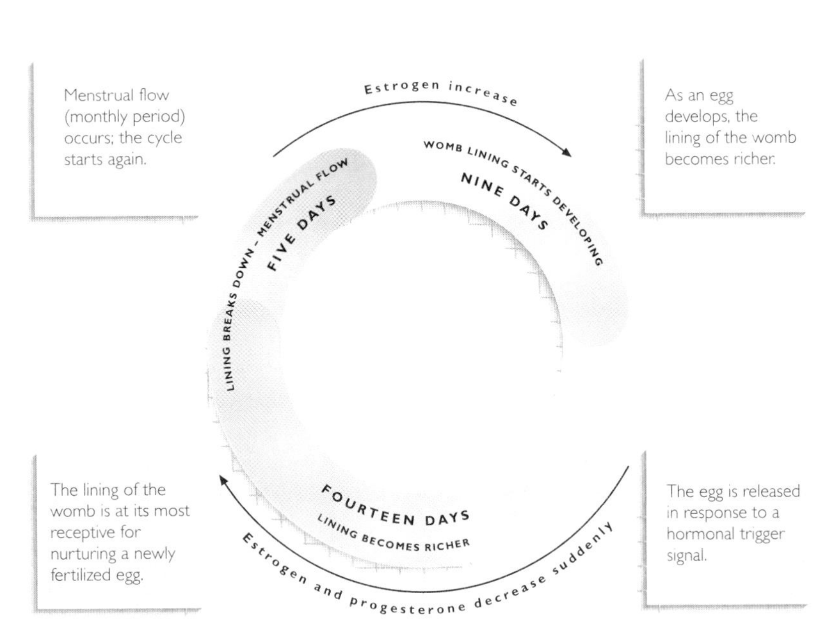

Fully Grown

THE TROUBLE with diagrams of sexual organs is that there is no way of showing their warm, moist, throbbing qualities. Even pop-up books fail. Bear with us, therefore, with these diagrams. What *we* want is to make sure that *you* do at least have access to what is known about body parts.

Of course it is much easier with men than with women. Sexually aroused, men's interest is pretty well advertised. Erections are not easy things to hide. Women's arousal, on the other hand, is much more contained within her body – though physiologically it is no less real and rather more complex.

The full processes of the sexual response cycle are described in the anatomy and physiology sections towards the end of the book. Here we want to make sure that men and women really do have an understanding of one another's sexual organs – at least so far as their structures are concerned, and how they are supposed to work. How you *make* then work, and enjoy them, is largely what the rest of this book is about.

It is worth remembering how it all started. All of us start out as female, sexually, and remain so until around the end of the first seven weeks as an embryo. Male and female are identical.

Then if, under the influence of the XY genetic code, the mother has a certain level of testosterone in her blood stream, the embryo starts developing into a fetus with male sex organs. Left alone without this hormonal stimulus, it continues developing female sexual characteristics. The male loses all the complexity of clitoris, vagina and labia for the simple structure of a penis. Sexual sensation stays focused in the penis for men. In women it is much more widely spread, often throughout all skin surfaces and into the deeper structures of the womb as well as the vagina, clitoris and labia.

Many women never really look at their sexual organs – and almost never have a chance to see any other woman's closely. So often women experience a great deal of fear and ignorance with regard to their sexual anatomy. Little boys have everyday experience of seeing their own genitals, and frequent sight of other boys' and men's genitals in locker rooms. Little girls do not have these experiences.

Ask your partner whether that's true in his or her experience. Little girls, of course, learn the little boys' language for penis. But little boys have scant chance to learn anything about little girls' sexual anatomy. Yet small children can grow up into sexually experimenting teenagers, and often become mature adults, without gaining any firm knowledge on which to base an understanding of their sexual selves, let alone their partner's self.

In some ways such ignorance does not matter too much when things are going well – and sex can go well, spontaneously, when driven by plenty of mutual desire. But that is not a state in which most people find themselves most of the time. It is when things are not going well, or there are real problems, that lack of knowledge becomes a serious disadvantage.

The best principle for both partners to adopt is that both will always have more to learn about sex than they already know; that each is the other's best teacher; and that if neither has the answers, there are reliable sources to which they can turn.

Which brings us back to sexual organs. Some people say the whole of the body is a sexual organ – all skin surfaces can be particularly responsive to sexual touch, given the right conditions. For the moment, though, we are concentrating on those parts of the anatomy which are particular to sex, and which are great sources of pleasure.

We can only look properly at a woman's sexual organs by getting her to lie on her back and open her legs for us. In love-making, that is a great gift to her partner.

Here is a picture of a woman lying on her back and we can see the *external* sexual organs which, when she is standing up, are otherwise hidden by the triangle of pubic hair and her closed legs.

The *mons* is a fleshy pad which covers the underlying pubic bone. Coming down the mid-line from the mons towards the opening to the back passage, the *anus*, there is first of all the *clitoris*. In an un-aroused state the clitoris may not be very

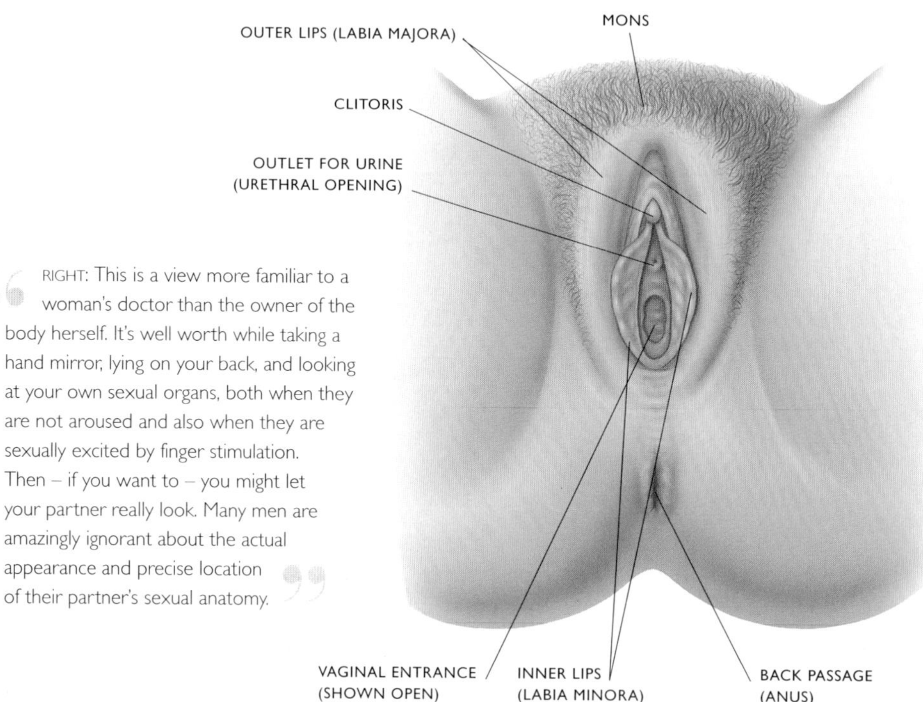

RIGHT: This is a view more familiar to a woman's doctor than the owner of the body herself. It's well worth while taking a hand mirror, lying on your back, and looking at your own sexual organs, both when they are not aroused and also when they are sexually excited by finger stimulation. Then – if you want to – you might let your partner really look. Many men are amazingly ignorant about the actual appearance and precise location of their partner's sexual anatomy.

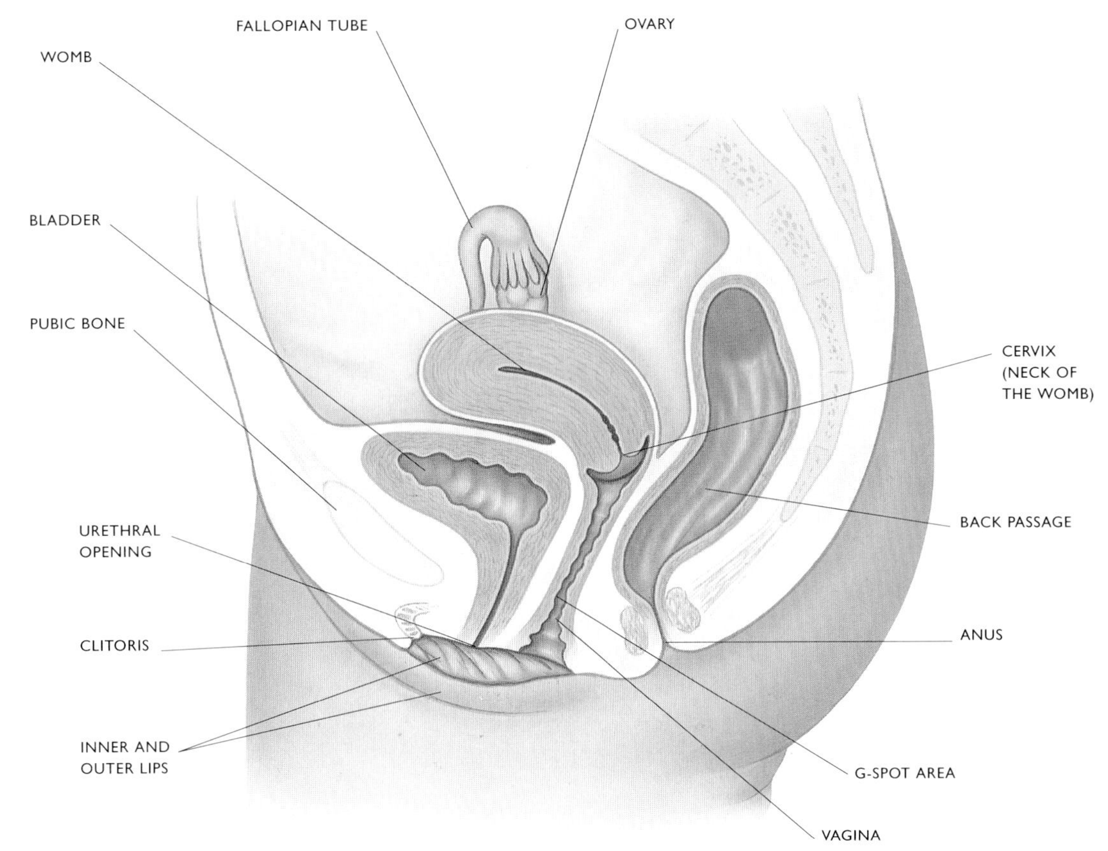

RIGHT: This side view of the female sexual and reproductive organs shows how low down in the abdomen they are. The bones of the pelvis protect them. The diagram also shows very well that the vagina is a closed space – rather like the back of the throat, until it expands to swallow something. The G-spot itself is a rather ill-defined area more than a very specific "spot," and not all women by any means experience G-spot sensations.

apparent in some women, though quite obvious in others. It is a small, pea-shaped fleshy structure, hidden in the folds at the top of the inner lips or *labia minora.*

The clitoris is very special in that its only purpose is to be a source of sexual stimulation. Interestingly, it is the tissue supply from which the male penis grows in the embryo, but the penis has reproductive and urine-disposal functions as well – it is a multi-purpose tool. The clitoris, on the other hand, is an exquisite receptor of sexual stimulation. However, remember that the wrong stimulation here can also easily produce pain.

Continuing down the mid-line we come to the opening which permits urine to flow away, the *urethral opening.* It is not discernible by touch, and sometimes cannot be seen by the naked eye, as it rests closed in the pink flesh above the vagina. It has no sexual significance at all – except, of course, if the urinary tract has become infected, when it may cause a good deal of discomfort and real pain.

Following the mid-line down, lying between the folded skin of both the inner lips and the outer lips *(labia majora)*, is the opening to the vaginal passage.

Men tend to think of the *vagina* as being an empty space for them to fill – as if there were a permanent tube waiting to receive a penis gratefully or otherwise. In fact in its unaroused state the vagina is really *potential* space – rather like the back of the throat when not being used for swallowing. When aroused, the vagina increases in length and width to accommodate an erection. In men, of course, excitement is obvious. They become erect. In women the signs are much less apparent, but a great deal is happening, nevertheless.

The most important sign of sexual arousal in a woman is that vaginal lubrication begins to happen. (There is more about this later in the book.) For now it is especially important to know that lubrication in a woman is the exact arousal equivalent of the beginning of erection in a man. Wanting a woman to make love without any lubrication is like asking a man to tie a matchstick on to a limp penis to stiffen it. Neither should be done!

At the end of the mid-line is the opening to the back passage, the *anus.* The surface area between the vaginal opening and anal opening, which is known as the perineum, as well as the other part of the anus itself, can give a good deal of sexually-sensitive pleasure to appropriate touch.

During sexual arousal all the fleshy areas of the sexual organs swell with blood. Tissues become engorged – just as happens, more obviously, when a penis becomes erect. One of the painful consequences of a woman becoming aroused but not having a climax is that frequently blood gets trapped in sensitive tissues. Without the flow-back from tissues into the main bloodstream that happens with a climax, it can only seep away very slowly, causing an unpleasant sensation of pressure pain before it goes, especially in the inner thigh area.

The *internal sex organs* are connected both to reproduction and sexual pleasure.

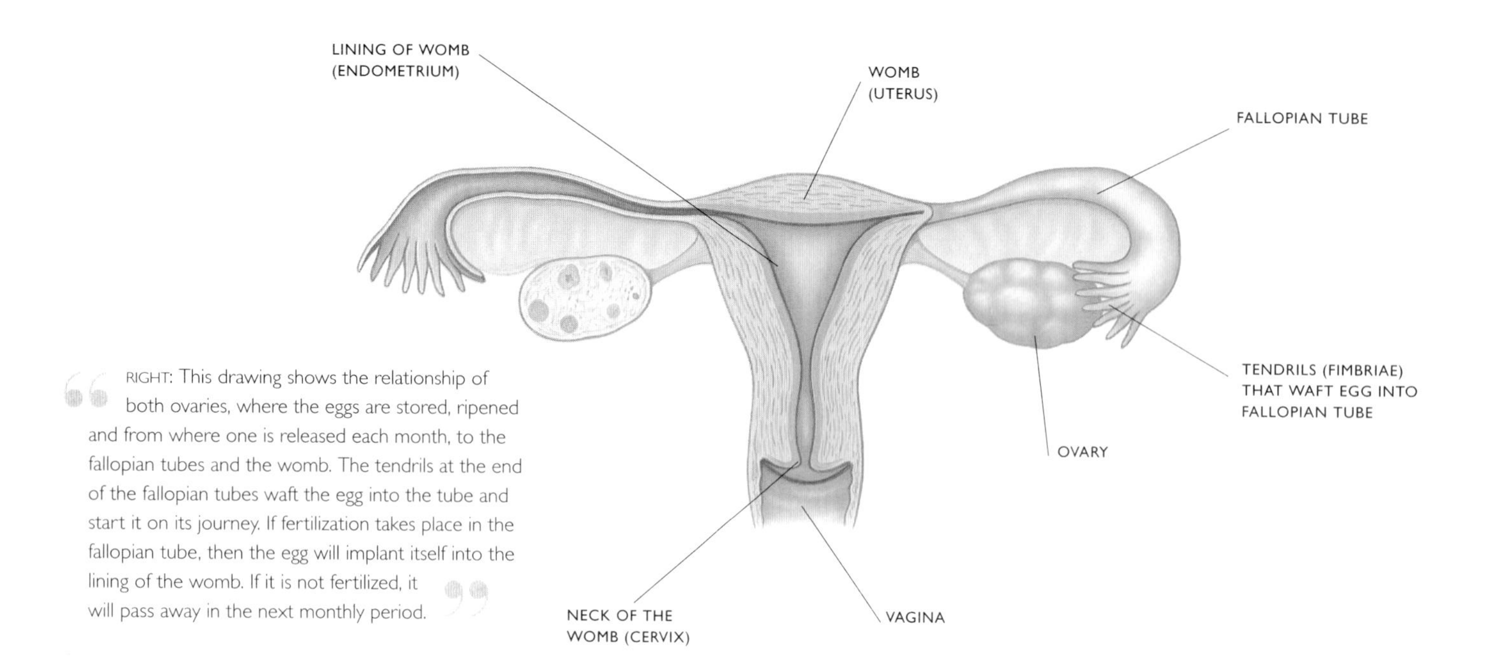

RIGHT: This drawing shows the relationship of both ovaries, where the eggs are stored, ripened and from where one is released each month, to the fallopian tubes and the womb. The tendrils at the end of the fallopian tubes waft the egg into the tube and start it on its journey. If fertilization takes place in the fallopian tube, then the egg will implant itself into the lining of the womb. If it is not fertilized, it will pass away in the next monthly period.

It used to be thought that the vagina itself had very little sensitivity. That has proved to be what men thought, not what women experience. Indeed, there is a special spot (called the G-spot after the physician who first described it, Ernest Grafenberg), on the front wall of the vagina which in some women is especially sensitive erotically.

Although the G-spot is very difficult to locate and account for anatomically, there is no doubt that for many women stimulation of that area of the vagina is highly pleasurable. Touch from either a finger or penis there will readily provoke a climax. In some women such a climax may also be accompanied by a flow of a liquid. Women may fear that they are urinating at this time, but the liquid is not urine. It seems to be a substance which is not unlike the milky fluid of a man's ejaculation, though not so sticky and much more copious. The origin or purpose of this secretion is not very well understood, but it is a well-described phenomenon, and not to be confused with the loss of urine *(stress incontinence)* that some women do experience during a climax.

At the inner end of the vagina is the neck of the womb (the *cervix*), which can easily be touched with a finger. It feels like the tip of a nose when rubbed lightly with the soft pad of a lubricated forefinger. The sexual sensation here comes mostly from deep thrusting during penetration of the penis. Recent studies using ultrasound techniques have shown that penile thrusting makes all the woman's internal organs move around a surprising amount. If there has been any tearing of deeper muscles during childbirth, this can cause some pain.

Any pain during intercourse *(dyspareunia)*, for either woman or man, should be properly investigated and understood. There used to be a fashion for labelling almost any pain during intercourse as being *psychogenic dyspareunia*, with the implication that the pain was only in the mind. Pain is represented in the mind, of course, but it has to come from somewhere.

All these sexual and reproductive organs in the woman are contained within a remarkably small area of the body, tucked safely away inside the boney protection of the pelvis. The floor of the pelvis is very rich in powerful muscles. They can be used to great effect for sexual pleasure. Contracting them squeezes the vagina and anything – especially a penis – lying inside it.

These muscles (called *pubococcygeal* or *P-C* muscles) can be strengthened by learning to stop and start urine flow while passing water. The effect of the muscles can also be felt by inserting a finger into the vagina and trying to squeeze around the finger. Tightening and relaxing the P-C muscles can be practiced anywhere.

Finally, the womb (or *uterus*) itself. A pear-shaped object, it is remarkably small considering how much it can swell to contain a baby (or two or more!).

While not directly involved in the sensations of sexual arousal, many women describe a very warm, spreading sensation in and around the womb just before and during a climax. Muscles around it tighten during a climax too, and help the cervix to dip down into any pool of semen that is lying in the top of the vagina after the man has ejaculated. Not surprisingly, therefore, although a climax is not in any way essential for becoming pregnant, if you want to conceive, becoming pregnant when having a climax is much more fun.

This brings us to a central difference between men and women's sexual organs. Women's internal organs are, first and foremost, designed for reproduction. Sexual sensation is an add-

RIGHT: The male genitals manufacture sperm in the testicles, store them in the epididymis, and deliver the sperm contained in seminal fluid, secreted by seminal vesicles, out through the same opening in the penis that is issued for passing urine. Two sphincter muscles near the neck of the bladder make sure that, during erection and ejaculation, sperm rather than urine is passed out.

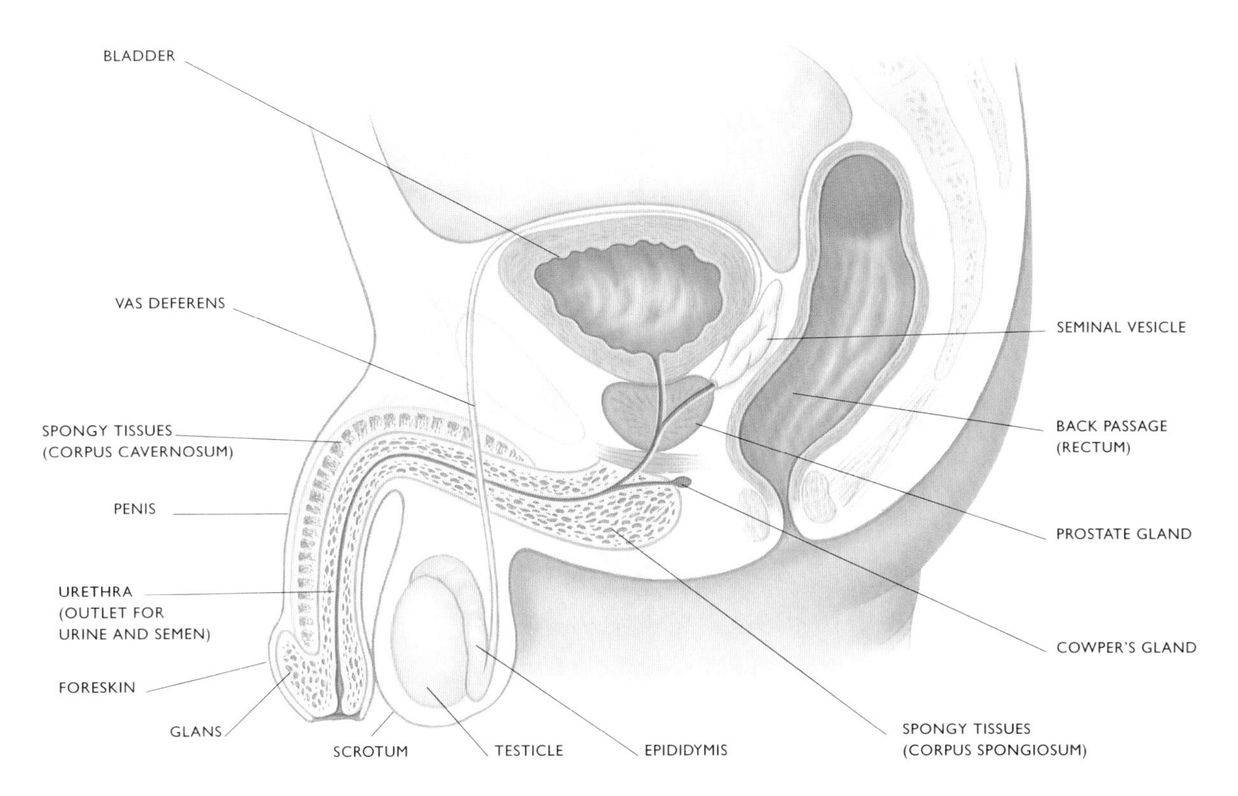

on. The pay-off for this seems to be that, when a woman is sexually aroused and has a climax, it is much more intense and wide-spreading throughout her body than is a man's. It is her external genitalia which elicit the most intense sensations, and which have no relevance to reproduction.

Men, on the other hand, *have* to be sexually aroused in order to be reproductive. Without an erection the possibilities of conception are very limited indeed – modern artificial methods apart, of course.

Which brings us to the male sexual organs. Let's look at the external structures first of all.

The *penis* consists neither of muscle nor bone. It is a mass of spongy tissues which have the capacity to fill with blood during sexual arousal – in much the same way that water fills the cell structure of a sponge. As penile tissues fill, however, they are contained and restricted by the outer sheath of skin covering the whole of the penile shaft. Increasing pressure as the tissues fill creates increasing resistance from the outer skin. This is the mechanism that makes the hardness of an erection.

Running through the penis is a tube (the *urethra*), through which both urine and semen flow at separate times. This urethral tube is connected through the prostate gland to the testicles and also to the bladder.

Surrounding the urethral tube are the spongy and the cavernous bodies called *corpus spongiosum* and *corpus cavernosum*. These tissues, when there is no arousal, are limp and flaccid; but when the blood of sexual arousal is flowing they fill to create an erection.

The penis is a well-designed delivery system for the sperms that travel in the seminal fluid of an ejaculation. By being deposited in the vagina, sperm have a flying start, as it were, which gives them an increased chance of getting to an egg for the great evolutionary purpose of fertilization.

That's really all there is to it, for men – getting hard and going soft. The internal sexual organs (the man's *testicles* and internal glands important to semen production) play no significant part in the man's conscious sexual experience. So important is penile sensation to him that almost all his sexual gratification is focused on sensations on the surface of the penile shaft; on the head of the penis itself (the glans); and in the experience of ejaculatory contractions inside the root structures of the penis. It is all much less subtle than in women, though no less miraculous.

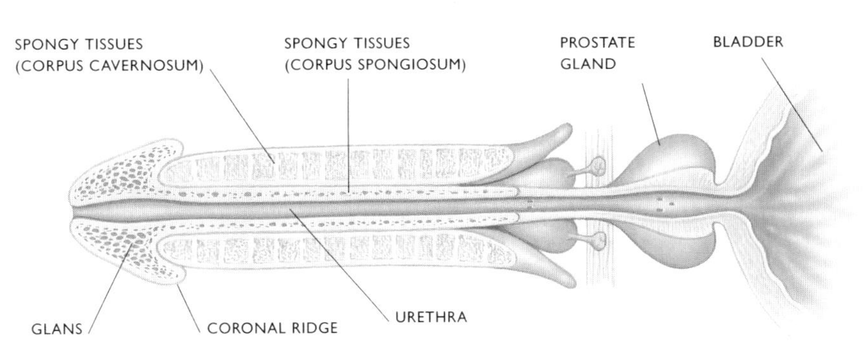

ABOVE: In this view we are looking down on a section through an erect penis. Sperm travel from the testicles, via the vas deferens, to be mixed with seminal fluid, and are then ejaculated from the penis down the urethra during orgasm. The prostate gland secretes a fluid that is added to the semen.

SECTION TWO

The Best of Sex

Beyond the remarkable story of how our bodies find their adult shape is the experience we have of being adults and (supposedly) grown up. Children wonder what it will be like when they grow up. Grown-ups know that it is a never-ending state; a constant process of finding out about being grown up.

This never-ending quality comes from our human need to be in relationships with others, and the fact that we only discover some aspects of ourselves through being in relationships, while still understanding that relationships themselves are fluid. An encounter with a driver exhibiting road rage will tell us things about ourselves that might be as surprising as when we first ran up against raw sexual jealousy, or fell head-over-heels in love.

Sex creates us, reproductively. It is also one of the main channels through which we know ourselves psychologically. We come into the world dependent upon our parents for nurture; we exist as adults in various kinds of inter-dependencies. Being adult is about being self-sufficient; but being really mature sexually is about losing that self and merging it with someone else's self in a process where both people paradoxically can be profoundly selfish and equally selfless all at the same time. Our bodies can do this physically more easily than our selves do it psychologically. Sex can be just an act. Or it can be a complete gift, willingly given and readily taken on both sides.

Good sex is based on skills, just like any other activity in which we might find pleasure. There are manners associated with it too. In managing a close relationship with another we regard as an equal, manners are the social process of recognizing the other's sensitivities and having proper regard for them. By such a process we help cement the other's knowledge that we do *have regard for them, and so contribute to their own self-worth.*

Good sex is about taking and giving. Loving sex is knowing for certain that those are good things to do; that they are life-enhancing; and that, because they can only be experienced fully through and with another person, we need to know how to share our own sense of loving sex with that other person.

Loving sex is also a positive statement about being healthy, psychologically and physically. At a time when there is great doubt about sexuality and its expression, when parents are often afraid to hug their children because it might be misconstrued, and when we are all afraid of AIDS, it is quite difficult to state an unequivocal positive regard for good sex.

Fear is a very corrosive emotion. Yet we know that good loving is the antithesis of fear. The two cannot exist together. Our bodies, at their most vulnerable when they are naked, are the means through which we can as adults, together, affirm the life-giving qualities of sex.

Eye Contact

EYES ARE the distance sense. We can see more accurately further than we can make out sounds, and pinpoint a location with our eyes more easily and at greater distances than with any other sense.

Although non-verbal signals differ in different cultures, eyes covered by lowered eyelashes are universally held to be a sign of submission. By contrast, a straight gaze has a challenge in it, especially if it is held steadily beyond the short time-scale required for recognition. Men look to women's eyes for sexual signals. Women look to men's eyes for honesty and truth.

Some sex hormones will increase the diameter of a woman's pupils by up to thirty per cent. This has a powerful effect on men. Low light also increases pupil size. What are colloquially known as "bedroom" eyes have this quality of enlarged pupils. Victorian women used to enlarge the pupils of their eyes artificially with a drug derived from deadly nightshade, *belladonna.* Although the Latin name means "beautiful lady," it was definitely *not* good for the eyes, even if men *were* captivated.

The eyes are the gateways to desire. They also express desire. They also have the advantage that the language of the eyes leaves no record. A person is not held accountable for what another interprets in their eyes. No signature follows a glance, no incriminating action necessarily comes from a longing gaze. Thus eyes are immensely powerful and immensely safe at the same time.

Looking at another person's eyes directly for more than two minutes can induce high levels of passionate interest. Lovers are well known for gazing deeply into one another's eyes.

Eyes, therefore, convey more directly than any other non-verbal signal what the *emotion* is that a person is feeling. Eyes are believed to reveal true feelings. No wonder then that lovers are so intent upon the eyes.

A gaze well held is challenging as well as sexually stimulating, and can provoke the other person into an intimate game of returning the gaze without a word having to pass or any incriminating action having to follow.

Head tilted towards him, eyes held in direct gaze and mouth slightly open, this woman conveys desire with tenderness, and just a touch of nerves. She has angled her head so that she has to look up into the man's eyes rather than stare more directly. Her smile welcomes and hesitates. Mouth and eyes tell them both of their interest in each other.

RIGHT: Sideways looks have a quite different implication than a straight, face-to-face look. The wider the eyes, the more interest is implied. If a woman accompanies this with half-open lips, then that is a very strong invitation of interest to a man. A man's half-closed eyes and smile convey secretiveness and intrigue.

LEFT: Men look at women, and women watch themselves being looked at... except, that is, when the woman is doing the chasing. Here a woman shows how she uses her eyes, as if in surprise, to widen her gaze, raise her eye-brows, show excitement. It is all the more potent for being indirect, and for coming out of an otherwise steady head.

EYES MEETING in mutual attraction make the stomach drop and the pulses race. A chance glance, the momentary registering of the other's interest, the look that's slightly more coy – leading to a longer gaze, pausing and then looking back, builds expectation. Eye contact in these circumstances becomes more frequent, lasts longer, and becomes more transparent in its purpose.

More commonly, women learn to avoid men's eyes. We have too many experiences of fear and humiliation, meeting leering and jeering on eye contact rather than warmth. We learn instead to look at the ground, avert our gaze, stare at advertisements, read magazines. If we consciously choose to meet the gaze of a lover – or a potential lover – we are showing our interest and strength as a sexual being.

In the safety of a familiar relationship, things are different.

Women notice the color, depth, sincerity in a man's eyes. A woman in love will spend hours gazing into her lover's eyes, hoping to see her own love, or her own self-image, reflected there.

Eye contact makes for mutual exposure. We can see and be seen. It makes us powerful and vulnerable. We use the other's eyes to register whether we are loved, admired, deceived, desired, objectified. Much depends on what a woman perceives in a man's eyes. If she sees desire but no recognition of herself, she feels diminished. If she sees urgent sexuality and passion, she feels excited or afraid. If she sees a leer or a wink, or an assessment of her vulnerability, she feels humiliated or angry. If she sees love, she feels at peace.

ABOVE: Head tilted forwards and slightly sideways, eyes under lids, shoulders hunched, arms crossed, all convey a defensive wariness, and an incipient sadness. It's the kind of lack of eye contact which can rouse a tender, mothering instinct in a woman very fast.

LEFT: This woman knows she is being looked at, and is enjoying it. If men knew how easy it was to seduce a woman, restaurants and pubs would be full of women talking and men listening. Women long to be listened to. Here the man encourages her by resting his gaze on her face and leaning towards her. Her whole body leans towards him in awareness and appreciation. The lowering of her eyes is pleasurably self-conscious, but it is his look of interest which produces the half-smile in her.

Talking

WOMEN CRAVE verbal initimacy with men. We want an exchange of experience that encompasses past lives, present preoccupations and deep feelings. Words comfort women. We need to be praised, loved and listened to – even if this comes in the form of small talk. Words help us feel connected with others, even across the gender divide.

One of the commonest seductions is for a man to say to a woman that she is the only one he can talk to. While this statement sends obvious warning signals – how come his capacity for trust and intimacy is so low? – women are often flattered by this image of uniqueness, and hopeful that real communication is imminent. Unfortunately, it tends to set us up as endless supportive listeners and, while most women have been trained to listen to others, even the most obliging woman will get bored by a monologue, or frustrated at being interrupted or ignored.

What women like is relationship-talk: emotion put into words, mutual listening, loving and praising, engagement in future plans, interest in each other's shared and separate worlds. Men talk with women in this way when they are first interested in developing a relationship. Do they then get embarrassed or anxious about such closeness that they have to withdraw into something more separate and excluding? Men's silence in the home is a major disappointment for women.

Women are just as embarrassed as men are in talking directly about sex: what we like, don't like, would like to try or change. Should we use biological words or the graphically sexual words, or coy, childish words to describe parts of our anatomy? Much depends on contact and intent as to whether sexual words are erotic or offensive. If they are used to enhance a passion already felt, or spoken with love and warmth, they are likely to be experienced as erotic. If they are used in public with aggression or dispassion, they are likely to be found offensive. But there are other questions too that make women reluctant to talk about sex – not least the anxiety that if we point out that something doesn't turn us on much, will he be so hurt or humiliated that he never has an erection again?

Talking can be a way of avoiding sex. Spending hours talking about domestic or work issues, or concentrating on areas of friction and dissent creates an atmosphere antipathetic to sexual intercourse. Both men and women do this.

The capacity to communicate is what makes us feel safe with a partner, particularly if we can keep talking when things get bad. Perhaps that's why men are so attractive to women when they are good communicators, while even the best-looking man does not keep a woman interested if he is boring. Few of us are so well-loved or so confident that we do not need the reassurance of a compliment or a direct expression of love, whether from a stranger, a new lover or a long-term partner.

“ABOVE: What words are passing here that she conveys doubt in her posture – shoulders forwards towards him willingly, but eyes and face turned away? The slightly pugnacious upward tilt of his chin suggests he's trying to convince her of something of which she is not altogether certain.”

“BELOW: Not every moment in bed has to be passionate. Talking naked in one another's arms feels warm and companionable. We enjoy feeling secure as well as desired in bed: sharing moments of the day, discussing issues, listening to one another feels as important as sex.”

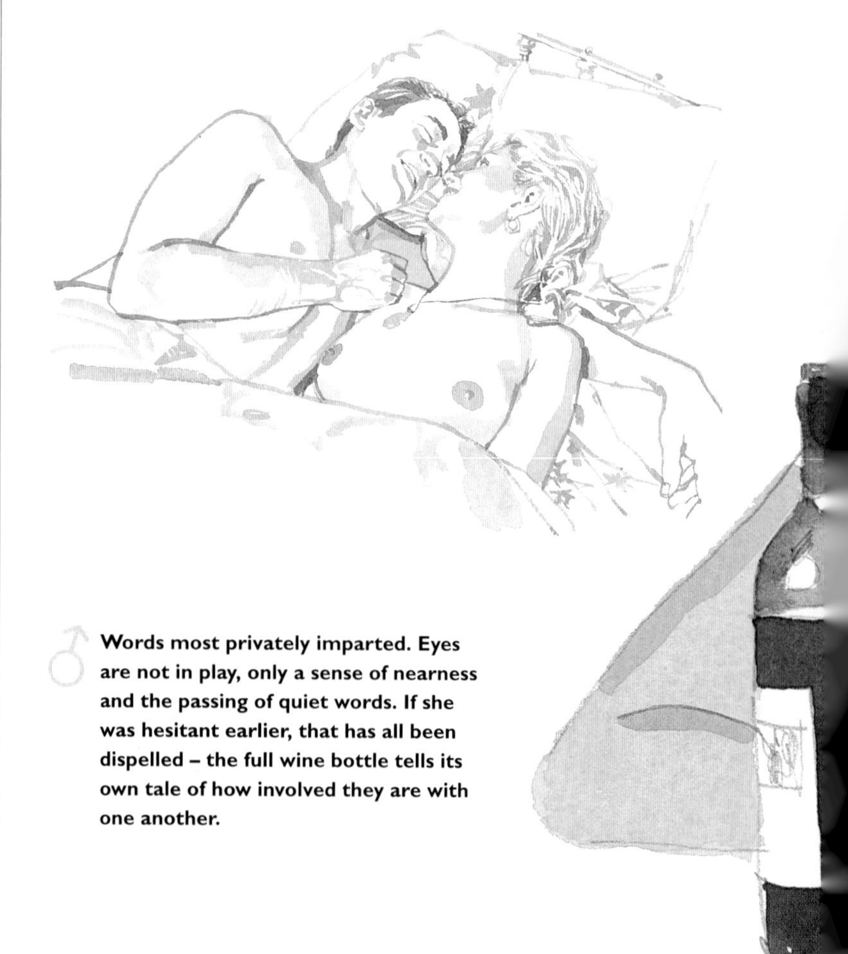

Words most privately imparted. Eyes are not in play, only a sense of nearness and the passing of quiet words. If she was hesitant earlier, that has all been dispelled – the full wine bottle tells its own tale of how involved they are with one another.

TALKING IS not just about what we say and how we say it. Even more importantly it's about how we listen and what we hear. In more than any other channel of communication one person's words can either be properly heard or not heard by the other. How that is done depends upon actual listening skills.

With the other four senses – touch, sight, taste and smell – many of the reactions we have are instinctive or reflexive. They just happen. But though we may have instinctive startle reactions to loud noises, most of what we use our hearing for is words. Words are learned, and our understanding of them is conditioned by intonations and emotions deriving from infancy. So words have the special quality of not only having a meaning of their own when spoken, but potentially a different meaning of their own when heard.

Words are so important in our culture that they tend to supercede our understanding and appreciation of our other senses. If we cannot find words – never mind if they are inadequate for the task – we tend not to believe in our experience. Yet though words have the capability of carrying ideas of profound subtlety and complexity, our basic feeling system is probably a much more reliable guide to what is going on in the world. Words can deceive, both by design and accident. Feelings, properly monitored, very rarely deceive, and never by design. Words may be very powerful tools both for good and evil – as every seducer knows, and anyone who has been seduced soon finds out.

Words of true lovers are the best words of all, for they are totally integrated with feelings. No wonder love inspires poetry, the most advanced word form of all.

BELOW: Men and women are good at talking their way into sex. We know how to create initimacy with words: we flatter and admire, cajole and tease. We want to be pursuer and pursued at the same time, so we advance and retreat using words, touch and eye contact to signal stages of the game. He comments on her appearance, and she responds with a touch.

Being wined and dined with candles may be a cliché, but women get high on romantic love, and rarely get enough of it. An evening out can be a good opportunity to talk about sex – to discuss what is good and what could be even better, safely away from the immediate pressure of the bedroom.

Holding Hands

EYES MAY be the organs of the distant sense, and establish the first contact with another person; but touch is what really conveys closeness. Touching brings one within arm's length of the other person. There, men know they are within a woman's psychological space. Women know that too. Danger and excitement lie within those boundaries. Emotions can take over from intellect.

Any part of the surface of the skin can become sexually sensitized to touch. At times of sexual arousal quite surprising connections can be made and unexpected areas of skin can become sexually charged.

Some regions of the body are especially connected to sexual function. They create sexual arousal when touched appropriately, rage and fear when wrongly touched. These are the erogenous zones – the skin surfaces of sexual organs, inner thighs, lips, ear lobes, breasts, neck and shoulders especially. When touched in an erotic way, they trigger arousal.

But that's a big step from holding hands – usually the first contact between lovers and sometimes so charged with sensation that people describe the experience of a longed-for touch as being like an electric shock. It is as if the skin stores up special chemicals in anticipation of such a touch, and they are suddenly released when the touch happens – much as in the way that sexual excitement will prepare erotic skin surfaces to be increasingly sensitive, and climax can happen very quickly in consequence.

Men long to touch. Holding hands starts with an exploration of whether the touch is welcome. It is hands that are joined symbolically too in marriage ceremonies. Hands are, thus, powerful and deep symbols.

“RIGHT: Almost unbearable if there is pent-up sexual tension, this delicate caressing of the center of the palm is like tickling, like stroking, but not quite. The small circular movements in the center of her palm charge the hand with eroticism. Do men enjoy this as much as women do? Her hand will naturally wrap around his finger after a few seconds, but only to find relief before taking more.”

♂ **Fingers interlocking, just as bodies might be later. In the signals that hand-holding sends, all the possibilities of touch all over the body are enshrined within a palm. Women know this, subconsciously, and men know in the same way what their finger tracings mean. It is not possible to play with the fingers or palm of someone with whom one is out of sorts or angry.**

“RIGHT: Warm and companionable, the swinging of hands held in the open transcends age and culture, and transforms a mundane shopping trip or a lengthy walk into a reverie between two people. It is the familiar act of a couple who have spent many years together, and the mutually possessive act of a new couple intent on excluding others.”

WHEN WE start a relationship we make tiny movements towards intimacy. Tiny movements like brushing fingers, like touching the back of a hand to make a point. Hand-holding may be the culmination of a hundred tentative touches. It is also the place we return to for love and reassurance.

We hold hands in public and in private. Requiring no eye-contact, no undressing, no other intimacy, the public gesture can hold within it warmth, comfort, sensuality, passion – or merely convince others of a closeness not experienced. We can hold hands in public for hours, the meaning of it changing with every moment.

In private we hold hands to feel connected. Watching TV, driving a car, talking, lying side by side in bed – reaching out a hand is an abiding pleasure. Where there is sexual tension, hands become hot, sensitive, moist. Fingers entwine and embrace, hands want to wrap around each other. Despite our difference, men and women seem to find ways of using their hands to simulate genital sex. A finger is sucked or stroked between two fingers, wrists are exposed for delicate rubbing, the palm of the hand reaches peaks of pleasure when it is massaged with a thumb or lightly tickled. Fingers tease and explore, evading closure then coming together in an interlocking that sets the heart pounding. Extraordinary that a part of the body so utilitarian can be transformed into the most sensitive, lovely communicator.

When hand-holding is for love, the holding feels as much emotional as physical. Women enjoy feeling held, supported, squeezed, enfolded sometimes. Do men allow themselves these feelings enough? As children, girls usually get to hold hands with parents and other children for safety, comfort, direction. Adult women too feel loved and cared for when their hands are held. There can be a profound sense of belonging in a hand firmly held; equally, a hand refused, or dropped too quickly, can leave a profound sense of loneliness.

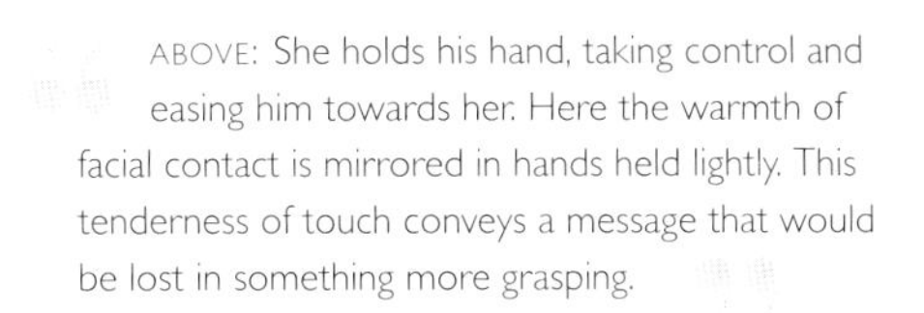

ABOVE: She holds his hand, taking control and easing him towards her. Here the warmth of facial contact is mirrored in hands held lightly. This tenderness of touch conveys a message that would be lost in something more grasping.

ABOVE: Hands parallel other movements of the body. Whoever encloses the other's fingers signals, for that time, who has the upper hand in the relationship. Fleeting though it may be, watch for it and respond. Passing control flexibly between you sends strong signals about what kind of lover you might become.

The distance between these two hands is held precisely to maximize tension and movement. With palms slightly curved, fingers taut and lightly touching, both hands are generating heat and sensitivity. Rarely staying still, they will soon move again – to intertwine, or clasp firmly, or move away.

Touching

TOUCHING CROSSES the boundary into the zone of real intimacy. From earliest days, touch is the sense that makes us safe. Skin sensors respond with lightning rapidity, knowing what any touch means. We are born with that capacity, and in all kinds of ways it keeps us safe and lets us know about the intentions of others.

Being touched when it feels all wrong is a danger signal that the body generates. Being touched when it feels all right creates signals mixed with excitement, pleasure, encouragement and an extraordinary mix of tension and relaxation. Anticipating touch, hoping for touch, creates tension. Welcoming touch creates relaxation and well-being. In sex, one touch can so readily lead on to another, and another, and another... Each touch can be both satisfying and tension-making at the same time. Wanting and not wanting come out of that.

ABOVE: Heart, head and body all in one place – no part of the self needs defending against. This picture shows mutual delight in meeting with the pelvis, arms and eyes.

Skin is the body's boundary between one's self as a person and the world. Being touched crosses that boundary – hence the capacity that skin has to signal both danger and pleasure. Lovers know that the first real touch heralds all the delights of exploring the other's boundaries, and the possibility of gradually crossing over them until it becomes possible to merge identities in the sexual act.

Never lose the excitement of touching. The wish to touch and the acceptance of touch keeps bodies sexually healthy. Finding that you do not want to be touched is a profound message about how you really feel about another person. Hence all lovers want the reassurance of touching and being touched, as well as the excitement and/or fear that the first touch might not be welcome.

Men's wish to touch erotically gets confused with establishing control. They also try all kinds of strategies to control in order to touch. Find out about this as a man by agreeing with your partner, for fun, that the next time you make love *she* will do all the touching and you will do all the receiving. It will heighten your awareness of what it is like to be the one who is touched, and help you understand what your touch means to her.

WOMEN ARE SO used to seeing their bodies through the eyes of others, sexualized and inadequate, that we have little everyday experience of how we really feel inside our skin. The shock of touch and the closeness of another person's body breaks through that habitual self-scrutiny. We regain a sense of the inside self – not just the outside – and become aware of emotion and physical sensation.

One of the great delights of being able to be close to another adult's body is to return to the fun and feelings of childhood. Couples enjoying being together often behave like puppies – chasing each other, rolling over, laughing while biting and scratching, pinning each other down, only to run off again to pursue more pleasure. They test each other's strength and speed, and explore differences in height and body weight. At quieter times, both men and women regress to more child-like needs. She might want to be rocked, carried, cocooned in strong arms; he wants to suckle at her breasts and nestle into her lap.

When women are in contact with a man's back, neck, legs, arms, waist, buttocks, chest we are in a world that has been hidden from us. When a man touches those parts of our own body, we are surprised by sensations we didn't know existed. The back of the neck tingles under caressing fingers, the waist contracts with an arm around it, arms and legs turn to fire if they are brushed against, shoulders soften and yield under his embrace. It is as though we get our bodies back – for some of us, for the first time.

Sadly this profound experience and the integration that accompanies it, is not necessarily matched by the man's experience. The stroking, touching and holding that women so much enjoy is not necessarily appreciated by men in the same way. Although some men have learned to sensualize their skin through massage, many men only focus on sensation through the penis. This is very disappointing for women, who then have to choose between pulling away from a pelvic clutch that feels too soon, or giving in to the man's demand for something more sexual. Perhaps this is where we have to teach one another something about difference. Women come alive with whole body touching, men in feeling hands on genitals. Neither exludes, nor is better than, the other.

"RIGHT: She pulls his mouth towards hers by reaching up with her body and caressing his face with her hand. The kiss is important to her, while the connection at the hips may feel more important to him."

♀ **Men pressuring women to be sexual results in rejection. Here the woman shows in body posture and touch that she welcomes his hand on her breast, while she protects her genital area with a hand on her skirt and keeps her knees held together.**

♂ **Clothes are only just managing to keep the appearance of a boundary here. Everything about her posture says: "My body is here for you to touch, but I'm going to be quite passive about it." She is both dressed and undressed at the same time. Make haste very slowly, it says.**

"RIGHT: A sunset pose. Her thumb is hooked into his waistband, and his arm is protectively around her shoulders, while hips are moving together. Perhaps they have made love in the grass, and are walking away glowing."

Hugging

IT IS THE NATURE of a hug to express warmth and friendship. Hugs make a welcome and seal a goodbye. Hugs mend hurt feelings after a fight. They console the sad and encourage the fearful. Hugs say "well done" or "I need you" or "don't leave me". And then there's the hug for sheer joy and delight in one another's presence.

ABOVE: This kind of hug can go on for ever. Both people feel safe, dependent, looked after – equal in the relationship. Both bodies are held still and very close at all levels, without sexual demand.

Women love to hug and be hugged. Hugging fulfils a deep need to have the body cuddled. Whether that's an echo of babyhood or the womb, there is no doubt that the giving and receiving of a hug makes the body calm and the heart light. It is different from sexual touching even if a hug moves on to something more erotic. This is important for women – that it is possible to have a hug without it leading to sex. Sometimes men seem confused or alienated by women's wish to separate these two needs.

Girls grow up learning that their bodies are not their own. Female bodies are the subject of scrutiny, desire, ridicule, mimicry, and even unwanted touch, from a very early age. Becoming a woman offers the chance to reclaim a body boundary that is essential for self-esteem and healthy identity. Being able to say Yes and No for herself about touch, and finding that there is a form of physical closeness which does not involve a sexual contract, can be a huge relief to some women. Some women take a long time to satisfy their need to hug and be hugged, and will postpone or refuse sexual contact until they feel free to enjoy it.

A really good hug lasts for a long time. It starts with eye-contact, and bodies are held close and still against each other with only slight movement of hands or head. Arms embrace warmly and confidently. When both people let this kind of hug continue, there follows an awareness of body rhythms. We hear each other's breathing and heartbeat; we smell each other's clothes and skin. The longer the hug continues the more the body rhythms seek to coincide. Such stillness and closeness feels emotionally and spiritually satisfying. Its wholeness, connectedness and love nourishes the relationship and the people within it.

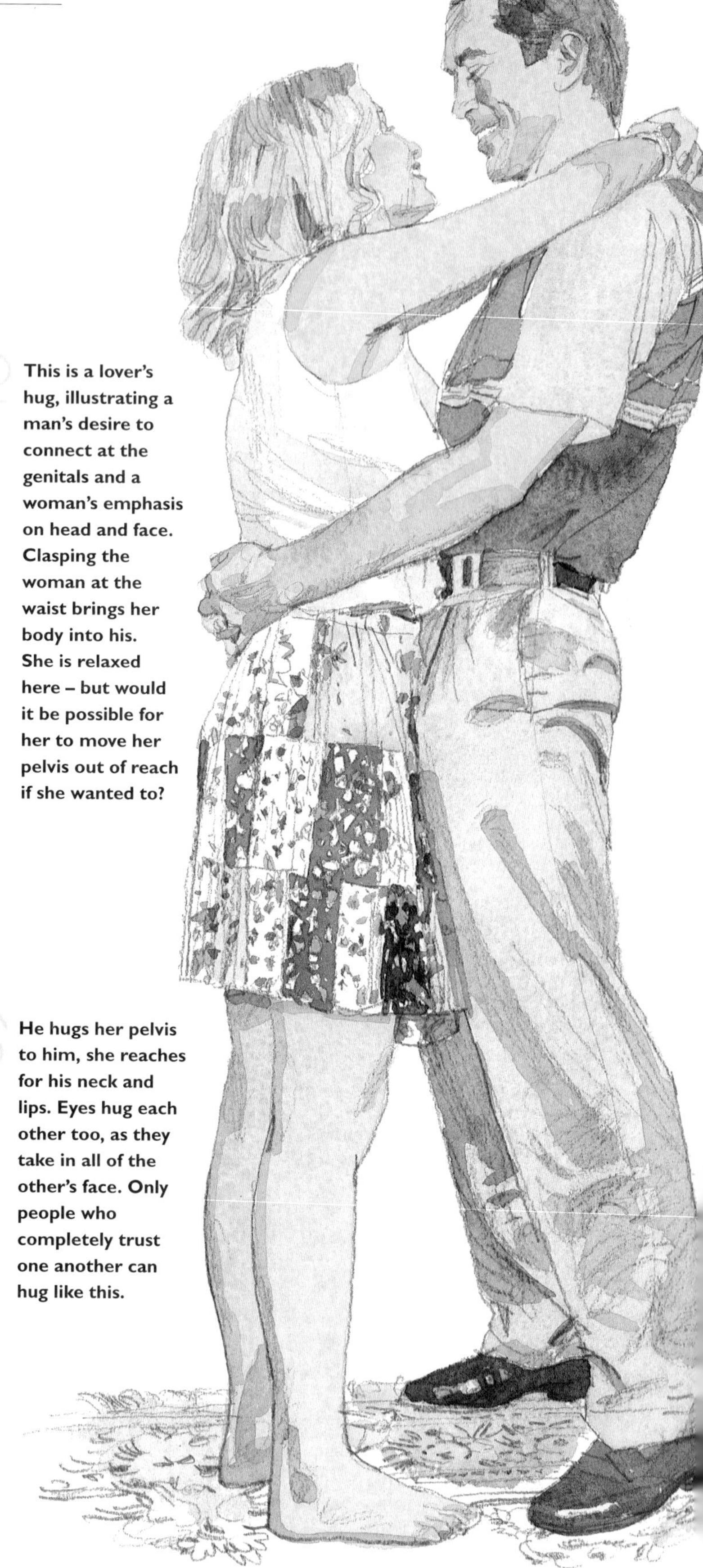

This is a lover's hug, illustrating a man's desire to connect at the genitals and a woman's emphasis on head and face. Clasping the woman at the waist brings her body into his. She is relaxed here – but would it be possible for her to move her pelvis out of reach if she wanted to?

He hugs her pelvis to him, she reaches for his neck and lips. Eyes hug each other too, as they take in all of the other's face. Only people who completely trust one another can hug like this.

HUG FOR safety, hug for love. It is the most natural of human gestures between people who are close emotionally. Arms protect, bodies give warmth. Softness and strength are combined together.

There is no other single act which helps us to deal with sadness or expresses joy in quite the way that hugging does. If we are lucky, from earliest infancy we are enveloped in hugs. For grown-ups the world can seem a whole lot safer if there's a plentiful supply of them.

Too often it is men who do the hugging, women who are hugged. Try it the other way sometime. Feel the safety of being cradled in the arms of someone who loves you. Give yourself up to feeling helpless, dependent, smaller and weaker than the woman you are with. Sink into those feelings. They will extend your range of awareness of how things are for her a lot of the time, how important it is that she knows your strength is there for her, and what a feeling of well-being it produces.

If being loved properly creates a feeling of being merged with another person, then hugging is also the simplest, everyday expression of that.

ABOVE: Tenderness lies at the center of hugging. It is the safest of all forms of human contact – good with music in the background, a video on the screen, or fires burning brightly.

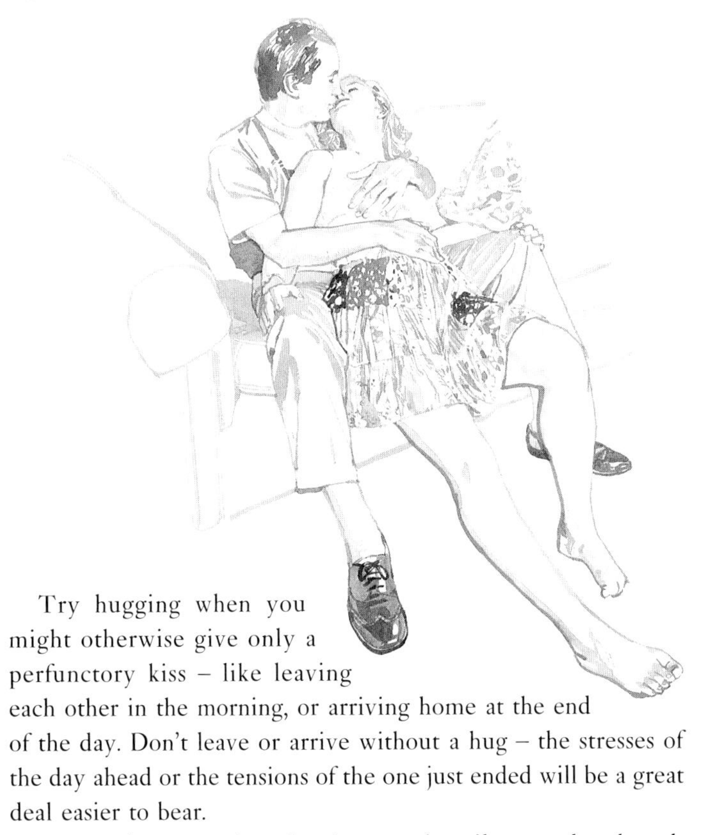

LEFT: This could become more sexual. Or she could talk to him, loosely cradled but close. It is a useful position to reverse: they both lie on the sofa, but with his heavier body lying back on her chest and shoulder.

Try hugging when you might otherwise give only a perfunctory kiss – like leaving each other in the morning, or arriving home at the end of the day. Don't leave or arrive without a hug – the stresses of the day ahead or the tensions of the one just ended will be a great deal easier to bear.

In a curious way, hugging is not primarily sexual – though the spine-crushing hugs of lovers meeting again after being separated too long might make one think otherwise. It is really about knowing that one is precious to the other person.

RIGHT: Hugged, held, kissed: both could be almost lying down together, so closely are their bodies pressed against one another as she stretches to him and he bends slightly to her in a timeless image of lovers locked together, scooping each other into the closest embrace possible, and taking a hug into passion and beyond.

Smelling

♀ WHAT LOVER has not wanted to preserve the smell of sex on fingers and groin, all day long? An after-sex mixture of semen and vaginal fluid gradually seeps out on to a woman's underwear to create an aroma, difficult to describe, but something like baked bread and salt. It is a smell so instantly evocative of sex that a whiff of it can restimulate her, or send her into a reverie for minutes – hours.

Women have been conditioned to fear their own body smells. We learn to deodorize armpits, groins, mouths – even the air in our rooms. There are no messages which counter this anxiety. Advertisements tell adult women they must smell "fresh" to feel confident. How could we not be anxious about our bodies? Men are not asked to do anything about their natural groin smells, except wash – and that seems fair enough. And it should be fair enough for women too.

Many men assume that all their body smells are instantly acceptable to a sexual partner. She might be happy kissing his fetid mouth when he wakes, but turned off by bad breath during the day. Perhaps we could negotiate?

We can, of course, have fun with perfumes. Civilized out of our senses, we have probably lost touch with the pheromones which other species use to attract each other. We can engage a lover with spicy, flowery, musky scents. Interestingly, the marketing of perfume is now aimed at men and women using the same scent.

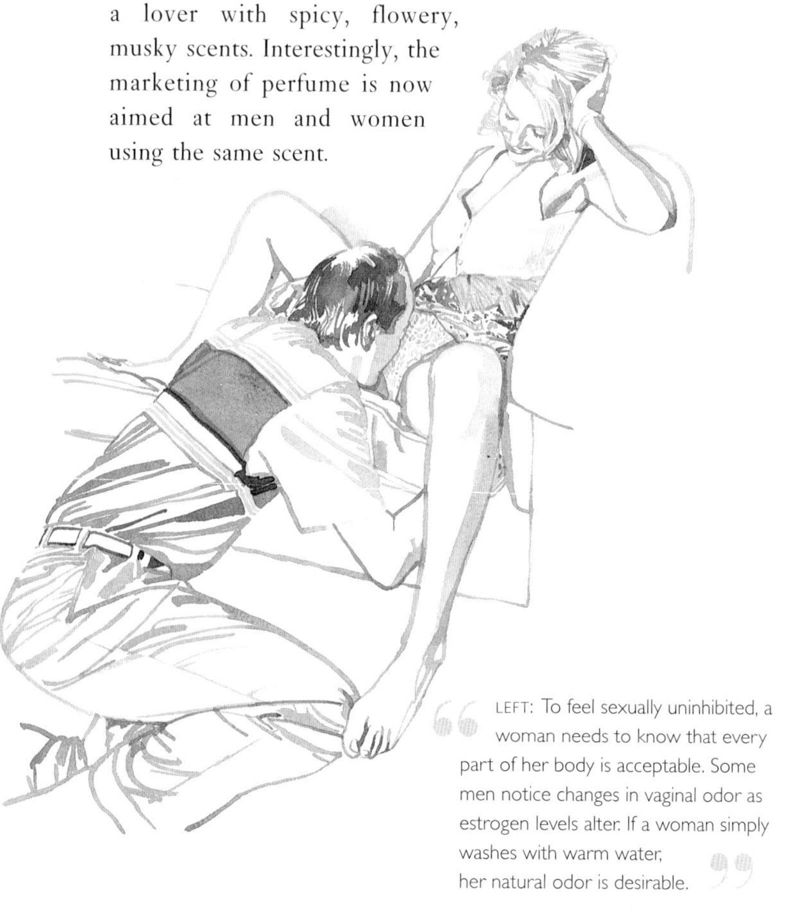

LEFT: To feel sexually uninhibited, a woman needs to know that every part of her body is acceptable. Some men notice changes in vaginal odor as estrogen levels alter. If a woman simply washes with warm water, her natural odor is desirable.

♂ THE BODY has an extraordinary sexual chemistry, some of which is secreted in bodily smells. It is probable that smell plays a much greater part in sexual attraction and desire than we tend to give it credit for – perhaps because it is so basic.

The portion of the brain that manages our capacity to smell is the first to develop and it is closely linked to the part of the brain which stores emotional memories.

A suddenly remembered smell can conjure a whole host of associated images in a way that is more powerful than with any other sense. Smells are the best way of getting into men's emotional selves – something the perfume industry knows very well.

Animals secrete special sex-stimulating hormones, called pheromones. They can attract a mate by smell over very considerable distances. Pheromones almost certainly have their equivalents in human beings, so that when people say: "It's the chemistry...," they are more right than they know. But pheromones are more easily created by humans than detected by them, for we tend to underrate and underuse our sense of smell, and so what we do pick up is at a subconscious level.

One of the favorite sites for the release of pheromones in humans is on the upper lip in women. Kissing may be no more than a device for getting your nose close to your partner's upper lip to take in her stimulating pheromones. That explains why kissing one person can be very much more pleasurable than kissing another, whatever the actual kissing skills being enjoyed.

Natural body smells can be enhanced by perfumes, most of which rely very heavily on the basic animal smells of musk and civet. But do not underestimate the subtlety and pleasure of natural body smells. The human animal is not so civilized that its basic fragrances are lost. There is especial delight in discovering body scents free of the perfumer's art.

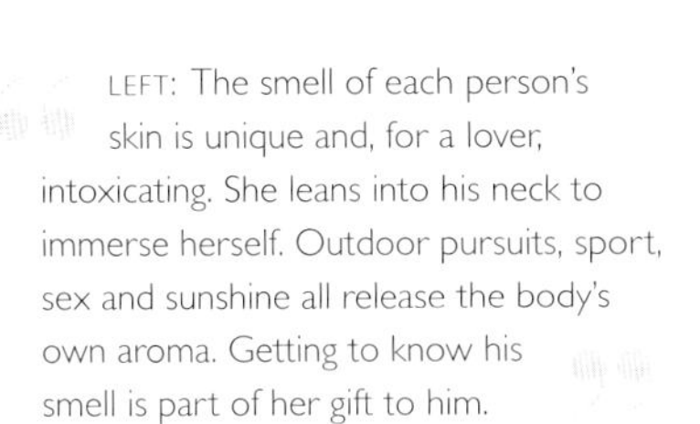

LEFT: The smell of each person's skin is unique and, for a lover, intoxicating. She leans into his neck to immerse herself. Outdoor pursuits, sport, sex and sunshine all release the body's own aroma. Getting to know his smell is part of her gift to him.

Wearing a perfume that they both like, she can luxuriate in his enjoyment of the scent worn behind her ears. This is a lovely affirmation from the man to the woman. He desires her, smells her, touches her – and she responds by closing her eyes and letting her neck yield in acceptance.

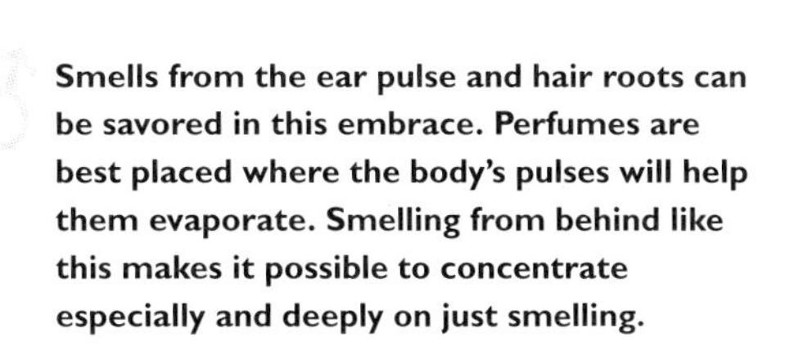

Smells from the ear pulse and hair roots can be savored in this embrace. Perfumes are best placed where the body's pulses will help them evaporate. Smelling from behind like this makes it possible to concentrate especially and deeply on just smelling.

LEFT: The smells from a naked torso, an armpit and hair roots will all combine for her, as he simultaneously picks up the scents released by the pulsing in her wrist.

Tasting

LEFT: Passing wine from lips to lips puts flavor at a premium, as well as skill and close contact! All flavors derive from the interchange between the source of the flavor itself and the person who is tasting it.

WE DO A LOT with our mouths. We use them to talk, to eat, to kiss, to brush over skin, to suck fingers, breasts, toes, vulva and penis. We swallow saliva, semen and vaginal fluid; we pass drinks from mouth to mouth. We lick labia, clitoris, glans, perineum, anus – and we eat food off each other's skin. We bite ears and nipples and necks, and blow cool air on to sweaty skin. We make more use of our mouths during sex than in any other activity.

The mouth is sensual, erotic and adaptable. Getting to know the taste of a lover's mouth is like getting to know his smell. It's unique, intimate, secret. Letting tongues explore deep inside the other's mouth is like trying to eat the other person.

The only drawback to this activity is bad breath. Lots of tastes become bearable in the right mood or with the right person, including nicotine, alcohol, garlic, but some tastes make even the most ardent lover turn away. If a taste makes you feel so uncomfortable that you cannot kiss him, it is better to say something, even if it is difficult. If you simply turn your head away, he may be hurt.

BELOW: He tastes that warm, private part between her legs; she relaxes into sensation and wetness.

Favorite foods can be smeared on the skin or genitals and then eaten. The vagina allows itself to be used for the temporary intrusion of foods, though it is inadvisable to insert anything which could get stuck or lost in the vaginal canal. The penis enjoys being covered in creams, jellies, jams and sauces. The pleasure of these experiments is two-fold: food eaten off skin tastes different and delicious. A mouth licking and foraging on skin or genitals is intensely arousing, and fun.

Women sometimes gag on semen. It tastes salty, warm and slightly viscous. If a man ejaculates into a woman's mouth the semen spurts into the back of her throat, whether or not she wants to swallow it. Men's erotic literature is full of women who like to swallow semen, so it is a turn-on for a lot of men, but not necessarily for a lot of women. This is something that should be discussed before hurt feelings occur.

Certainly it is important for women to feel that their genitals and body-fluids are acceptable to a lover. A woman needs to feel uninhibited enough to allow and want a man to lick her crotch. Although it is sensually and sexually arousing, if she is embarrassed she will lose touch with the physical pleasure and only be concerned with how she must taste or look or smell. Similarly, she must know that her lover will not humiliate her.

As with other aspects of sex, there's attraction and revulsion in tasting body-fluids and orifices. Sex is like that. We need to overcome civilized sensitivities in order to give ourselves up to sexual pleasure. We can help each other do that, with generosity and love.

ABOVE: The taste is skin and sweat. She takes his glans (head of the penis) in her mouth, and controls movements.

How rare and lovely to have the back of the neck attended to ... the base of the neck is surprisingly sensitive to biting, producing a thrilling and primitive submission.

Special treats; only with a lover is the nape of a neck accessible. Smells come from the roots of the hair, and tastes from the accumulated, microscopic particles of sweat on the surface of the skin at the top of her spine.

TASTE MAY not be the most important of the sexual senses, but there are lovely minor pleasures to be had from it. And considering how important taste is elsewhere in our lives, is it not a little surprising how under-explored it is in connection with the body and the variety of flavors it offers.

Closely linked to smell – which is why tastes get so dull if one has a cold – tasting also involves us in the extremely erotic area of mouth and lips. The whole of the human body, properly used, is available for the pleasures of sex.

The most direct sources of taste are found in bodily fluids – seminal fluid from a man, vaginal secretions from a woman. Neither of these are waste products. Quite the contrary; they are connected with the making of life. Not surprisingly, then, they have very distinctive flavors.

Vaginal flavors, from the lubrication that arousal creates, can vary from being quite salty to quite sweet. Over a few hours, left on probing fingers, the taste can become faintly sharp as the smell loses its immediate freshness. End-of-day vaginal tastes are quite different from newly bathed, delicate, hardly perceptible tastes.

Try them and find out. Your partner may herself want some encouragement to let you explore this aspect of her femininity. There are so many pressures these days for high standards of cleanliness that over-sanitized sex can lose its natural earthiness. Just as there is a great difference between the flavor of mushrooms newly picked from a morning field and the vacuum-packed, regulation size products of the supermarket, so the flavors of sex can be earthier or more bland. Try more of the natural bodily flavors, with their organic processes unimpaired.

Similarly with the fluid from an ejaculation. Try your own, and find its slightly ammoniac flavor. Your bodies are full of taste delights, there for you to discover.

ABOVE: The man caresses her and then puts his fingers, sticky from the vagina, into her mouth for her to taste. She confronts the taboo of oral contact with her genitals.

Kissing

SURPRISINGLY kissing erotically, lips to lips, is not a universal custom. Some cultures find it sexier to concentrate on exchanging saliva, while others prefer nuzzling, smelling facial contact, cheek-to-cheek.

In our culture, though, kissing is of enormous erotic significance. The lips are so well-endowed with sensitive nerve endings that they can feel the lightest touch of a single hair and the gentlest brush of another person's contact with them.

Women's lips are also emphasized and adorned for the purpose of sexual attraction, through the application of lipsticks and glosses. Women's lips also symbolize to men the presence of those other lips surrounding the vagina with which women are so deliciously endowed and with which men so seek for contact. Both represent the entrance to the warm, secret, moist parts of a woman's body.

Kissing conveys a vast range of messages. The welcome from lips that are offered encouragingly, as against the hesitation of lips that are not responsive, are signals that will be simultaneously occurring throughout all the other muscular systems of the body. For such a small area of the body they are extremely powerful receptors and communicators.

RIGHT: Holding her face in his hand while kissing her mouth lets this woman know her face, not just her groin, attracts him. She responds by holding his arm in place.

Perhaps the most special aspect of kissing is that speech is prevented. Hearing is taken off the agenda, and touch is at a premium. Hollywood is credited with teaching the world that serious kissing involves closing the eyes. Try finding out what the difference is between kisses with eyes open and closed.

A soft mouth represents a soft heart. His gentle kissing of her upper lips asks her mouth to open slightly. Excitement builds in taking time over little kisses, feeling each different sensation grow and develop.

Touch, taste and smell make a kiss completely absorbing – an intimacy equalled only by the physical act of insertion and being entered sexually. Eyes closed convey total trust, eliminating any distractions.

WOMEN LIKE kissing – before, after and during sex. We tend to consider ourselves more expert at kissing than men; certainly we like to spend more time doing it. We're often more interested in kissing his mouth than fondling his penis.

A woman knows she is loved when she is kissed. Sexual intercourse may produce words of love, but kisses do not lie. The mouth is either hot or cold, gentle or hard, responsive or closed. It is easier to fake an orgasm than a kiss.

Kisses are conversations as well as sensations. There is a build-up of expectation that comes from lingering over kissing.

Lovers kiss with their whole mouths, not just their lips. The softest, most sensitive area of the mouth lies beyond the lips where the inner flesh is moist and warm. Open-mouthed kisses require a mutual yielding of facial tension, so that warm breath and saliva are freely exchanged, tongues can explore each other, and teeth bite and clash a little. A tongue forced into a mouth too soon is unpleasant, but a tongue welcomed in mutual desire resembles sexual intercourse, and is extremely erotic.

Passionate kissing moves from penetration by the tongue to teasing to caressing, and back again. Tender kisses which cover a woman's face, neck and eyes and kisses which gently brush her mouth and pull at her lips, are likely to be received with love and appreciation.

“LEFT: Butterfly kisses almost always cause smiles, as an eyelash deliberately flutters against a cheek or forehead. Light kisses, deliberately avoiding the lips, tease the other into desire.”

“BELOW: Mouth to mouth kissing often seems most satisfying when the man is on top and the woman underneath – even if he is shorter than she. He sits more upright as she slides down a little.”

“LEFT: We kiss our friends, relatives, children – even our pets – but this is the kiss for lovers. As with the penetration of any other part of the body, we need to be excited enough and receptive enough to enjoy the movements of a tongue in the mouth. Some people never like it. While it is often given male to female, women can do this to men too. One tongue is sucked by the other in movements that mimic sexual intercourse, with the tongue thrusting or flicking rhythmically inside the other's mouth.”

Undressing

UNDRESSING TAKES us past the outer barriers of clothes. Nakedness makes us our most vulnerable selves – but also our most free. What a boundary to play around with.

Undressing also brings back parent/child experiences. Learning to dress ourselves as children is a crucial part of the development of independence and self-identity. By the age of five or thereabouts most children are dressed less and less by their parents. Only the difficult bits – like doing hair and maybe tying shoelaces safely – gets left to them.

Undressing for a child usually implies intimacy, fun, or both. For many children it's a very special time associated with bathing, stories and being tucked up safely in bed.

Undressing connected to sexual feelings comes as part of our developing sexuality. But it also carries all our unconscious childhood associations. We can still want to be cuddled and kept warm, no matter who is undressing whom.

Typically men are undressed sexually by their partners much less frequently than women are by their men. Being made to feel vulnerable contradicts many men's ideas of being masculine – even though it may release maternal feelings for women and so help balance an encounter. Not wanting to feel vulnerable and dependent, men resist being undressed. They also feel that it is their role to be the pursuer or the undresser. Women can start to feel the man is only interested in getting at her sexually if the balances are not equalled.

Nakedness also brings into play all the doubts about whether or not one is attractive. This is a very pervasive part of feeling vulnerable, and perhaps its worst aspect. Men are very much less conscious about whether they are physically attractive than are women, except for anxieties about muscle mass and penis size, which is where the male ego feels most threatened.

Kissing is important before, during and after undressing. Some men stop kissing when the clothes start coming off – a signal which can feel like a mood change from closeness to goal-seeking. Here she responds to the kiss by lying back acceptingly, pulling him towards her with her hand to his neck.

Everything in the line of these bodies says she is wanting to pull him towards her. He is responding with his hands moving to feel the boundaries of her clothing. He wants to remove barriers to make close contact with her skin.

RIGHT: Being helped off with garments combines the vulnerability of being a child, with the excitement of adult desire. Some women shave under their arms; others don't if they find that more sensual.

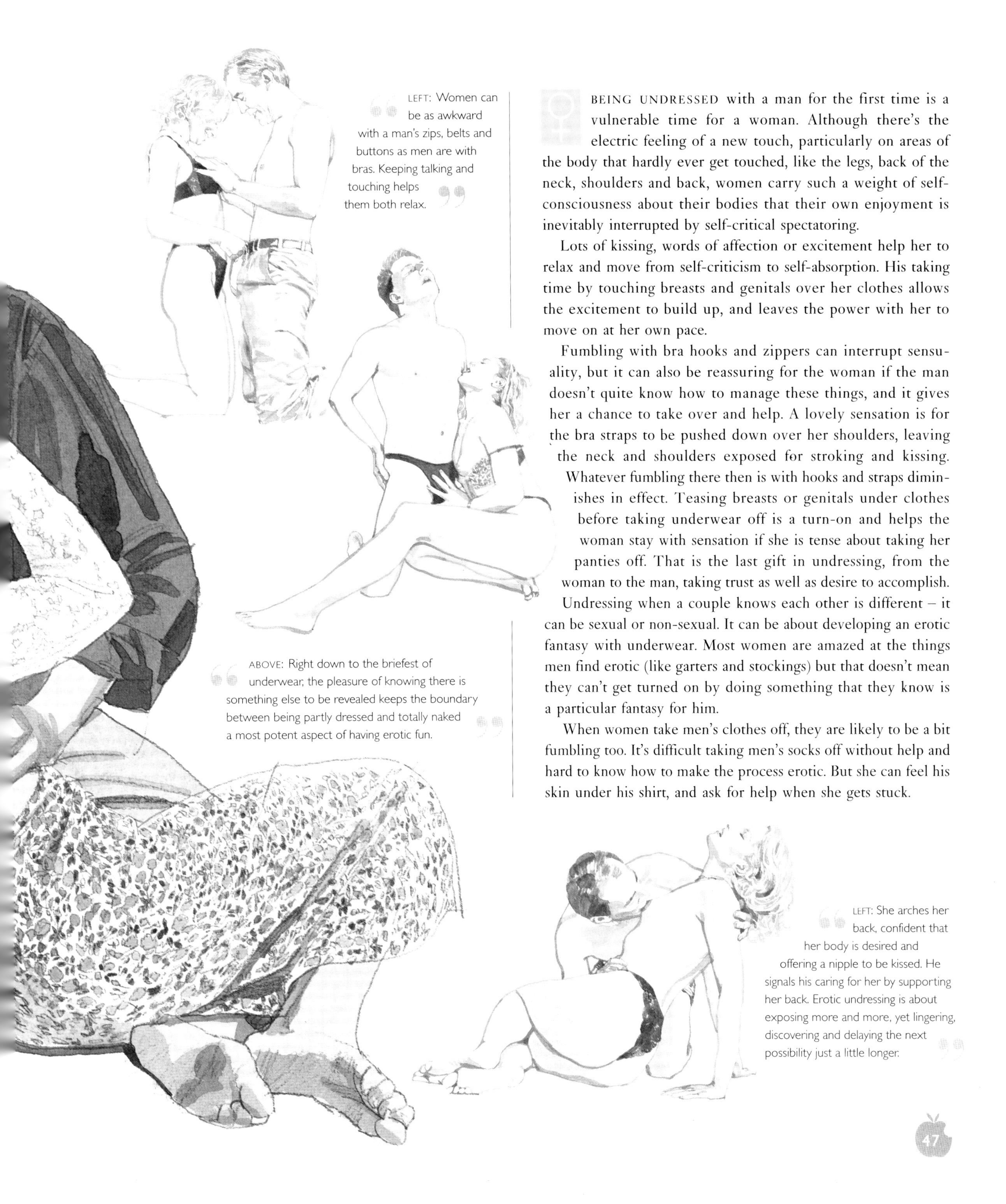

LEFT: Women can be as awkward with a man's zips, belts and buttons as men are with bras. Keeping talking and touching helps them both relax.

ABOVE: Right down to the briefest of underwear, the pleasure of knowing there is something else to be revealed keeps the boundary between being partly dressed and totally naked a most potent aspect of having erotic fun.

BEING UNDRESSED with a man for the first time is a vulnerable time for a woman. Although there's the electric feeling of a new touch, particularly on areas of the body that hardly ever get touched, like the legs, back of the neck, shoulders and back, women carry such a weight of self-consciousness about their bodies that their own enjoyment is inevitably interrupted by self-critical spectatoring.

Lots of kissing, words of affection or excitement help her to relax and move from self-criticism to self-absorption. His taking time by touching breasts and genitals over her clothes allows the excitement to build up, and leaves the power with her to move on at her own pace.

Fumbling with bra hooks and zippers can interrupt sensuality, but it can also be reassuring for the woman if the man doesn't quite know how to manage these things, and it gives her a chance to take over and help. A lovely sensation is for the bra straps to be pushed down over her shoulders, leaving the neck and shoulders exposed for stroking and kissing. Whatever fumbling there then is with hooks and straps diminishes in effect. Teasing breasts or genitals under clothes before taking underwear off is a turn-on and helps the woman stay with sensation if she is tense about taking her panties off. That is the last gift in undressing, from the woman to the man, taking trust as well as desire to accomplish.

Undressing when a couple knows each other is different – it can be sexual or non-sexual. It can be about developing an erotic fantasy with underwear. Most women are amazed at the things men find erotic (like garters and stockings) but that doesn't mean they can't get turned on by doing something that they know is a particular fantasy for him.

When women take men's clothes off, they are likely to be a bit fumbling too. It's difficult taking men's socks off without help and hard to know how to make the process erotic. But she can feel his skin under his shirt, and ask for help when she gets stuck.

LEFT: She arches her back, confident that her body is desired and offering a nipple to be kissed. He signals his caring for her by supporting her back. Erotic undressing is about exposing more and more, yet lingering, discovering and delaying the next possibility just a little longer.

Time and Place

ABOVE AND BELOW: Candles, soaps, mirrors and wine – a tranquil setting for talking and loving. Candles are the most seductive of light sources.

CONSIDER HOW much time you take preparing a table and dining room if guests are coming for dinner. Then think of how much time you might spend preparing the setting in which to make love.

For the first time of making love to a new partner, a man may well pay all kinds of attention to detail. Fast forward to the fiftieth time, though. The man who can say he still pays as much attention to setting the mood as he did the first time is either a wonderful lover or as great a liar.

Yet each time we make love, the gift of one another's body is as precious as it was the first time and deserves an appropriate setting to reflect that fact. Too much love-making happens last thing at night, in tired time, and with no sense of surprise, or discovery or real excitement left. The lights get switched off in more senses than one.

Champagne every time might be more than the housekeeping can stand, but if you only splash out once a year it reminds you both what a special occasion making love really is. Candles are a good investment. Soft lighting costs no more than hard lighting. And a bed that invites needs only imagination in folding the covers back. Flowers placed in a bedroom instead of being offered to a receiving hand also make the point that creating mood and setting is a great turn-on for a partner. Clothes are no less a part of mood creation than flowers, candlelight and an inviting bed. *Everything* that is sensual needs emphasizing for good sex. Women know this very well. They dress not only for the man who interests them, but because of the sensual quality of particular clothes too, for their own enjoyment. Although the leisure fashion industry has not yet designed clothes especially for sex, a little imagination will make it clear that some clothes can be much more sexually appealing than others.

In the latter part of the 20th century men do not generally dress for display. They dress for function. In the 18th century and before, men's clothes – like many male animals' display – were gorgeous and highly colored. Let clothes connected to sex be real display clothes.

Regrettably the printed page of a book prevents us demonstrating smell. Flowers may or may not perfume a room. Try especially to find ones that do. But give real thought both to the way a room can be scented and the way you can be scented too. Women love sweet-smelling men. It's a quality worth savoring.

The best kind of cast-offs! Place and time give way to the urge to be completely wrapped up in the other's body.

THERE IS NO one perfect setting for sex. Given the right amount of passion, we will all make love in a broom closet. Sex meets needs which vary with time, place and partner – and the mood and the setting do not always coincide.

Women do not mind the occasional grope in a broom closet, but mostly we like an environment which reflects our self-worth. What feels good is when a man has put care and thought into making arrangements. His cooking a meal is therefore a greater treat than always being taken out to dinner. At a basic level, women like protected time – free from intrusions like work, children, phones – clean sheets, the answering machine on and the phone off. No old socks and dirty coffee cups. And he buys the condoms.

When we move naturally from talking on the sofa to making love, all the movements in transition allow a woman's body to open.

ABOVE: A bed can be entirely welcoming or quite forbidding – just like human beings. Warmth and softness are very encouraging.

Men often seem to want to make love first and talk afterwards. Women like it the other way around. We want to feel close and trusting before we take our clothes off. An harmonious emotional climate is good; an honest emotional climate is better. It does not matter whether it is the first night or the tenth year of a relationship: women want to be listened to, want to be loved, and want emotional language. It does not need to be "I love you." "I hate you" said with passion can be just as much a turn-on. But a day-to-day sense that a man cares enough to ask us how our day has been, to remember birthdays and events that matter, to say "I've been thinking about you," rather than not saying anything, is more likely to make a woman feel like sharing her body than any amount of meals out, attempts at flattery or bunches of flowers.

When it is just about setting the scene, a woman will often go to a great deal of trouble to make sure that things look good, sound good, smell good, taste good. We will buy flowers, and light candles, wear new clothes and cook expensive food. Men often seem oblivious of this effort: perhaps it means nothing to a man; are there other things he would prefer?

On the whole women expect to pay their own way these days, unless he earns an enormous amount more than she. Even then she will want to treat him sometimes, so as to share in the giving and the power. Money can be a turn-on or a turn-off; it depends how it is used. Generosity of thought and money is definitely an aphrodisiac. Meanness and excess are turn-offs.

Other turn-offs include drunkenness and over-eating, whether it is the man or the woman who over-indulges. The greatest turn-ons are often the ones we create ourselves: the talking over of past memories and shared hopes; doing something that both people love; a touch that shows you care; taking time to listen. Very simple, very ordinary, but they work.

Clothes To Be Dressed In

♂ AT THAT TIME of adolescence when I was engaged in the sorts of activities that were later dignified in the film *Dead Poets Society*, one snippet of verse fixed in my mind the sexuality of clothes for ever. In 1648, Robert Herrick wrote:

"Whenas in silks my Julia goes
Then, then (methinks) how sweetly flows
That liquefaction of her clothes."
(UPON JULIA'S CLOTHES, 1648)

At much the same time a piece about stockings appeared in one of the Sunday newspapers. It was in the form of a lament about the limitations of tights which had made their appearance not long before. There were two characteristics of stockings whose passing the writer, a woman, mourned. The first was that a stocking with a seam always conveyed the message that a line led somewhere. In my adolescent sexual fervor that seemed the most licentious thought imaginable. The same adolescent has enjoyed it for forty years.

The second was that she had always thought there was a way of improving the design of a stocking top. What intrigue it could have, she thought, if a Braille message could be fashioned into it. Again my adolescent fantasy went wild. Stocking tops were very much forbidden fruit, and full of allure. Messages in Braille would have made some rudimentary language instruction for the fingertips very necessary indeed.

Indeed, to a great degree the special quality of clothes is connected to the sensation of touch. Sight will intrigue, as Herrick's verse implies, but touch builds the excitement.

Clothes are in one respect a substitute for the surface of the skin and are sources of sensation in their own right. But most especially clothes act as barriers to be breached, boundaries to be crossed. They will yield more or less easily depending on the circumstance.

We understand the nature of such boundaries because of the delicately different sensations that our body signals to us in response to another's touch. A hand slipped inside a shirt or bathrobe to caress a chest, or inside a dress to cradle a breast, is quite differently experienced from the hand that strokes a bare chest or breast. Clothes protect. However welcome touch inside them is, the body knows that protection is in place. When the protective boundary is crossed – and when that crossing is welcome – the body sends a little frisson of excitement that frequently isn't experienced when the body is quite naked and exposed to the touch.

Explore these fine differences of sensation. Becoming aware of them adds great enjoyment and delight to lovemaking. Pause at the barriers. Extend the boundaries. See them not so much as hurdles to be jumped in going for the goal of sex, but as sources of satisfaction in themselves. Don't lose awareness of them just because a relationship or a body is familiar. Value them. Know them. Enjoy them.

LEFT: High heels make the legs and ankles taut, throwing a woman's body forward. Elegant or outrageously sexy, her unsteadiness also expresses vulnerability.

♀ THERE IS A SADNESS in women spending so much time and money on clothes. We have been persuaded that if only we can look good enough, our lives will somehow magically be transformed. Hooked at an early age, as much by our mothers as by men, we believe that what we look like is who we are.

Interestingly when women spend time on their own or with other women, their clothes become looser, warmer; of mixed colours and mixed materials. We become less concerned with how we look and more concerned with how we feel. Sexuality switches, no longer dependent on how we think we look, to something more internal.

Most of us live in cultures where the female form is seen in a particular way. We dress with an awareness of "bits" of ourselves – breasts, legs, waists, buttocks, thighs. If we are proud of our bodies we may wear clothes that fit closely. We hide the bits of which we are ashamed under loose-fitting and drab clothes.

While we have taken in the idea that we have strong and weak points (i.e. firm thighs, tight abs), we also know that our own sexuality is not broken down by specific areas. We feel sexiest when we are fully aware of our whole body and our clothes reflect that. Whether walking down a hallway or running on the beach, it is the vibrancy of skin and freedom of limbs that feels exciting. In countries where we do not have to hide from the elements, we might wear shorts, leggings, flowing skirts, short skirts that leave the legs free, and tops which move with

Nightwear for lovemaking: not for keeping warm in, nor for cuddling up with a good book.

The most alluring clothes combine formality with the possibility of intimacy – treats to be offered only to the chosen lover.

RIGHT: What jeans, a shirt and a belt really mean – tight buttocks and thighs, and male sensuality. Clothes for men who like being watched by women.

our breasts. Standing or sitting, walking or talking, a woman comfortable in her own skin – big or small – is a sexy woman.

The man who appreciates his looks is as attractive to women as he is to other men. Women love to look at men who feel attractive. Some heterosexual men seem to want to make a statement about heterosexuality by "dressing down," as though it would compromise their maleness to wear clothes of character, color or gloss.

Women often do not care much about a man's body shape. We care about the way he walks and carries himself in the world. The man we stop and look at is the one who has his feet on the ground, his head in the air and bears his own bodyweight with confidence. Only then do we notice his clothes.

Clothes To Be Undressed In

ABOVE: Tantalisingly, underwear separates covered and uncovered flesh, keeping private the most intimate aspects of the body. Fastenings make for seductive delays.

WE HAVE come a long way since 18th century clergymen sermonized against the wickedness of women wearing knickers at all. Better the 17th century poet, Robert Herrick, who wrote: "A sweet disorder in the dress/Kindles in clothes a wantonness."

Underwear is especially the boundary between clothes and nakedness. No better place then for perfect order which hints at the possibility of disorder to come. This is exactly what the most erotic underwear does – it hides, reveals, and makes promises all at the same time.

Men's underwear, alas, has not received the same attention to erotic detail in its design as has women's – though with recent attempts to bring back the codpiece, perhaps it will. In the 20th century it is only quite recently that men have taken as much interest in scents and fashion as they now do, taking their lead from women. Perhaps male underwear will be the next fashion breakthrough.

But then again, perhaps it is in the different nature of male and female that women are not so interested in unwrapping men as men are in unwrapping women. Consequently, concerns about the packaging are different. Men's is utilitarian, with a minor interest in appearance; women's is much more involved with appearance, sometimes at the price of comfort.

It seems to be that women have a stronger visual impact on men than men do on women. Women set out to enhance their visual appeal. Covering and un-covering various aspects of the female body is the continuing work of fashion, but it services a deep underlying need for men to be attracted to the female form, and for women to want to attract them.

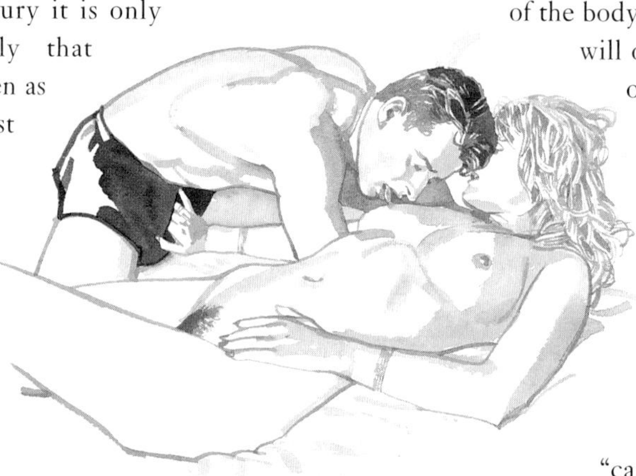

ABOVE: The only smart and sexy underwear for men – black or navy shorts. Her nakedness accentuates his semblance of control in remaining relatively unexposed.

IT IS HARD for a woman to separate out what is truly erotic for herself and what might be erotic for a man. Her sense of what is feminine derives almost entirely from commercialized images of madonna and whore. It is the whore-image which evokes sex, not the girl-next-door to or the prospective mother.

Men are turned on by women's underwear in a way that few women understand, but most accommodate. Of course it is exciting to be able to seduce him with what she wears, but women are amused and bewildered by an obsession with bras, stockings and garters. While men like it trailed seductively over the floor, women think more of the laundry basket. Women do not exhibit an equivalent interest in men's underwear, although the young are more conscious of the male body than ever before.

The aim of sexy underwear is to accentuate particular areas of the body. Women buy it to excite a man, but they will only wear garments which appeal to their own vanity. No amount of pleading from a man will induce a woman to buy garters if she cannot bear the look of her own thighs or stomach.

Underwear shops offer permutations on the bad-girl theme, but little more. They have wired and unwired bras (wired ones push up the breasts); "panties" or "thongs" (bikini or G-strings); "teddies" or "camisoles" (a bra-corset which fastens at the crotch, or short silky vest); tights or stockings from very fine texture to opaque; garter belts or corsets (corsets tighten the waist and include suspenders); slips, petticoats and, finally, vests and large panties. It is the latter which are now kept hidden behind the counter.

While dressing up satisfies exhibitionist tendencies, underwear can also be exciting if only one person wears it while the other remains fully clothed, or goes naked. There is a sexual frisson in the power-play of covered, and exposed, bodies. In addition, the feel of certain materials like silk or satin add sensuality to the experience, even if most of us have to make do with nylon. Secretly, though, some women keep buying plain cotton underwear for themselves.

LEFT: All clothing associated with being undressed can acquire erotic possibilities – even a loose-fitting night gown. Being naked and warm in bathrobes is a delight for the body and a simple prelude to sex.

RIGHT: White corset and suspenders mix purity and experience: her elaborate underwear is noticeable while his shiny briefs barely register.

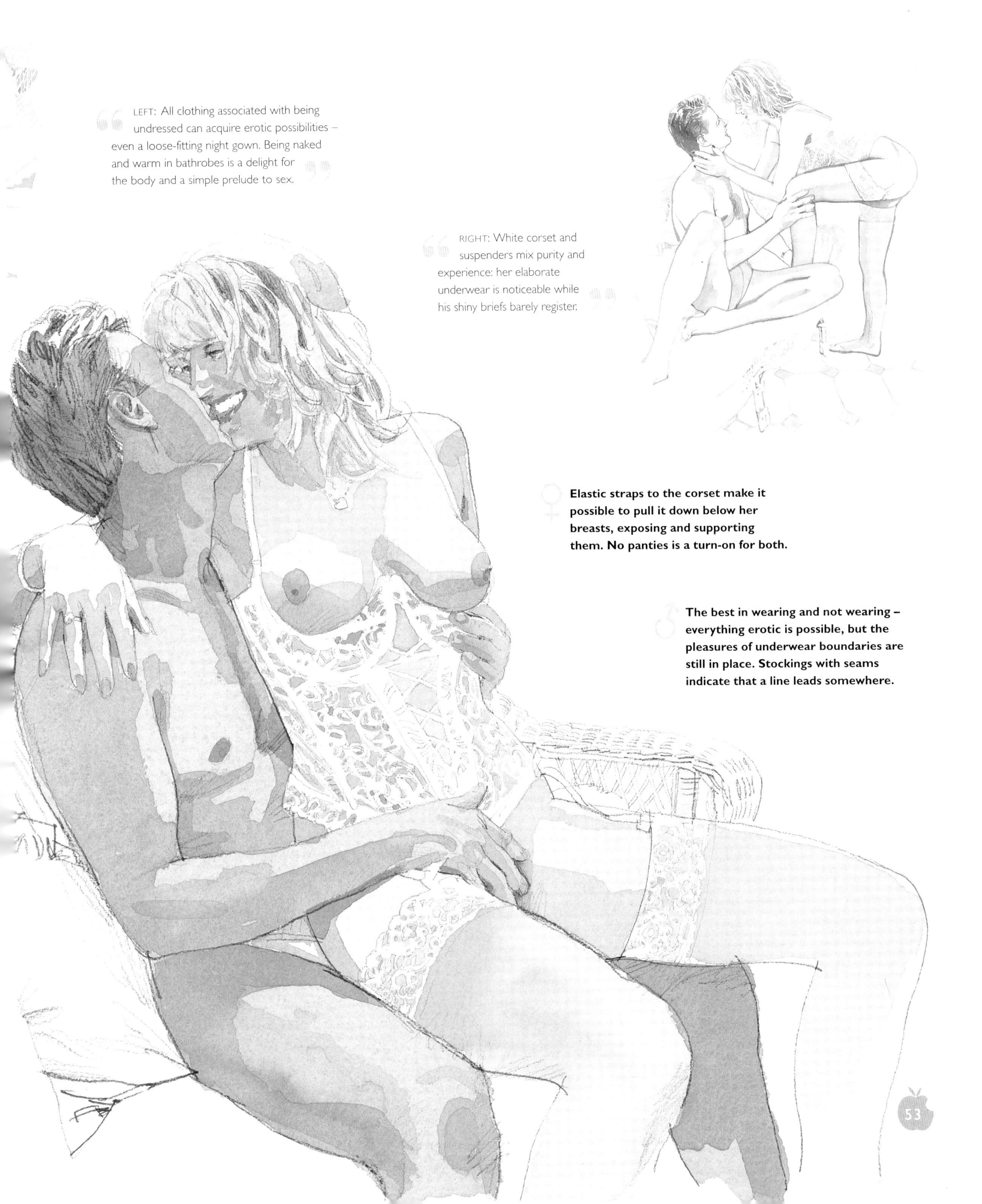

Elastic straps to the corset make it possible to pull it down below her breasts, exposing and supporting them. No panties is a turn-on for both.

The best in wearing and not wearing – everything erotic is possible, but the pleasures of underwear boundaries are still in place. Stockings with seams indicate that a line leads somewhere.

Breasts and Nipples

BREASTS AND NIPPLES can be full of sensation or have little feeling in them. If a woman is excited she is more likely to push out her breasts and arch her back, so that the breasts swell more. Many women do not touch their own breasts in a sexual way, so they have to learn – along with the man – what turns her on, otherwise there is a tendency to skip over this part of a woman's body and miss the enjoyment they can bring.

Breasts respond to all sorts of touching – soft, hard, biting, sucking, stroking – and the nipples can be squeezed quite firmly because their pleasure is in the zone between excitement and pain. Getting that pressure right can be difficult to convey to the man because he has no physical equivalent on his own body, and because his hands are often hard and large in comparison with the tenderness of breasts. The woman can help him by showing him with her own hands what she needs, and by moaning appreciatively when he gets it right. The intensity of pleasure from nipple-sensations is sometimes combined with what feels like a chemical rush from nipple to vagina.

Giving him pleasure back, and taking part in the breast-sucking too, means that she might also want to suck his nipples and stroke his chest. Some men seem to find that erotically exciting, and others not. Using breasts as a pretend vagina for a man's penis is another way of giving to him – the sensation being more visual than physical for the woman. It's also a good way of him climaxing if there's reason for non-penetrative sex, or just because it's exciting to do something different.

The best way for breasts to be stimulated is to take time with them. One way is to tease – for the man to use a tongue or wet finger in circular movements around the breast working in towards the nipple. If he leaves the nipple untouched whilst caressing and teasing the fullness of the breast, the woman is likely to be very excited.

“LEFT: Sitting still and taking a pause during lovemaking to stimulate a woman's breasts can be important for his ejaculatory control, and for her increase in arousal.”

“BELOW: This picture shows how hands and mouth can be used simultaneously on a woman's breasts, giving contrasting sensations of firm hands and light tongue.”

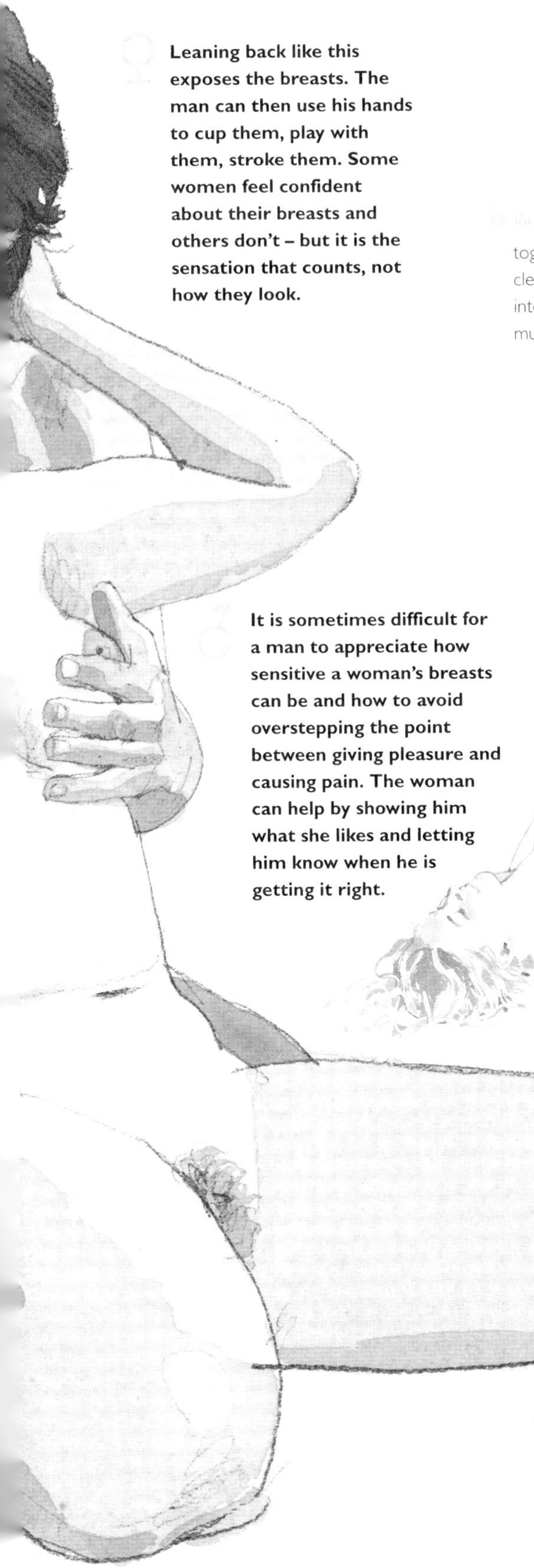

Leaning back like this exposes the breasts. The man can then use his hands to cup them, play with them, stroke them. Some women feel confident about their breasts and others don't – but it is the sensation that counts, not how they look.

BELOW: If the woman squeezes her breasts together, this can make a firm cleavage for the penis to thrust into, and she's very much in control.

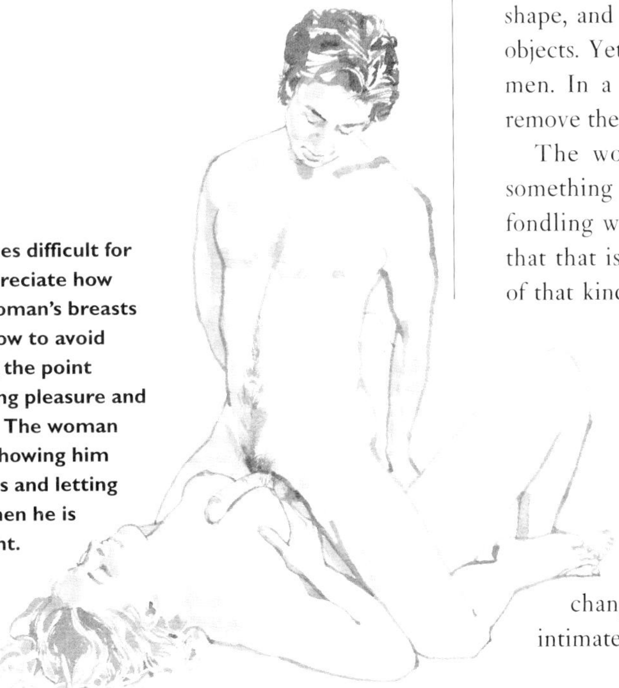

It is sometimes difficult for a man to appreciate how sensitive a woman's breasts can be and how to avoid overstepping the point between giving pleasure and causing pain. The woman can help by showing him what she likes and letting him know when he is getting it right.

NOTHING QUITE expresses the mystery of being a woman so much as her breasts. To a man they are so privately parts of her and yet so publicly an aspect of her shape and attractiveness. There is no aspect of a man's body which has similar qualities of being a source of nourishment, delight, comfort and fascination all at the same time.

We are attached to these beautiful physical features from the first day of our lives, both for feeding, and for safety. As a grown up, one of the most satisfying things men can ever do is learn how to enjoy them fully and bring that pleasure to our partner too.

Women hate being defined for men by their breast size and shape, and quite rightly too. To do so turns women into sexual objects. Yet women's breasts are sources of endless attraction to men. In a relationship, the pleasure that they give men can remove the social anxieties that so many women have about them.

The worst thing is to think of your partner's breasts as something to do with "foreplay." It implies that a bit of breast-fondling will somehow switch a woman on to intercourse, and that that is always the goal of making love. The predictability of that kind of approach is a major sexual turn-off.

Enjoy finding out about the sensitivity of breasts. Light holding can become stroking. Light stroking can become very intense holding. Pressure is good. See how they change shape as your partner's sexual arousal increases. Learn how the nipple will become erect at one stage, and then seem to disappear as the breast itself becomes fuller in shape. Look at the way the dark area surrounding the nipple changes color and enlarges. The breasts send all kinds of intimate signals to a lover who really understands them.

RIGHT: The woman can be both tender and demanding in her sucking and biting of his nipples. He's showing her that he's responding and allowing himself to be the receiver in this position.

Massage

SEXUAL MASSAGE is about making contact with the surface of skin lubricated with a scented oil or cream, and focusing on the pleasure of the person who is being massaged.

Be the masseur. Pour scented oil into the palm of a hand, and make your hands slippery with it. Explore your partner's body in a rhythmic and systematic way with your finger tips and the whole of your hands without the urgency of wanting intercourse. Your partner can luxuriate in having nothing to do but receive the sensory pleasures you give.

Sexual massage should not be confused with therapeutic massage or anything designed to affect deeper muscle structures. Sexual massage is centred only on the pleasure of sensation from the skin's surface.

Make sure the room is warm. Be naked yourself. Sexual massage is deliberately designed to create sensation that arouses but does not necessarily signal intercourse. If you do become aroused and erect, enjoy it. If your partner wants you to massage her to climax, get there gradually.

Start on your partner's back. Let her feel the rhythm of your hands up and down her spine, around the curves of her buttocks and hips, and between her legs. Or start with the soles of her feet and her toes. Gradually work up her legs, her inner thighs, around the curves and crevices of her behind. Stroke her spine and smooth the palms of your hands along her body to her neck and shoulders.

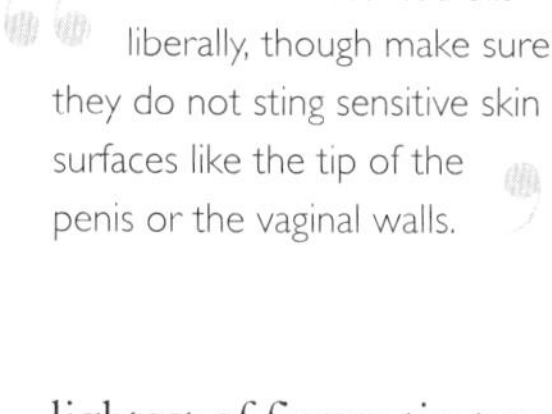

ABOVE: Use scented oils liberally, though make sure they do not sting sensitive skin surfaces like the tip of the penis or the vaginal walls.

Turn her over. Sit with your back against the bed and cradle her head in your lap. Smooth all the muscles of her face with the lightest of finger-tip touching. Cup her breasts in your hands, and stroke them for her pleasure. If she wants you to massage her clitoris especially, do it for her not for yourself. Work out the rhythms she really wants. Let her take your fingers and use them as her own while she teaches you what suits her mood.

Sexual massage can be surprisingly exhausting – not from the physical effort, but because of the mix of arousal and relaxation it can create. End your massage session cuddled closely together.

LEFT: We often hold tension in the lower back and shoulders. A back massage is a therapeutic and sensual way of caring for each other.

IT'S AMAZING how some people are turned off by the idea of massage. It must be one of the few experiences that is better in reality than fantasy. Having the person you love stroke and massage your body is truly exhilarating.

Lying naked on a sheet, prone under someone else's hands, is certainly exposing. It requires a lot of trust. At its best, it involves an exchange of energy between one person and another which results in deep sensual relaxation and tenderness on both sides.

It is not necessary to be highly skilled at massage for it to work well. There just has to be willingness to try, and an understanding of the basics. Be sure your hands are warm before you touch another person's naked skin. Oil is essential. Take time to go slowly, whether your hand movements are large and sweeping, small and circular, lightly tapping or powerfully kneading. Go gently around bones (and particularly anywhere near the spine), smoothly on skin, deeply into muscle. What you do to one side of the body, do to the other – otherwise it feels lop-sided. Minimize talking, except to communicate about touch.

Massage can lead to sex, if both people want that. Massage can also substitute for sex. Massage is a pleasure in its own right. Lovers who enjoy it will spend a whole evening massaging one another in front of a fire or on a bed, whether or not sex is wanted too.

RIGHT: Massaging around the genitals, but deliberately avoiding them, can be more arousing than touching them. The mind focuses on those parts of the body that are untouched, leaving them sensitized to the point of frustration and excitement.

Women are often a little afraid of the strangeness of the male body: it is harder, thicker, hairy and unfamiliar to the touch. Giving a man a massage is a good way for a woman to relax with his body.

It is also good for women to be massaged by a man. Women sometimes find it hard not to be in control. A massage demands that she gives in, gives up, and allows herself to take and receive.

Most women do not know their bodies very well. We have little experience of sensual touching. Muscles we did not know we had protest under pressure. Skin feels vibrant. Tenderness, gratitude, and love grow out of sensitive, generous touching. As the body lets go into deep sensual relaxation, our minds open up to images and reverie, bringing us closer to our lover and ourselves.

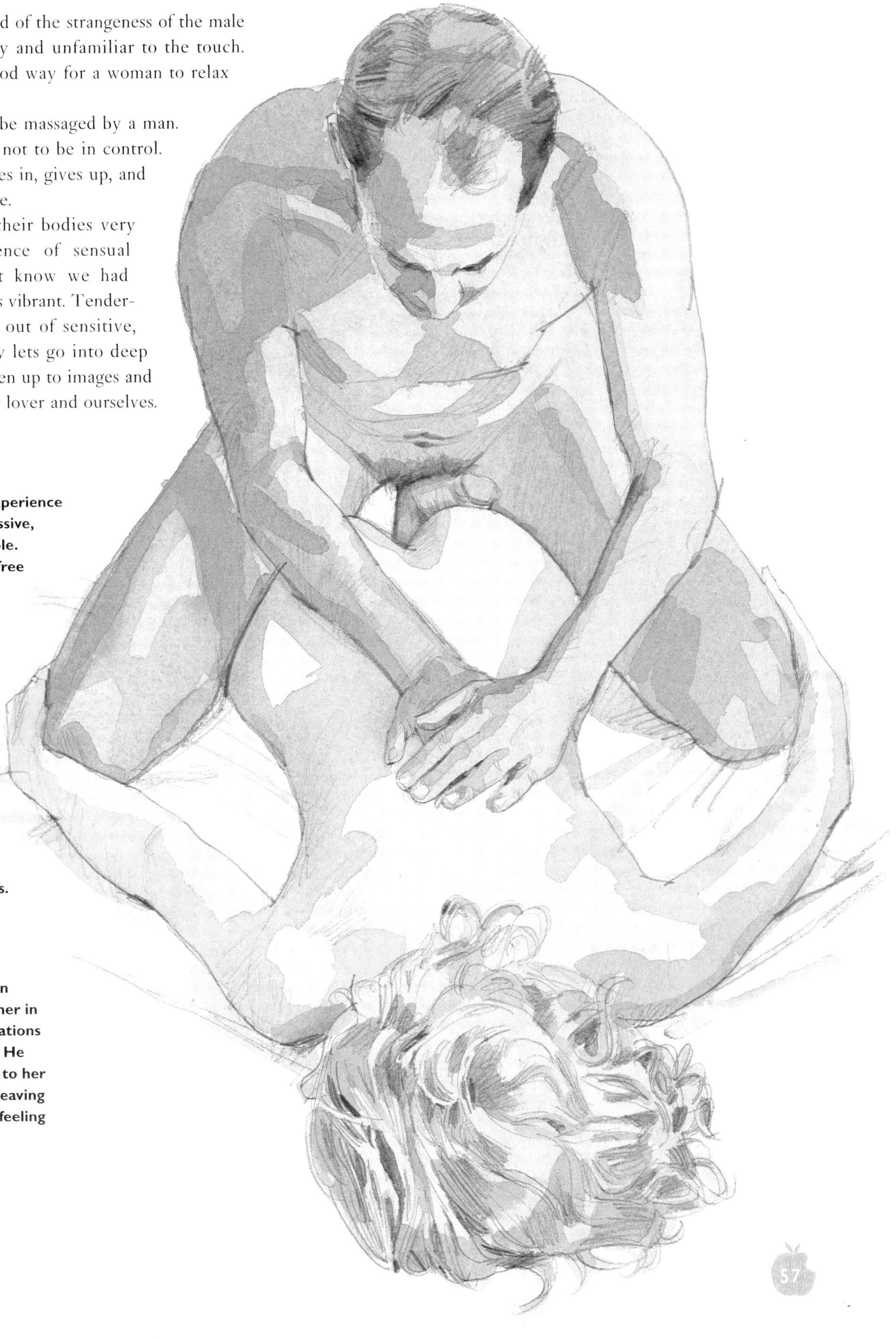

Massage allows a more separate experience than sex, one person taking the passive, while the other takes the active, role. He has positioned himself to have free access to her whole back and buttocks and she is free to absorb herself in sensation. Unexpressed emotion is stored in our bodies, so massage sometimes arouses feelings we did not know we had – from tenderness to rage, tearfulness and joy. The body does not forget things, and with deep relaxation and the power of touch, powerful memories can return.The release of these feelings is healthy, and often leaves a feeling of peace afterwards.

Here is the classic massage position for lovers – one on top, and the other in contact erotically with all the sensations that hands on bodies can produce. He will work gradually down her back to her buttocks, her calves and her feet, leaving the whole of the back of her body feeling closely in touch with him.

Men's Fingers, Women's Bodies

THE FIRST touch of his fingers on her vulva is a moment worth leading up to, again and again. He can feel underneath her clothes to stroke the entrance to her vagina; he can use his whole hand on top of underwear to vibrate the vulval area; he can reach down under the top of her panties to stroke pubic hair and gently caress around her clitoris.

With panties off, he can see her pubic hair and beneath it, two folds of darkish fleshy skin which hang together. If he parts these lips, he can see the clitoris like a small protrusion at the top, a tiny hole for the urethra below that, and further down a triangle of flesh over the vaginal opening – not a gaping hole as is often imagined – but just the glimpse of an entrance. An inch or so below that is the anus. In looking at her, her lover may be seeing more than she has ever seen of herself. Women cannot see their genitals just by looking downwards, and it is only relatively recently that we have been brave enough to hold a mirror between our legs and look.

Clitoral and vaginal sensations are different. The very lightest stroking around the clitoris, or the effect of a finely vibrating hand over the pubic bone, can cause the most exquisite pleasure. It may take a while to locate an exact point of arousal, or just the right speed of movement but – with help from her – the effect of his touch can be electrifying.

At the entrance to the vagina, and for an inch inside it, she feels other sensations – more like deep heat, throbbing and pulsing – than the electrification of the clitoris. As he gently circles the rim of the vagina, she feels herself opening up and wanting more pressure, or a finger or two inside her.

These genital sensations come and go as a woman's focus changes with excitement. This can be hard for a man to follow as there are few external changes he can see. She must communicate well, and not leave responsibility for her arousal solely with her lover.

"LEFT: Direct touch on the unaroused clitoris can cause sharp pain. She lets him know that the movements of his moistened fingers increase her excitement, and she pushes her pelvis forward for more pressure."

He knows that a sharp fingernail can graze her, and that genital sensations are heightened by lubrication. He holds her thighs apart while lightly brushing over the pubic bone. She communicates what she enjoys specifically.

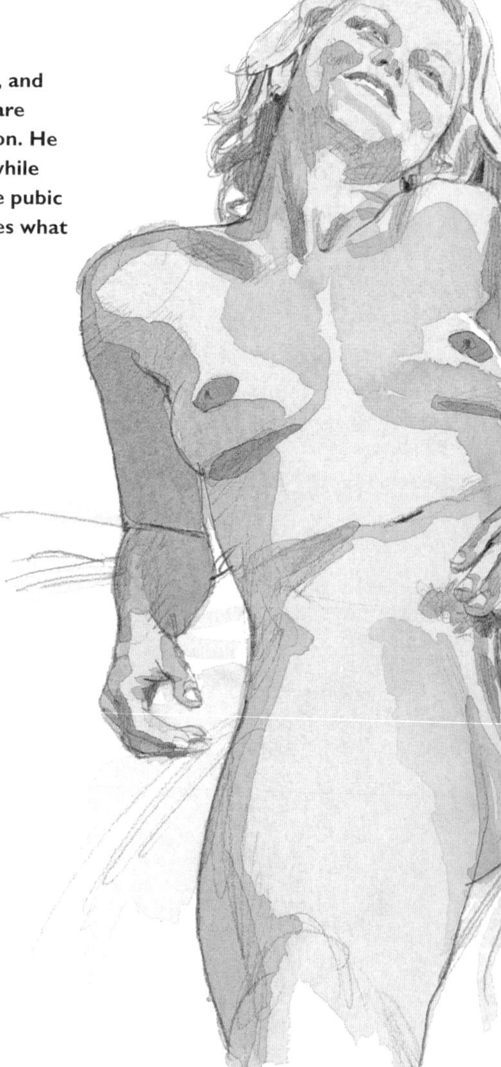

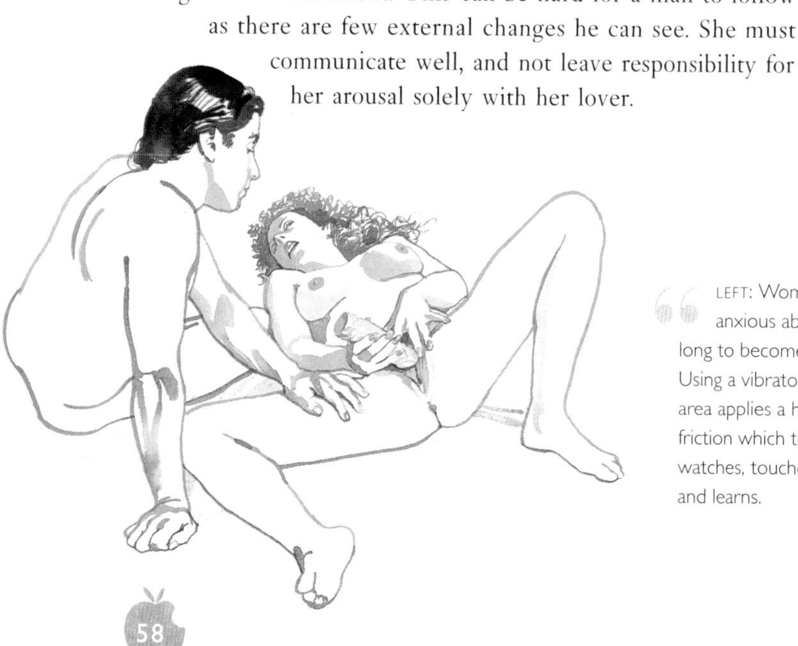

"LEFT: Women can feel anxious about taking too long to become genitally aroused. Using a vibrator over the clitoral area applies a high speed, delicate friction which turns her on. He watches, touches and learns."

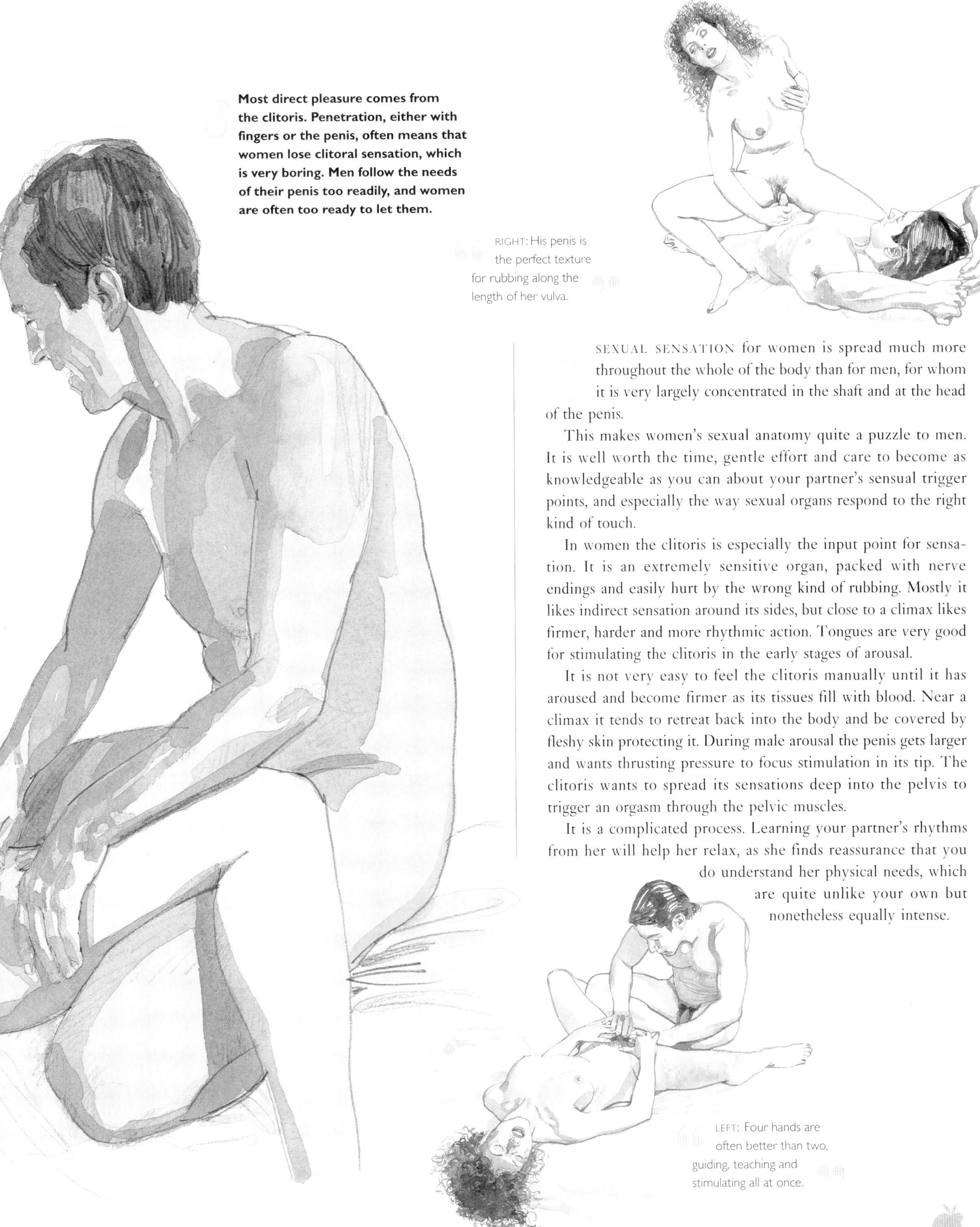

Most direct pleasure comes from the clitoris. Penetration, either with fingers or the penis, often means that women lose clitoral sensation, which is very boring. Men follow the needs of their penis too readily, and women are often too ready to let them.

RIGHT: His penis is the perfect texture for rubbing along the length of her vulva.

SEXUAL SENSATION for women is spread much more throughout the whole of the body than for men, for whom it is very largely concentrated in the shaft and at the head of the penis.

This makes women's sexual anatomy quite a puzzle to men. It is well worth the time, gentle effort and care to become as knowledgeable as you can about your partner's sensual trigger points, and especially the way sexual organs respond to the right kind of touch.

In women the clitoris is especially the input point for sensation. It is an extremely sensitive organ, packed with nerve endings and easily hurt by the wrong kind of rubbing. Mostly it likes indirect sensation around its sides, but close to a climax likes firmer, harder and more rhythmic action. Tongues are very good for stimulating the clitoris in the early stages of arousal.

It is not very easy to feel the clitoris manually until it has aroused and become firmer as its tissues fill with blood. Near a climax it tends to retreat back into the body and be covered by fleshy skin protecting it. During male arousal the penis gets larger and wants thrusting pressure to focus stimulation in its tip. The clitoris wants to spread its sensations deep into the pelvis to trigger an orgasm through the pelvic muscles.

It is a complicated process. Learning your partner's rhythms from her will help her relax, as she finds reassurance that you do understand her physical needs, which are quite unlike your own but nonetheless equally intense.

LEFT: Four hands are often better than two, guiding, teaching and stimulating all at once.

Women's Fingers, Men's Bodies

ERECTIONS ARE very obvious, hard, insistent aspects of the male anatomy, designed for thrusting with sensation focused in the tip of the penis. That's the official story, anyway.

Try thinking of your erection much more as a sensitive, exploratory, inquisitive, alert guest in the lubricated sheath of a warm and welcoming vagina.

Then take that thought into penile exploration, and let your partner take control. Map out with her where the sensations are, how they are different at various points of the shaft, and what kinds of pressure and touch you most enjoy at various stages of arousal. Don't forget the sensations in your scrotum – especially as you get aroused and testicles are pulled up into your body and the scrotal skin loses its normal slackness.

Around the head of the shaft – the glans – sensations are very variable. The underside is especially sensitive to stroking. The coronal ridge, on the other hand, which is where the glans joins the main skin-covered body of the shaft, can become extremely sensitive to touch in the later stages of arousal so that pleasure and pain there are closely allied. At this stage the coronal ridge sensations are probably much like those of the clitoris when it is fully aroused. Both need lots of lubrication for the best sensations to occur.

ABOVE: With plenty of lubricating cream around, try running one hand down the shaft immediately followed by another. It feels like continuous penetration.

In an unaroused state, the penis has very little immediate sensation. It responds to pressure and contact – which are the first signals it might be touching something interesting like a partner's pubic bone. But once blood starts flowing into it and erection enlarges the skin surfaces, a positive feedback loop forms so that it seeks further stimulation to become even more erect.

Despite its erectile size and strength, the penis is vulnerable to psychological doubts about its capacity to perform. Worries, anxieties, feeling devalued, poor self-image can all play their part in deadening an erection, despite the most favorable conditions of a willing and sympathetic partner. Under these circumstances a negative feedback loop can occur. The more you try to get an erection, the more resistance there is to one happening. Once this has occurred, doubts set in for the next time.

If ever you sense an erection is unwilling to appear when you want one, stop trying. Trying harder is seriously counter-productive. Just back off. Relax. Come back to it some other time.

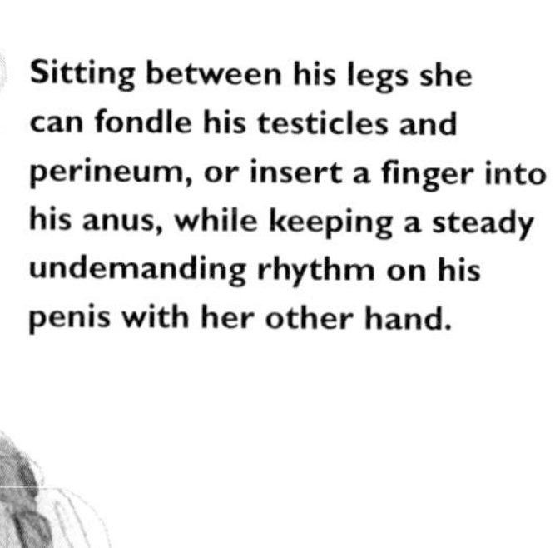

Sitting between his legs she can fondle his testicles and perineum, or insert a finger into his anus, while keeping a steady undemanding rhythm on his penis with her other hand.

ABOVE: Stroking the shaft, up and down, creates the sensation most like insertion. Pulling down too hard can hurt. Women complain of aching wrists too.

Sensation right at the base of the penis, especially gentle squeezing, helps the penis feel full and strongly erect.

MANY WOMEN have to learn to love a man's penis. It is hard to see his penis as a gift, his erection as splendid, if a woman has had bad experiences in the past. This is usually manageable over time.

What is not manageable is coercion. A woman will find it unwelcome if a man asks her to masturbate him when she has indicated she does not want to make love. She need not make amends for her preferences or feelings.

When we do want to hold a man's penis, it might be a playful tease, a gift to him, or a mutual exploration of sensation. What is a surprise to women is the instant arousability of the penis and its vulnerability. Even a fully erect penis, of whatever size, is not huge compared to the size of a man's body. It is sensitive, pliable and soft to touch even when erect. Potency is in the mind rather than the flesh. What then do women do with this awareness?

We tease. We go slowly over his well-lubricated shaft when he is desperate to go faster. We take our hands away just when he is on the brink of orgasm. We make him ejaculate in our hands when he is wanting intercourse. We tell him fantasies so that he loses control. And we giggle.

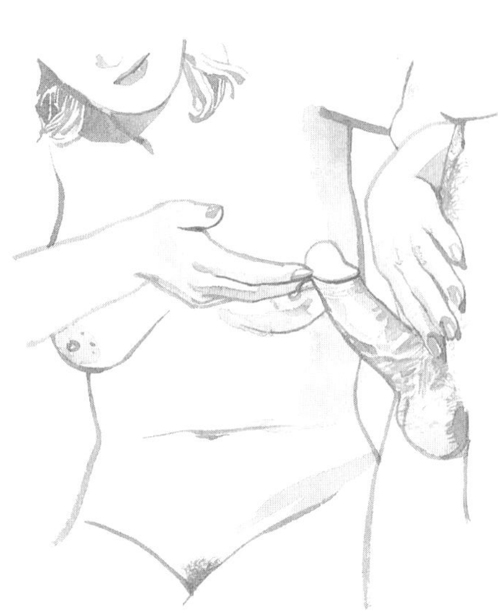

ABOVE: She touches his glans with great care, only applying pressure below the coronal ridge.

We also feel tenderness. When we hold his penis in our hands we are holding him. He and it become precious. The effect of our fingers, with his guidance, is visible and rewarding. It is lovely to see him submit and succumb, or to feel him thrusting into our hands, as though we partly own his penis and have power over him. In the moment of his ejaculation, his penis becomes his own again, wherever the semen has been shed. This is both a gift and a loss to us. His flaccid penis lets us know that his body and his arousal are his own again.

Men's Mouths, Women's Bodies

THERE IS often something to be overcome in tasting another person's genitals and being tasted. Sanitized and civilized out of behavior that is too animal-like, undignified or – worse still – "dirty," women have to fight anxiety and incipient shame. We wash so as not to offend, but are more deeply reassured when we sense that a man really wants to know every inch of our body because he loves the whole of us – not just the sanitized parts. Once we have made the switch from inhibition to something more carnal, ordinary, sensual, and neither disease nor rejection nor shame ensues, we become more able to feel the quite extraordinary and exquisite sensations of his mouth on our genitals.

More difficult for her to manage, but this can be a turn-on for both; she sits over his face so that her vulva is in direct contact with his mouth.

She lies down and opens her legs; he licks her crotch. She flinches, sighs, shudders. He continues. She feels the wetness and softness of his tongue and begins to relax. This is not a feeling she could induce in herself. He takes his time exploring her, noticing her reactions. She relaxes more and begins to feel excitement in her clitoris. She puts a hand to his head and pulls him in further, wanting him to eat and slobber, suck and brush all the areas or the vulva.

ABOVE: A sight a woman is unlikely to see properly for herself is one of the special gifts of cunnilingus, and the reward is tongue-probing.

Whether we kneel over his face or lie down, we are aroused by his saliva making us really wet, little tugs at the outer lips, light brushing (with or without a beard) of closed lips over the clitoris, licks and flicks at the vagina and clitoris with his tongue. If he moves between clitoris and vagina, he can tease both into excitement and then use a finger on one area and a tongue in the other. If she has washed and he is adventurous, he licks around the outside of her anus. As she focuses on the build-up of sensation, it changes of its own accord to the swell and rush that precedes the sudden, pounding discharge of the clitoral orgasm. Sometimes she might pull his head up towards her so she can kiss his mouth, and taste herself on his lips.

Here you are at the absolute point of the triangle of her pubic hair and the separating of her legs. Wonderful!

Men often want to penetrate a woman immediately after licking her to orgasm, when her body needs resolution and her mind needs time to reconnect with him. Although we are capable of more than one orgasm it does not mean that women have no need to rest. The pleasure of oral sex is that it is a gift and like any other gift, it sometimes needs time to enjoy.

Women's capacity for external and internal genital excitement is underscored by oral sex, each area of the vulva being experienced separately and simultaneously. Clitoral and vaginal sensations differ. Both feel satisfying, frustrating, intoxicating. Both feel necessary and different. Sensitivity to arousal in either area changes with each sexual experience, and develops throughout her life.

ABOVE: Anus and vagina are available for probing. The vaginal and anal rims respond to licking and gentle penetration of the tongue.

CUNNILINGUS IS AN awkward word for an act that is one of the most intimate that sex together offers. From the Latin it means, literally, "cunt tonguing," and that's not a bad description.

The wet warm softness of a tongue around the labia, clitoris and entrance to the vagina is quite unlike any other sensation you can give your partner. An erection usually wants to push its way inside. A finger can be too insistent or rub too hard. A tongue is simply moist, warm and exploratory – even tickly, which can be quite distracting.

As with fellatio, sight, taste, smell and touch are directly involved with your partner's sexual organs. You can look at them much more directly than ever she can herself. The taste and smells of a warm, clean, excited body, with the damp fur of pubic hair, swelling vaginal lips and glistening clitoris are all there for your tongue and lips and eyes and nose. What a gift! The smooth skin of inner thighs, usually unseen and certainly untouched except for sexual pleasure, contrasts with the slight roughness of the pubic hair which surrounds the beauty that lies between a woman's legs.

Many women are themselves uncertain how to feel about their vaginal area, and whether or not the man in their life *really* likes that part of their body. Nothing is more unkind than to convey to your partner that this most private aspect of herself is unpleasant or unacceptable when, at the same time, you want her sexually. If as a man you have any doubts about loving every aspect of her sexual body, sort out your own feelings and get your attitude straight. If you cannot love every aspect of her, you cannot really love her. And if you cannot really love her, then a lot of the deepest pleasures that come from sex will be ones you never really know.

Sucking gently at the vaginal lips, the entrance to the vagina and the clitoris is also part of having your lips and her labia close together. Never *blow* into the vagina, though. It can cause air to be trapped in her body, and in extreme cases can cause death.

The best thing about cunnilingus is finding out what she most wants – the kind of rhythm in stroking with your tongue, for instance; and whether a firmed-up tip of the tongue or its wider blade is best; and exactly where the best sensations are. If you can learn all these things for her, she will know for certain that she is loved and wanted and can then respond totally in kind.

BELOW: Totally engaged with lips in contact with each other's most private bodily aspects, managing to explore as well as be explored, makes this mutual experience one of the most tantalizing in sexual play.

Women's Mouths, Men's Bodies

♂ LET YOUR partner take control. Give yourself over completely to total concentration on the sensations she can create. Her mouth has all the softness, warmth, firmness and slipperiness of the most excited vagina. Let her use it on you. Her tongue brings into play very specific points of sensation. Follow them as her tongue touches upon them.

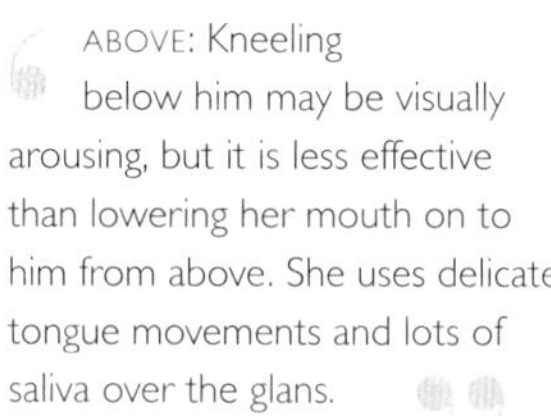

ABOVE: Kneeling below him may be visually arousing, but it is less effective than lowering her mouth on to him from above. She uses delicate tongue movements and lots of saliva over the glans.

Here you are, having nothing at all to do but relax into the most exquisite sensations. A penis inside a vagina hunts and thrusts for specific feeling. Inside a mouth, no action is required. With firm lips wrapped around it, or a tongue putting soft pressure across the tight surfaces of your erection, no thrusting is necessary. Indeed, thrusting might be quite unpleasant for your partner and cause her to gag if your erection presses against the back of her throat. Never hold her head when she has your penis in her mouth, in case you are tempted to press your penis deeper into her mouth than she wishes. Rather, learn in this position to give over control completely.

Giving over control takes the responsibility for creating sensation away from you entirely, and gives it to your partner. Instead of your penis being part of you that enters her, it can start to be something which she can stimulate and control how she takes it into herself; and how she uses her lips and tongue around it.

In this fellatio position she can clearly see what she is doing, and feel her body free to move around yours. "Fellatio" means "sucking." The pressure of lips can produce great varieties of sensation, and licking can create even more.

Your partner enjoys the sensations of taste and smell, as well as touch and sight, in the act of taking your penis into her mouth. In some positions her head will lie on your stomach, and she can hear your body's working too. So every sense she has can be involved in fellatio.

It is better not to let teeth touch the highly sensitive skin of the head of the penis. Teeth are sharp, and what feels like gentle pressure to the person nibbling can very easily cause a slight tear in the surface of the skin. The possibility that a bite *could* happen is infinitely more exciting than it taking place.

And what about ejaculating in her mouth? Well, that is for her to decide. It is possible to create the most exquisite sensation of ejaculation imaginable through a woman really wanting to kiss, lick, lip-caress and suck her way to your climax. Equally there is not much worse than forcing your climax into someone's unwilling mouth. In fellatio, it is what *she* feels able to do that counts first of all. When confidence is gained then freedom really starts.

♀ MANY WOMEN do not like the idea of oral sex at first; they do it because they want to please. They share in his enjoyment and gradually find that they like it, both erotically for themselves and as a gift to him. As with any other sexual experience, familiarity and skill changes our attitudes and capacities for sexual experience. This learning to love something is different from the self-abuse that some women feel when they mentally cut off from an act they hate.

We know how much men like oral sex because they tell us so. They fantasize about it, beg us for it and love us for it. To suck and lick a man's genitals is to feel a mixture of incompetence and power. Incompetence because we cannot imagine ourselves having a penis and having it sucked, and power because he wants it so much and is physically vulnerable. We protect him from our teeth, physically by being gentle, and emotionally by not rejecting him. Licking a flaccid penis into life also feels powerful, though a fully erect penis in the mouth can choke us.

ABOVE: Both mouths in touch with the other's genitals at the same time – in French, *soixante-neuf*, and in English, sixty-nine.

The feeling of having something firm to suck must

Here a man gives up control entirely to his partner's enjoyment of his erection. What she does with her lips can create the most exquisite penile sensations a man will ever know.

There is a spot on the underside of the coronal ridge which is particularly sensitive, which her lower lip is touching. She can suck the whole penis easily from this position, using her hand to retract the foreskin and to provide stimulation to the shaft while she concentrates on the glans.

BELOW: Lost entirely in his own fantasies, stimulated by her oral contact with the whole shaft of his penis, she can control what she does while he has a private sensory trip.

meet an infantile need since there is relief in the sucking. Perhaps sucking breasts is like this for men? We have to hold our lips and throats wide apart to allow full penetration, so we are liable to get jaw-ache and neck-ache. The action that seems to work best for him and for us is to corkscrew down over the whole penis, using saliva as lubrication. Holding one hand on the base of his shaft frees the mouth to concentrate on the delicate glans, which is more tender in the uncircumcized penis exposed in full erection than the circumcized.

Licking is easier. We can slobber and kiss him from glans to anus, taking in the testicles on the way. The taste of a penis and testicles is slightly salty, but semen is much saltier, has a sharp after-taste and is a little slimy, making it difficult to swallow. One compromise is to hold his ejaculate in the mouth and then let it run down the sides of the penis.

Sex Alone – Women

WOMEN, WHO carry most of society's shame about sex, have a hard time feeling good about masturbation. Girls masturbate furtively and in isolation. We do not learn until adulthood that it is our own self-knowledge that makes the difference in good sex. Masturbation is good for stress reduction, getting to sleep, relieving menstrual cramps and sexual tension, and for sharing with a partner.

The female body is anatomically designed for masturbation. A relaxed hand rests easily in the crotch, just touching the clitoris. Inserting fingers in the vagina requires some slight contortion. Unless we have a mirror in front of us or are sitting up to look, we masturbate by feel. We are free then to fantasize – while fingers circle, vibrate, stroke across, up and down the labia and clitoris. We moisten the vulva with saliva, vaginal or artificial lubricants. What we feel is the small mound of the clitoris, as near pain as pleasure to touch until fully excited, moist flaps below and then the vaginal opening which can just be penetrated by a finger. Inside we feel its ridges and soft patches, its wetness and heat. We use a mattress or cushion to rub against on our front, or squeeze our thighs together. We might want something penis-shaped in the vagina and something other than hands on the clitoris. We might want to touch breasts, mouth, belly, thighs, buttocks – anywhere – at the same time. The advantage of masturbation is the freedom to choose exactly what works.

Orgasm requires fantasy, friction and focusing inside. A woman's fantasies may be actual events or imaginary happenings that could not be enacted and that she would not want to happen. Her fantasy world is a private world of inner story-telling which changes as her own psyche develops and changes. Women who are frightened by their fantasies could reflect that this is one of the ways we have of working through our least pleasant experiences, and triumphantly enjoying ourselves.

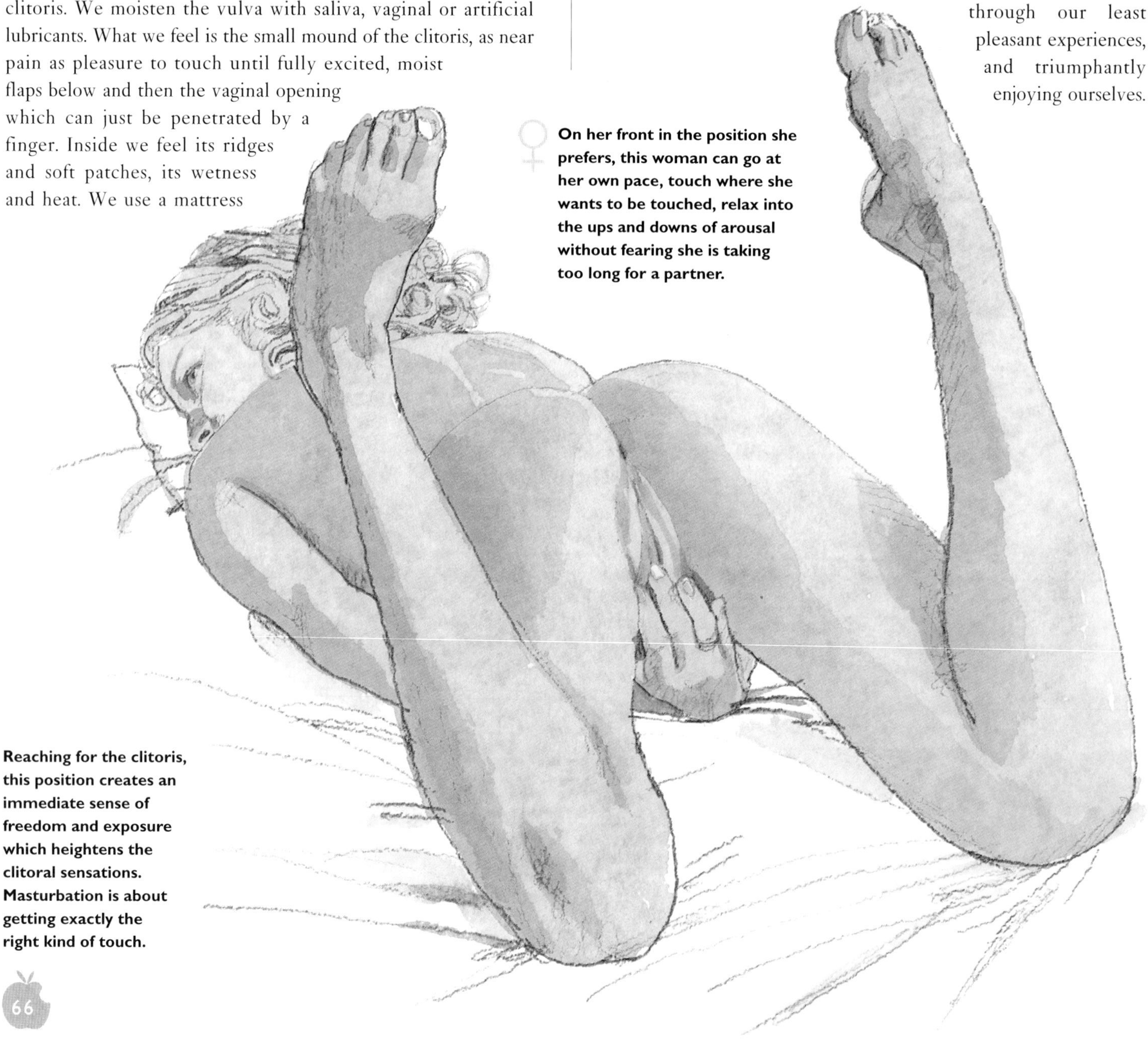

On her front in the position she prefers, this woman can go at her own pace, touch where she wants to be touched, relax into the ups and downs of arousal without fearing she is taking too long for a partner.

Reaching for the clitoris, this position creates an immediate sense of freedom and exposure which heightens the clitoral sensations. Masturbation is about getting exactly the right kind of touch.

ABOVE: Left finger pressure stimulates the clitoral hood, while a right finger explores the vaginal opening. She uses both hands so that each area is simultaneously excited.

MASTURBATION has had a very bad press over the centuries. Even in the medical textbooks of the 1960s it was still associated with insanity. Happily that is now seen for the nonsense it always was – but a lot of misery has been caused over hundreds of years simply because individuals wanted to give themselves pleasure in a way that we now know is not only harmless, but a good way of learning about one's body.

Actually, most of the issues about controlling masturbation have been to do with growing boys. Growing girls were never considered sexual beings in the same way. "Nice girls didn't ....", and that was that.

What really blew the whistle on the fallacy that "masturbation makes you mad" were observations that Alfred Kinsey, the American researcher, made in the 1940s. He showed that, when questioned, over 90 percent of American males admitted to masturbating. Clearly there was some discrepancy between this finding and the general social observation that, contrary to the elementary school fables, most men did not seem to be mad – or have gone blind or have hair on the palms of their hands.

LEFT: This vibrator is penis-shaped, but its function is to provide a soft buzzing sensation externally. She uses it around the vaginal rim with her other hand on the clitoris.

Then William Masters and Virginia Johnson, in the late 1960s, created an understanding that women really were sexual beings in their own right. They had sexual needs of their own but were often terribly ignorant of the sexual functioning of their own bodies (and men knew even less about them). They could learn a lot through self-pleasuring.

So now we have no doubt at all that women really can enjoy their own bodies sexually through masturbating – if they want to. There are a lot of advantages to it, not least for the pleasure of sexual relief, and for finding out how one's body works. That's very useful if at some stage it is to be entrusted to a man. Expert about women's bodies most men are not! Where would they learn anyway, but from a woman who knew?

If your partner feels able to let you watch her and to use your fingers while she masturbates, you will discover things about rhythm, pressure and speed that no book can ever describe. It also creates the most extraordinary sense of sharing.

It also firmly establishes the fact that women are not sexually *dependent* on men for all their sexual satisfactions, but that good sex is about *inter*dependency. Men and women can become more as a couple than they are alone – but they can also be self-sufficient alone.

BELOW: Cucumbers and other vegetables and fruits are safe to use in and around the genital area, provided they are washed.

Sex Alone – Men

THINK OF masturbation as being a bit like having a meal on your own – it is a pity not to make the same sort of occasion of it as you would if entertaining a loved one.

Masturbation does not deserve the condemnation it has suffered over the years. On the positive side, it seems to be a profoundly important way for growing boys to learn about the ejaculatory potential of their bodies, and above all *not* to feel guilty about the enjoyment connected with it.

ABOVE: Men are aroused by pictures, women by stories. He focuses his mind on images which may offend or arouse a partner.

Because masturbation can happen in all sorts of odd or hurried situations, it often gets associated with being secretive and quick. That is a pity, because those feelings of guilt and secrecy can all too easily cloud feelings about sex in general; and then be an inhibiting factor when engaged in sex with a partner. Worst of all, such negative feelings can be transferred *to* one's partner, who has the man's guilt for being sexual dumped upon her. As many women suffer real uncertainty about being sexual, echoing the man's bad feelings too can make sex an awful burden.

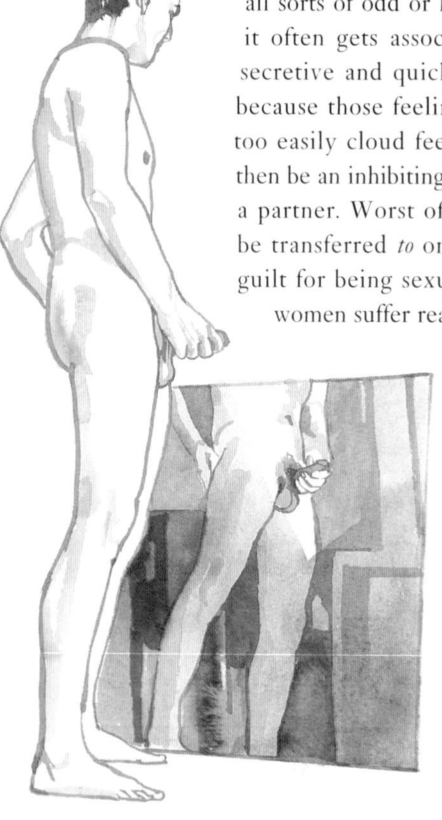

ABOVE: A mirror can let us see reflections of ourselves that we would not otherwise observe. Masturbating this way gives us the view our partner enjoys.

So in learning to masturbate enjoyably, and for pleasure, as well as the relief of sexual tension, there is the prospect of being able to bring positive, enjoyable feelings into shared sex. That can only be a good thing.

Watching oneself in a mirror is a very good way of getting rid of furtive feelings. It also tells you a good deal about how your partner sees you physically when aroused. Developing fantasies while masturbating about what you would enjoy when next with your partner is a good way, on the next occasion, of letting your partner know how your imagination is fixed on her. Sharing masturbation fantasies with your partner gets rid of sexual guilt very enjoyably.

What masturbatory fantasies do you have? Is it fair to use magazines to help them? Some people think that in doing so the women who have posed for the photographs are degraded in some way. When matters of sex are under discussion we all-too-easily find ourselves caught in moral dilemmas without first having worked out whether or not we *are* allowed to enjoy our capacities to feel sexual, or whether we have to feel guilty about it.

Magazines which are published for their erotic potential contribute to the fact that erotic stimulation has been a great source of fascination throughout recorded history. Using *people* as objects (not thinking about and responding to their feelings) is quite a different matter from using an object (like a photograph) *as* an object. Guilt-free masturbation is a way to start exploring your erotic potential. Try it.

WE ARE ALL envious of men's contentment with their own bodies, and their blithe disinterest in standards of appearance. Unselfconscious masturbation is part of this natural ease with the male body. Orgasm comes quickly and easily and – apart from cleaning up the mess afterwards – presents none of the intricate difficulties of having two genital zones and several psychological zones to deal with.

Men love watching themselves in a mirror or in their mind's eye, and they want women to admire them too. We do. We also find it funny, appalling, different. What we love is his inner confidence. Watching him masturbate is part of witnessing that.

Women do not want the pressure of a man who insists on sex when he becomes aroused. It is a relief if he takes his penis in his own hands. We can join in, or not, without feeling we have to – or masturbate ourselves.

Watching a partner masturbate we notice what a fast response he gets, using a more forceful action than we would. Do women see the penis as too vulnerable? He uses saliva for lubrication. He works up to a jerking rhythm very quickly, with one hand or two. He touches his nipples, buttocks, anus at the same time. He watches himself in the mirror.

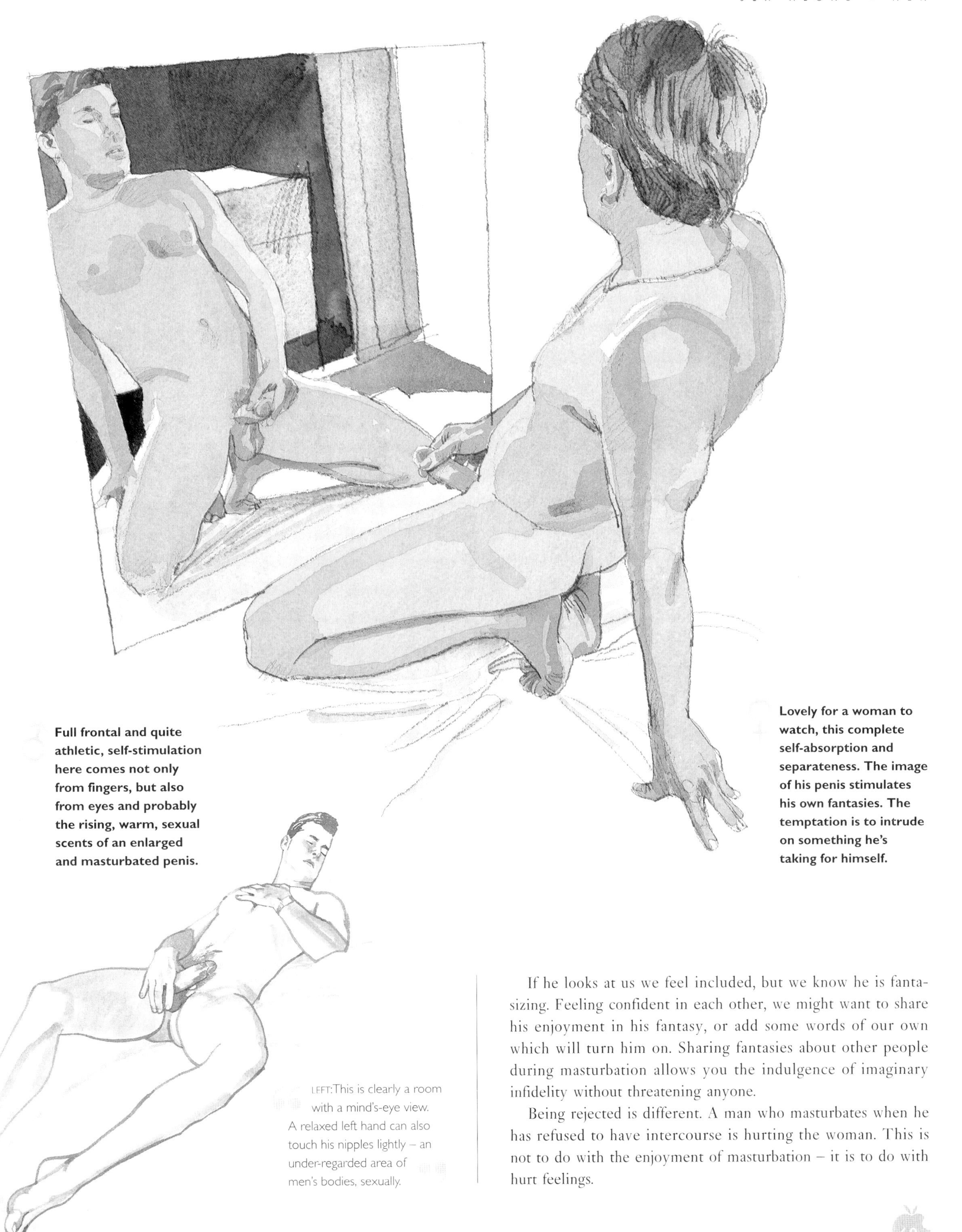

Full frontal and quite athletic, self-stimulation here comes not only from fingers, but also from eyes and probably the rising, warm, sexual scents of an enlarged and masturbated penis.

Lovely for a woman to watch, this complete self-absorption and separateness. The image of his penis stimulates his own fantasies. The temptation is to intrude on something he's taking for himself.

LEFT: This is clearly a room with a mind's-eye view. A relaxed left hand can also touch his nipples lightly – an under-regarded area of men's bodies, sexually.

If he looks at us we feel included, but we know he is fantasizing. Feeling confident in each other, we might want to share his enjoyment in his fantasy, or add some words of our own which will turn him on. Sharing fantasies about other people during masturbation allows you the indulgence of imaginary infidelity without threatening anyone.

Being rejected is different. A man who masturbates when he has refused to have intercourse is hurting the woman. This is not to do with the enjoyment of masturbation – it is to do with hurt feelings.

Men Get Superior

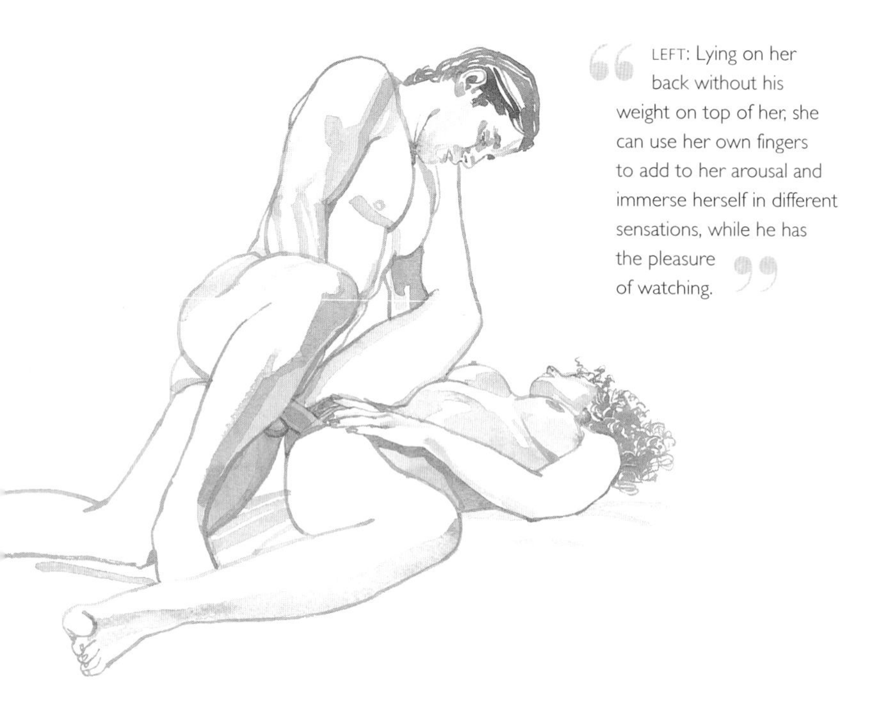

"LEFT: Lying on her back without his weight on top of her, she can use her own fingers to add to her arousal and immerse herself in different sensations, while he has the pleasure of watching."

MAKING LOVE at its most basic. This is the position in which almost everything is under the man's control, and also interestingly where he has least control over the timing of his ejaculation.

Perhaps those two facts are not unconnected. From the point of view of efficient reproduction, the quicker a man comes the better. For primitive man at risk of being attacked by predators while carelessly taking his pleasures in the new-fangled face-to-face position of intercourse, reaching orgasm quickly might well have been life-saving.

But once we abandon primitive actions and experience sex as the merging of two equal people, this position comes pretty low on the sexual pleasures agenda.

So the missionary position has its drawbacks. But that is not to say that *sometimes* it cannot be fun.

Nothing gives quite the same sense of possessing or being possessed. No other position gives such total body contact. In no other position is the woman quite so helpless.

These are good feelings between consenting adults. The disadvantages are that the woman may have very little control of the direction of entry of the penis and no control over its thrust; she may have very little clitoral contact; and can feel totally squashed if the man is careless about supporting his own weight. Moreover, if the man has uncertain control over his ejaculation, and is inclined to come too quickly, there is less chance of establishing good ejaculatory control in this position than in many others. And while she can stroke his back and buttocks, he can hardly use his hands in stimulating her body.

Yet for most people this is way they first make love. If that was a good experience then it's usually held in some tender regard. It is also the position in which it is possible to have the best eye contact. Eyes are so important to both men and women sexually, and this position emphasizes that advantage. Kissing is also an option, so is whispering in your partner's ear and sucking her nipples.

♀ **The first thrust of penetration feels emotionally and physically electrifying. It can be good for women to have it repeated over and over, by withdrawal and re-entry. Kissing and caressing complete a picture of physical and emotional togetherness, even if she risks cramp in her calves or aching hip joints from widely angled legs.**

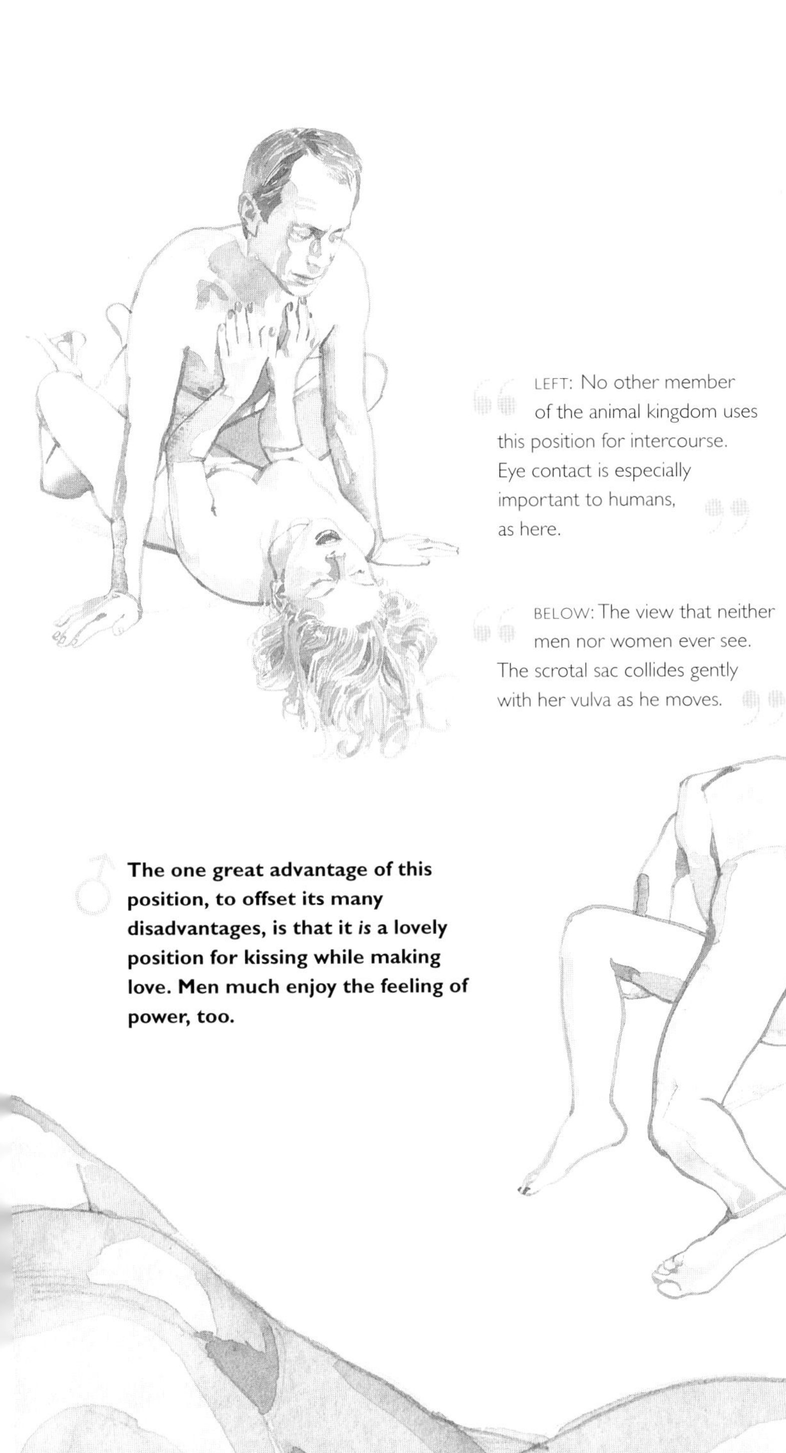

LEFT: No other member of the animal kingdom uses this position for intercourse. Eye contact is especially important to humans, as here.

BELOW: The view that neither men nor women ever see. The scrotal sac collides gently with her vulva as he moves.

The one great advantage of this position, to offset its many disadvantages, is that it *is* a lovely position for kissing while making love. Men much enjoy the feeling of power, too.

LAZY, DOMESTIC, loving, familiar – this is easy sex for women. It is the kind of sex that takes place at the end of the day, in bed, when both people are tired.

It is not *that* easy. It requires us to surrender a bit. We feel anxious about submission, trapped by immobility. Lying on our back with someone heavy on top of us requires a lot of trust. Flattened breasts and open legs make us feel vulnerable, but when trust is there, this is a position in which women can learn to love the look and feel of a man's penis. What is lost in the inability to move is gained in the sense of enclosure and intimacy.

Women like to feel fully entered, fully taken and fully needed by a man's penis. However, her own emotional needs and physical arousal do not necessarily combine. The deep thrust of a penis reaches places which are less sensitized inside her. Finding the right spot for arousal can be difficult. The outer rim, outer third and G-spot (half-way along the roof) of the vagina are better endowed with nerve-endings, but sensations come and go with friction, distraction and arousal. If she is willing to communicate she can guide the depth and angle of his penis by adjusting her own hips, by asking him to move or stay – or she uses her own hand, or his, on her clitoris while keeping his penis inside her.

Sometimes women want a slow build-up of clitoral and vaginal stimulation in this position, sometimes vigorous and deep thrusting, sometimes mutual pelvic movements, sometimes a penis held immobile or very gently moving just inside the vaginal opening. There is no right way, no best way – only the way that feels good at that moment.

Women want emotional bonding, not just physical fulfilment. The combination of penis in vagina, arms encircling each other, kisses on the mouth, talking and gazing enables a closeness and unity that feeds the heart as well as the body.

Women Get Superior Too

BELOW: Bending her knees she can move her pelvis backwards and forwards, in charge of the friction to her own vagina. He lets himself receive pleasure.

THIS CERTAINLY reverses the roles, though the male muscular system is not well adapted to the legs-apart-and-bent position; and pelvic movement is difficult for the woman. The man can thrust by lifting his pelvis to whatever extent he finds possible, but by and large it is the least satisfactory of the possible sexual positions.

Except, that is, for the really interesting experience for a man of learning what it is like to bear someone's weight entirely; and to find oneself on one's back, legs splayed apart, relatively helpless in the sexual encounter.

It's also a great position for enjoying a quite different view of the body of the woman you love. The whole of her front is displayed to your sight. Her pelvic muscles work for their own enjoyment. Her breasts take the shape of their own unsupported weight, and are available to your hands and your mouth. Her hips and buttocks are free, and their curves fit snugly in your palms.

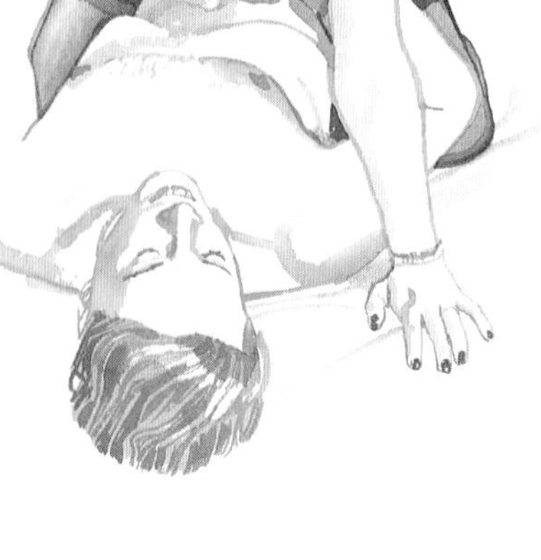

LEFT: He plays with her breasts while she is absorbed. She might guide his hands on to her buttocks, or reach back to feel his scrotum.

This position is also especially about what is going on in your head as much as it is about what your senses are telling you. Here you are, lying back and typically thinking of nothing; conscious only of the weight and warmth of another person above you, and trying to find a convenient way of spreading your legs far enough apart to accommodate that person's body between them.

Try, in your imagination, slipping into the feeling of being a woman. Imagine her breasts are yours, and the pressure you feel against those breasts. Imagine what it would be like to have a vagina, opening your legs for the person you love to insert themself into your body.

Now you will be beginning to have some sense of what a woman's experience is, much of the time, when making love.

Evolution designed men and women sexually for procreation, not for fun. But most sex is for fun, not procreation. Any body-on-top position leaves one person disadvantaged – unless it's an occasion for really enjoying being squashed.

With her legs outstretched, it is he who pushes up gently inside her. She lies still. Squeezing him with her vagina, there is a sense of activity without vigorous thrusting – a gentle appreciation of each other. His hands massage and squeeze her buttocks.

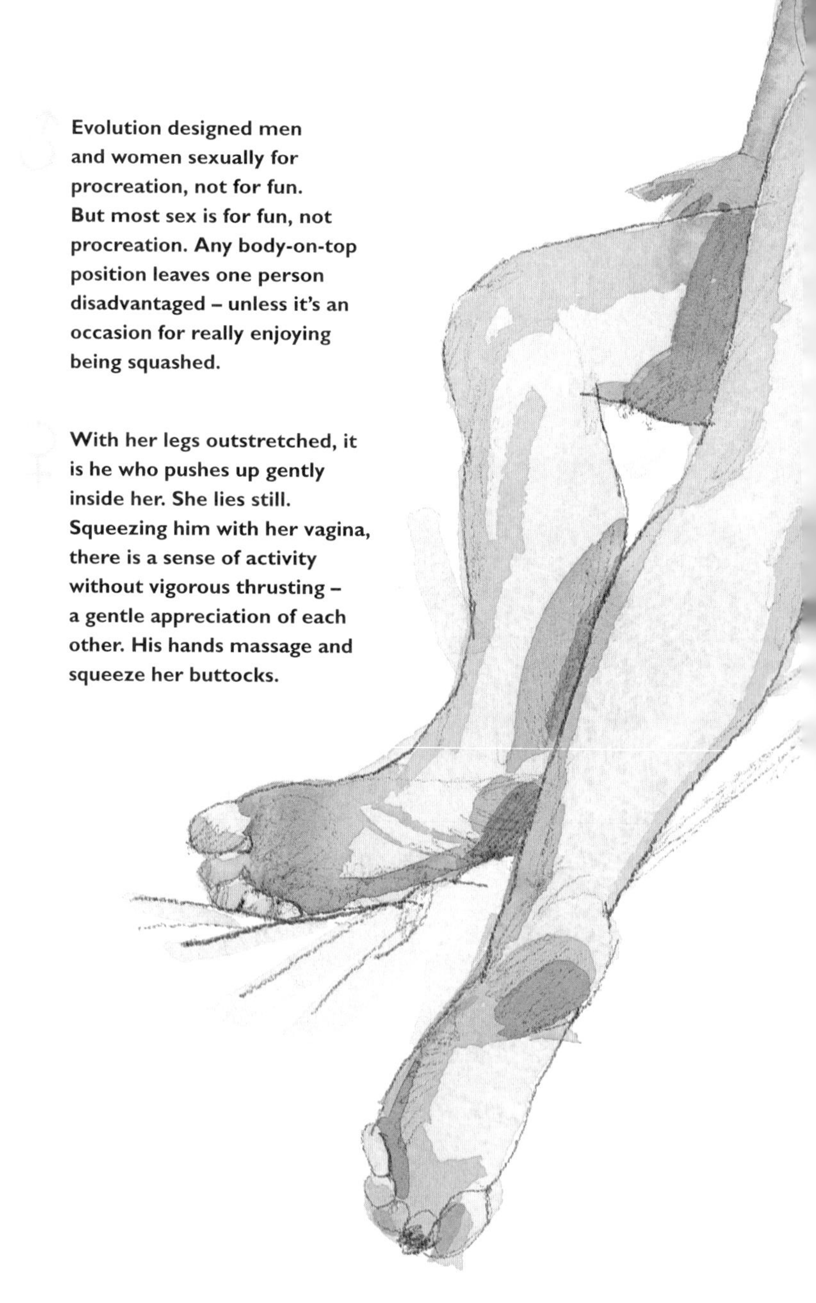

RIGHT: He takes the initiative to maneuver her backwards and forwards on an erect or flaccid penis – both being enjoyable. He increases friction for himself and she experiences both vaginal and clitoral stimulation.

BEING ON TOP, stretched over him, gives a woman a sense of what it might be like to be a man who takes this position. There is both power and tenderness in it, and a sense of responsibility – as though the one on top carries the burden of initiative and skill. For a woman to sustain this position for more than a minute, she does need a supple back, strong arms and strong legs to bend and make movement possible.

Having said all that, this is also a good position in which to relax. She can feel his penis inside her just by squeezing it, and there is little chance that he will slip out. Some of us get more genital sensation from keeping our legs together – the vagina feels narrower and more enclosing over the penis and there is a tightening up of the clitoral area. All she has to do while lying in this position is notice the build-up of sensation from very slight movements – something which is reassuring for women who doubt that they have many vaginal sensations. She can use her P-C muscles to squeeze his penis, and he only needs to thrust a little to maintain an erection. The sense of holding him is very different from active thrusting. And unlike the (usually) heavier man, she can let herself fully relax on to his chest, and even go to sleep in this position.

As his hands fall naturally on to her buttocks, he can use them to pull her weight up and down on his penis, or let his fingers squeeze and caress her; he can dig his nails in slightly and scratch a little. Some women like to have their buttocks slapped during intercourse. Others like a finger encircling the rim of their anus, or gently inserted. It is worth experimenting.

After a play-fight it can be fun for a woman to experience pinning a man down. However, when lying over his body in this way – rather than sitting up – it is still he who has the power to thrust into her, simply by pulling up his knees.

Lying on top means that our breasts, chins and stomachs droop in front of him. It helps if he looks up and likes what he sees, and he takes the opportunity to fondle breasts, kiss and talk.

Woman On Top

THE MOST obvious thing about this position is that the woman can be quite powerful in her action upon the man. She can clench her vaginal muscles whilst sitting astride him; she can move up and down on his erection; she can change the angle of her body; offer or remove her breasts from his reach. As many women experience greater sensitivity on the front upper wall of the vagina, she can angle her body forward to increase friction at the right spot.

Some of this takes energy and physical fitness, and it's easy for women to get cramp in this position. But even if she isn't particularly fit, many women enjoy this position for the different sensations, the pleasure of monitoring his excitement level from above, the ability to move her body more freely. There can be enjoyment in being aggressively thrusting, or in being passively receptive to his upward thrusting inside her. She can touch her own clitoris quite easily and he can touch her breasts. She will probably need lots of pauses in this position, so that she does not get sore, so that she can rest if her legs are tired, so that she can regain closeness through kissing.

Commonly men lose their erections in this position and slip out. It can be good to sit there and wait, and for the woman to stuff the penis gently back inside her until it grows again. Or for her to move her vulva gently backwards and forwards on his testicles, feeling the sensations of the testicles rubbing against the outer rim of her vagina. She can use his erect or half-erect penis and guide it manually to rub against her clitoris or round the outside edge of her vagina.

Just occasionally, this can be a position where an erection feels too long. If the woman is sitting too upright and the man thrusting upwards with a full erection, it can hit the cervix causing pain. It's another reason why it's important for the woman to keep control of the sitting angle.

“ABOVE: This is both very tender and very secretive – worth trying fully dressed, except for her pants, and in the open air somewhere. It's a lovely position for the penis feeling contained and the vagina feeling it surrounds the man. It's the closeness which is special to this.”

BY SIZE, weight, and all kinds of social conditioning, men typically expect to be on top sexually. What a lot is gained by lying back. Not only are normal positions changed, but the psychological perspective changes too. She is in charge – well, pretty much so. There is a fair bit of thrusting a man can do in some of these positions if he wants to. But the real thrill is finding out what it's like not having to be in charge or be the one directing the speed or rhythm of what is happening.

Not only that, but visually a quite different landscape of her body comes into view. Breasts can be held; inner thighs can be stroked; and her back can be enjoyed visually too.

Most especially, however, the man has the sensation that her vagina is enfolding his penis, rather than that he is thrusting into her vagina. She is the one doing the seeking, trying out thrusting, making the movements, dictating the pressure and length of each thrust.

Everything about this position is to do with the man making his body, and especially his erection, available and accessible to his partner for her enjoyment. She is the one doing the taking. He is at the receiving end of her seeking pleasure. Try and imagine what it is like for her to feel more exposed, more in charge, managing the angle of thrust to suit her.

As with all other positions, of course, it is very important too to know what state of arousal she is at. If there is fear for the man that he will come too quickly and before she has reached her climax, talk with her to find out how her pattern of arousal can be developed before she takes the penis into her vagina.

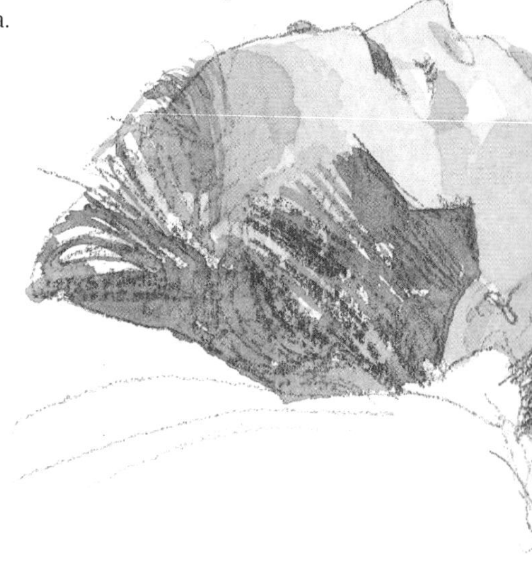

“RIGHT: Not the easiest of options, but very good for getting the penis to press against the front wall of the vagina which in some women is very sensitive indeed and is known as the G-spot. Unless you are very fit, it's not a position that can be sustained for long.”

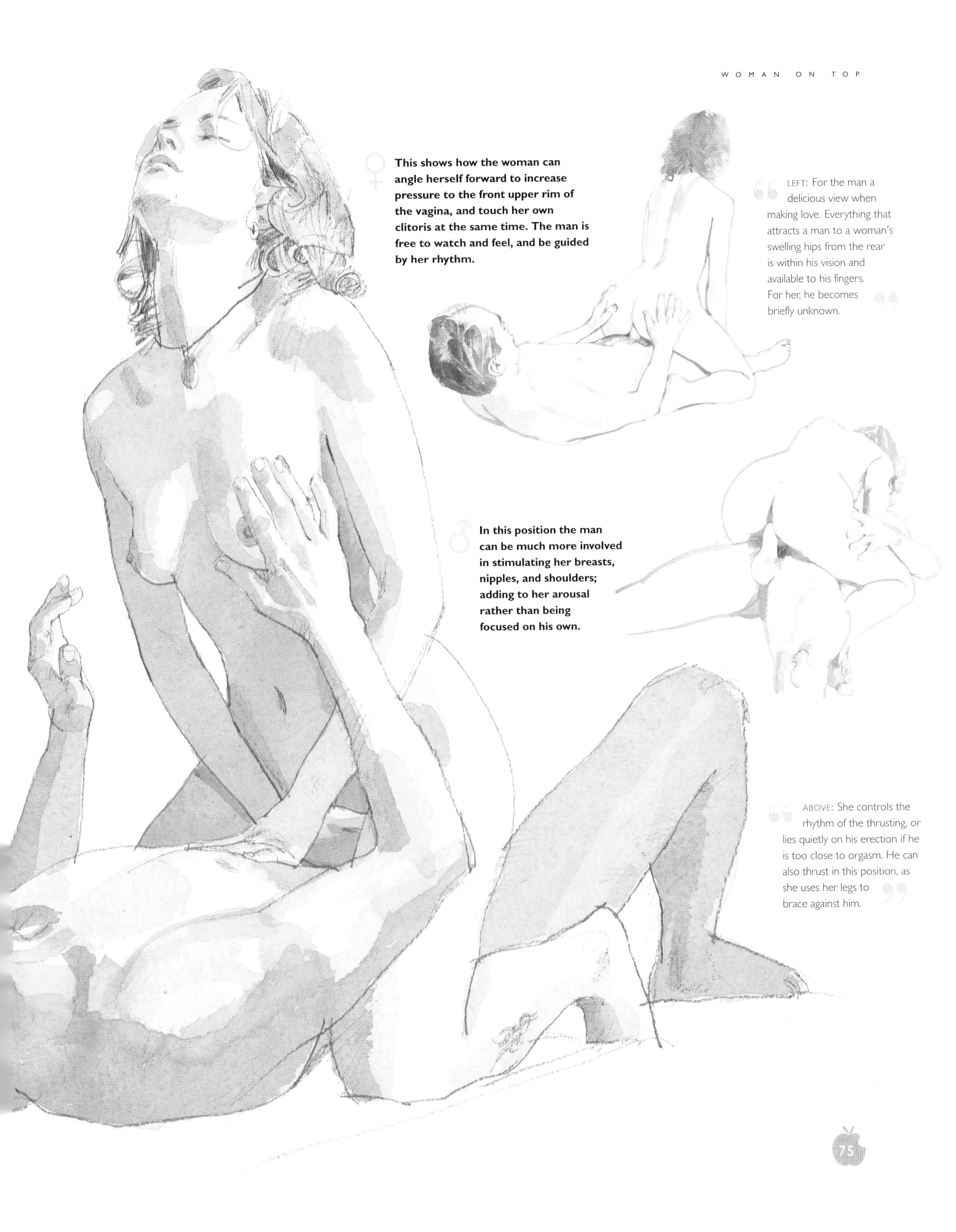

♀ **This shows how the woman can angle herself forward to increase pressure to the front upper rim of the vagina, and touch her own clitoris at the same time. The man is free to watch and feel, and be guided by her rhythm.**

"LEFT: For the man a delicious view when making love. Everything that attracts a man to a woman's swelling hips from the rear is within his vision and available to his fingers. For her, he becomes briefly unknown."

♂ **In this position the man can be much more involved in stimulating her breasts, nipples, and shoulders; adding to her arousal rather than being focused on his own.**

"ABOVE: She controls the rhythm of the thrusting, or lies quietly on his erection if he is too close to orgasm. He can also thrust in this position, as she uses her legs to brace against him."

Under and Over

LEFT: She lifts her leg over him to allow deeper penetration and contact with the upper vaginal wall; he massages her breast for his own pleasure.

THIS IS the freest position of all. The woman has a great deal of freedom of movement, and is not pinned down by the weight of a man on top of her, while he has all the erotic parts of her body available to touch. She can move her pelvis, rotating around an inserted penis as she will. He can thrust with his pelvis too.

Here men and women are completely equal in the sexual act. They share their bodies, but neither dominates. Each is able to appreciate the other without being submerged by the other. Nothing could be further away from the woman as object; nothing could be closer to full co-operation.

The woman is entirely free to move – both away from the man, if she wants to; and equally as close as she wants to. A quick twist of her body will release her completely from the situation. But she also bends her legs and in this action makes the gift of herself to the man.

In this position a man will never experience the feelings of power and control that he does in the missionary position. Rather he will feel a sense of being a supplicant for a favor that he is not able to take, but which might be given by a willing partner. This is the most romantic of all the sexual positions as it involves consent and trust on both sides.

Here then is an expression of the central theme of this book – a woman who wants to be as much involved sexually with a man as he does with her, but out of freedom, not out of constraint.

A REAR-ENTRY position is erotic and animal-like, but this particular way of making love has tenderness and sensuality in it too. The intertwining of arms and legs, the closeness of heads, is as much loving as it is sexual.

Each intercourse is a new exchange, neither a debt accrued from the past nor a promise for the future. Waking up after the passion of the night before, it can be good to feel gently prodded back into life by an erect, inviting penis – and equally awful to experience this as a demand before consciousness really allows repudiation. As with all positions, it is up to the woman whether she welcomes and receives his penis inside her, or not.

Rear-entry seems to make the vaginal opening fractionally more resistant. There is excitement in such tightness, but potentially also soreness. He has to persist with an erect penis if he is to broach the outer rim, and this tightness can be increased if she finds it pleasurable by keeping her knees together. Sometimes the gradual forcing of his entry is erotic enough for her to lubricate spontaneously; at other times – after a long sleep for example – she might need to be prepared first, with artificial or natural body lubricants, or by his rubbing his penis gently between her outer vaginal lips.

We are fully exposed in this position, displayed and uncovered, lying naked on our backs. It requires trust to be so open. Curling up around each other can be a relief after such openness. Such enfolding brings other feelings too – like those of a young child, even a baby, curled up against a parent. There is something of a child-like quality to much of adult sex – neediness, tenderness and playfulness all being part of our experience.

There is little that we have to be energetic about as women here, and lots of room for kissing, talking, caressing and looking. With access to our own clitoris, a woman can be fully involved in all her sensations and fully involved with him. Taking his penis at different angles arouses us into fresh awareness of the variety and mobility of vaginal sensations – a millimeter can sometimes make the difference between ecstasy and mere delight – but then again it can change and move on elsewhere.

LEFT: She opens her legs slightly more to enable his penis to move more freely inside her. He can curl round her in a fetal position. Their hands are free to hold and touch.

Gentle feelings are expressed in kissing and facial touch, quite in harmony with deep genital union. She keeps her knees together, possibly for increased vaginal sensations, but also to demonstrate a child-like response to his closeness and tenderness.

Totally entangled and equally free at the same time; knees bent in a way that feels protective without being defensive; this is the sexual position of greatest equality and tenderness. His hands are free to touch over the sensitive parts of her body, without any loss of penile pleasure for either of them.

ABOVE: He penetrates her mouth with his tongue, her vagina with his penis, and plays with her breast. She holds on to him in appreciation.

Back To Front

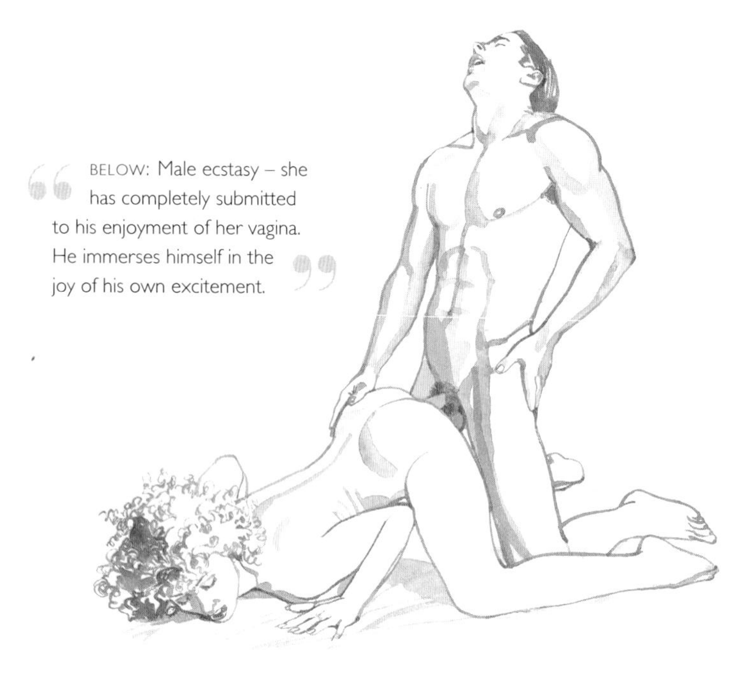

BELOW: Male ecstasy – she has completely submitted to his enjoyment of her vagina. He immerses himself in the joy of his own excitement.

BASIC ANIMAL instincts are operating here. The special human qualities of eye-to-eye contact, delight in facial expression and holding each other in an embrace are lost almost completely. He can take pleasure in the shape of her hips, and can see the line of her body. She can only choose to submit, and feel the thrusting erection.

Some caution is called for in thrusting in this position. With hands on her hips, the man can pull her towards him as well as make very strong pelvic movements. Make very sure she is comfortable with the depth of thrust and power that can be gained in this position.

The woman is making an act of complete surrender here. There is very little contact with her clitoris but the penis is very likely to be pressing against the more responsive, sensitive parts of her vagina, so it is possible for her to have a climax in this position. She will feel very vulnerable, displaying her vagina and anus completely to her lover.

Be careful with the stretched and exposed opening of her back passage. Light touch there, especially with a lubricating cream, may be very enjoyable for her. Or she may feel shy and ill-at-ease about any sexual interest you have in that particular part of her anatomy.

Find out together. But do not insert into the anal passage without her consent or enjoyment. It carries risk of spreading micro-organisms of the *E-coli* variety which can cause inflammation and pain if spread around the vaginal area; and they are very unpleasant if they get inside the bladder. Use a condom. The sensitive tissues of the anal passage can be easily scratched or torn.

WOMEN DISPLAY themselves without difficulty through dress, hairstyle, make-up – but it takes a different kind of instinct for exposure to raise up our haunches and display hips, buttocks and genitals for a man's delight. Images of animal mating abound. Female exhibitionism is a part of the bestial spirit. We kneel on all-fours, buttocks in front of him, our faces often buried in the bed.

Vaginal penetration – including having to withstand ardent pummelling from a very excited penis – makes the arms ache if a woman has to support her upper half for long. It is easier to subside on to shoulders provided we do not suffocate in the pillows. We can raise or lower buttocks, gyrate them around the penis, squeeze him or use his erection as a fixed object on to which to draw ourselves backwards and forwards. This is a good position for his penis to hit that soft place midway along the roof of the vagina which provides instant excitement and an emission of clear fluid into the vagina.

The usual gasps, grunts and cries tend to increase in this position: it is not easy to remain silent. There are sex words, begging for more, descriptions of what can be seen or felt, a vocal desire for orgasm. This is unrestrained lascivious sex, entered into when a couple is confident enough to move freely between all planes of body, mind and spirit.

Mental imagery affects eroticism, and this is a position in which men love to see themselves. They want a mirror, a camera, a film-recorder and, if none of those is present, they will delight in seeing themselves in their imaginations. Perhaps this is because the woman is in no position to gaze at him herself? However, visual impact is not just for him. Women are voyeurs, exhibitionists, narcissists. We only feel bereft if he is more interested in seeing himself in a mirror, than he is in relating to us.

RIGHT: In full enjoyment of her own raunchiness, she turns her head and reaches out an arm to touch him. He watches himself penetrating her.

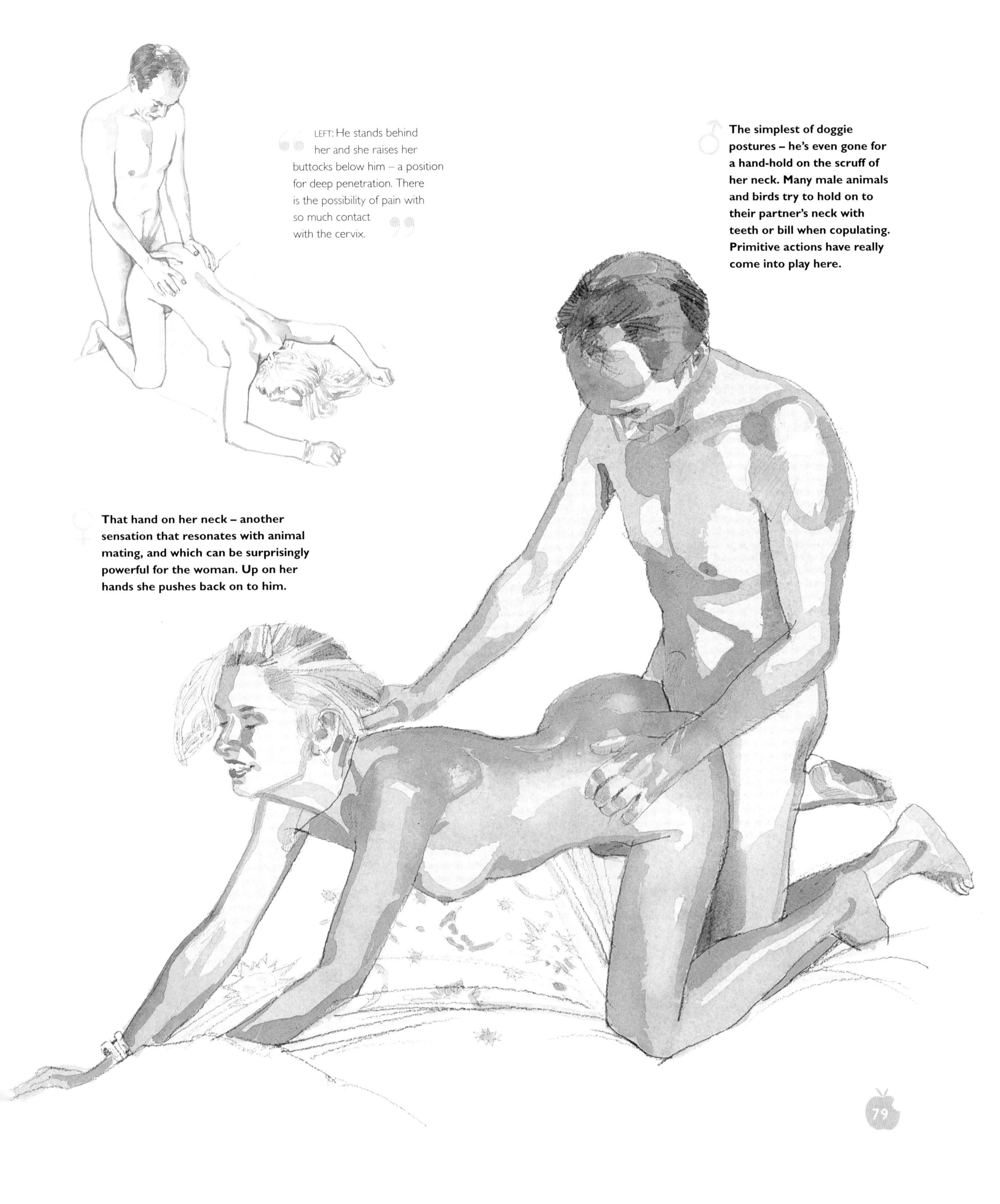

LEFT: He stands behind her and she raises her buttocks below him – a position for deep penetration. There is the possibility of pain with so much contact with the cervix.

The simplest of doggie postures – he's even gone for a hand-hold on the scruff of her neck. Many male animals and birds try to hold on to their partner's neck with teeth or bill when copulating. Primitive actions have really come into play here.

That hand on her neck – another sensation that resonates with animal mating, and which can be surprisingly powerful for the woman. Up on her hands she pushes back on to him.

Lying Like Spoons

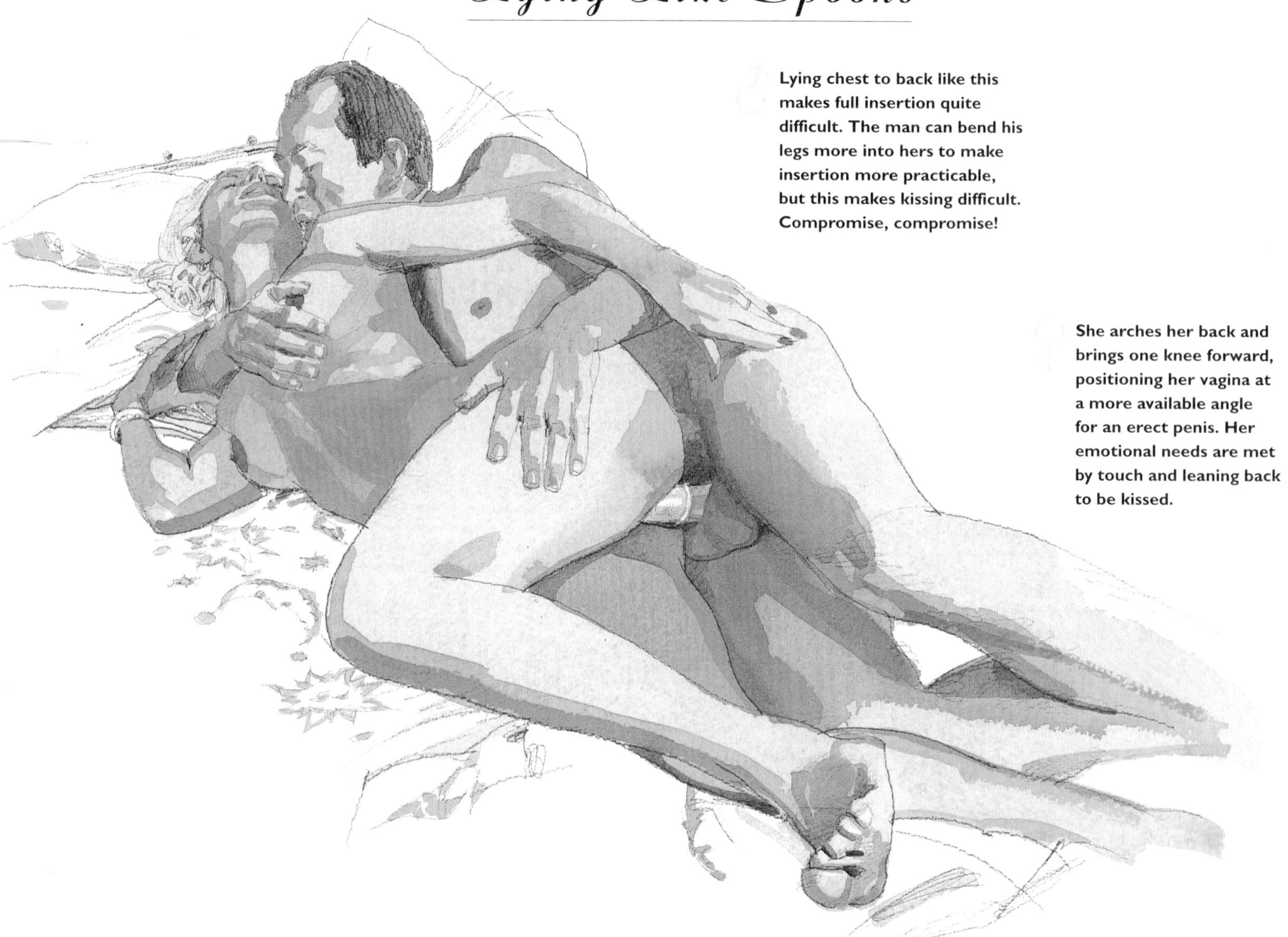

Lying chest to back like this makes full insertion quite difficult. The man can bend his legs more into hers to make insertion more practicable, but this makes kissing difficult. Compromise, compromise!

She arches her back and brings one knee forward, positioning her vagina at a more available angle for an erect penis. Her emotional needs are met by touch and leaning back to be kissed.

TRY INSERTING your penis, and both of you slipping off into sleep, like spoons lying side by side in a cutlery box. It is difficult, but very delightful – difficult because the man typically wants to have a qüickie climax, once inserted. The spoon position lets you practise restraint.

Lie curled, the knees of man cupped into the knees of the woman who lies in front of him, back to him, on her side. She can wriggle down on to his erection; he can gently ease himself inside her. Drift off to sleep bonded together.

Spoon positions can also be a bit more energetic than that. Any attempt to kiss means quite a lot of twisting around; and legs can be raised or lowered to ease entry or just for fun. But the spoon position is mostly about resting closely together, and feeling a connecting penis without expending any energy in thrusting. It is a pleasant method of making love when you are both too tired to be energetic, but want closeness.

In this position, the possibility of anal intercourse is also present. Some modern authorities are quite clear about encouraging entry into the rear passage. It is a fact that it is an area well-endowed with sensitive nerve endings. Surveys over the past fifty years have shown that anal sex between men and women is a practice that has increased substantially. Some women describe it as being highly pleasurable and capable of producing orgasms. Some also report that they enjoy a finger being inserted into the anal passage to heighten the sensation of a climax.

Heterosexual couples are also reported as finding pleasure in using an instrument like a vibrator which the woman can insert into the man's anal passage, so that he can experience a sensation of intercourse and of what penetration feels like.

Using the anus sexually feels to many people like breaking a taboo. Those feelings should be respected. Equally there are others for whom anal intercourse is a special delight.

RIGHT: Men and women are excited by her opening her legs and stretching the vaginal opening.

LEFT: A lovely way to wake up – cuddling against one another, deciding whether or not to have slow, lazy intercourse, keeping in close emotional contact.

REAR-ENTRY positions are better for pregnant women. They are also better for tired women, women who have eaten too much and women who, at that moment, prefer to turn their backs on their partner. This is not to condone resentful sex – it is just a fact that it happens. In most sexual relationships it does not happen as often as warm, appreciative sex, fortunately.

If a woman is curled on her side, or lying with her legs out straight on one side, he is not going to find a way in very easily. She can help him, or not. She needs to project her buttocks towards him at an angle, arching her back, or to move her upper half diagonally across the bed away from him. Or she might try wriggling herself up the bed slightly so that his penis enters her from below. Or she can raise her top leg to widen the angle of penetration. If she just stays alongside him, her vagina lies horizontally to him. If he tries to penetrate her from a parallel position, he will not get much further than the vaginal entrance. It is probably better if he slides down the bed a little so that his erect penis comes from below her. He can then move up beside her again once he is inside, and cuddle her.

Women love cuddles, so she may just want to lie like that, enclosed in warm arms, spoon-breathing in harmony, feeling his heart beat against her back, his breath on her neck. Held tightly like this, she might even want to fall asleep joined at the genitals.

Letting it develop more sexually, he or she can reach down to her clitoris or hold her breast in one hand. She can push against him, or allow small sensations to grow with slight movements. This position is good for furtive sex, when to engage in vigorous activity would attract unwelcome attention.

This is also a position in which anal touching and anal penetration is fantasized about – whether or not it actually happens – an image which can be a turn-on or turn-off. A woman's anal sphincter is tighter than her vagina and needs care if it is to be broached at all, whether by a finger or a penis. Unlike the vagina it does not lubricate itself; nevertheless the anus is an erogenous zone which some like to include in love-making.

RIGHT: Athletic and quite hard. Her knee gives him the pulling power he needs to keep this position working, though without much potential for thrusting.

Stand and Deliver

MEN HAVE fantasies about this position much more than they ever experience it. Women too!

We are back to the basic design again. Men are driven to ejaculate within the vagina as a reproductive urgency. But men and women are much more complicated than being just reproductive creatures. Yet their basic survival programming requires them to be sexual in making sure that genes are passed on to another generation. What better ways of playing that scenario out than this? It is the complete opposite of that fully-engaged-as-a-couple experience illustrated on pages 76–77.

In this picture he says: "I want you" and she says: "Have me, now." Or she might have said: "I want you," and he might have said "What, right now? In the kitchen? We'll get caught." And she could have said: "Dare you," and he's risen to the challenge.

ABOVE: The urge to interrupt each other's domestic tasks with a quick sexual thrill is a powerful aphrodisiac for both.

For every occasion that a man wants to come, ideally there should be a woman who has the opposite feeling that she wants to be filled. Alas this is rarely the case. For every time that a man wants to come, there is frequently a woman who feels obliged to give in, despite her own wishes and desire for sexual fulfilment. Modern sexuality is re-organizing this imbalance. It recognizes that both are equal in the respective needs, *different* though those may be.

This position illustrates better than any other the complete interdependence of men and women if they are both to enjoy their sexual lives. Once it was taught that nice women wouldn't (because nice women were not supposed to be sexually needy in any way at all), but now it is quite apparent that nice women really would (as long as the terms of the relationship are equal and understood by both partners).

A "QUICKIE" in the real world of relationships and domesticity is not very satisfying, particularly for women who need undistracted time, emotional rapport and a slow build-up to feel enthusiastic about sex. On the other hand, a quickie in the fantasy world of instant turn-ons and easy orgasms is exciting for many women. We fantasize that we are so irresistible to a man, and the urge to have sex so compelling, that it happens standing up, there and then, in whatever improbable situation, all underwear and other impediments having miraculously disappeared.

A compromise between this fantasy and reality is the well-orchestrated occasion for standing-up sex. A woman prepares for it by not wearing pantyhose or pants and she might lock the door of an otherwise public room, before bending over invitingly. The half-planned, half-spontaneous "uncontrollable urge" can then be acted out at the kitchen sink, in the bedroom, over the office desk or up against the garden fence.

It is a quickie because it is a hard position for a woman to hold for long. It works slightly better if he is a little taller than her – otherwise she has the strain of bending her knees or standing on her toes trembling. It is also not so good on an unstable surface like a mattress. She needs to lean against something solid to stabilize herself and to offer him a more horizontal angle. It is quite impossible if both people are trying to stand up straight.

Excitement is at least as much in the image of her buttocks exposed for penetration, as in her physical pleasure. She is only in touch with the man at the genitals, so she feels separate, free, powerful, womanly. There are images of animal-mating, but also of detached (human) sex. Women may want emotional union much of the time but we are capable of enjoying something completely genital, physical and almost anonymous. All we need is self-confidence and confidence in our relationships.

There is much potential for hilarity with this kind of sex. We might fall over or buckle at the knees. We become entrapped at the ankles or the thighs in half-removed clothing. We narrowly avoid being discovered. If her buttocks are held apart to ease penetration, the noise of air being expelled from the vagina can erupt. All in all, a recipe for ending up in a joyful heap on the ground.

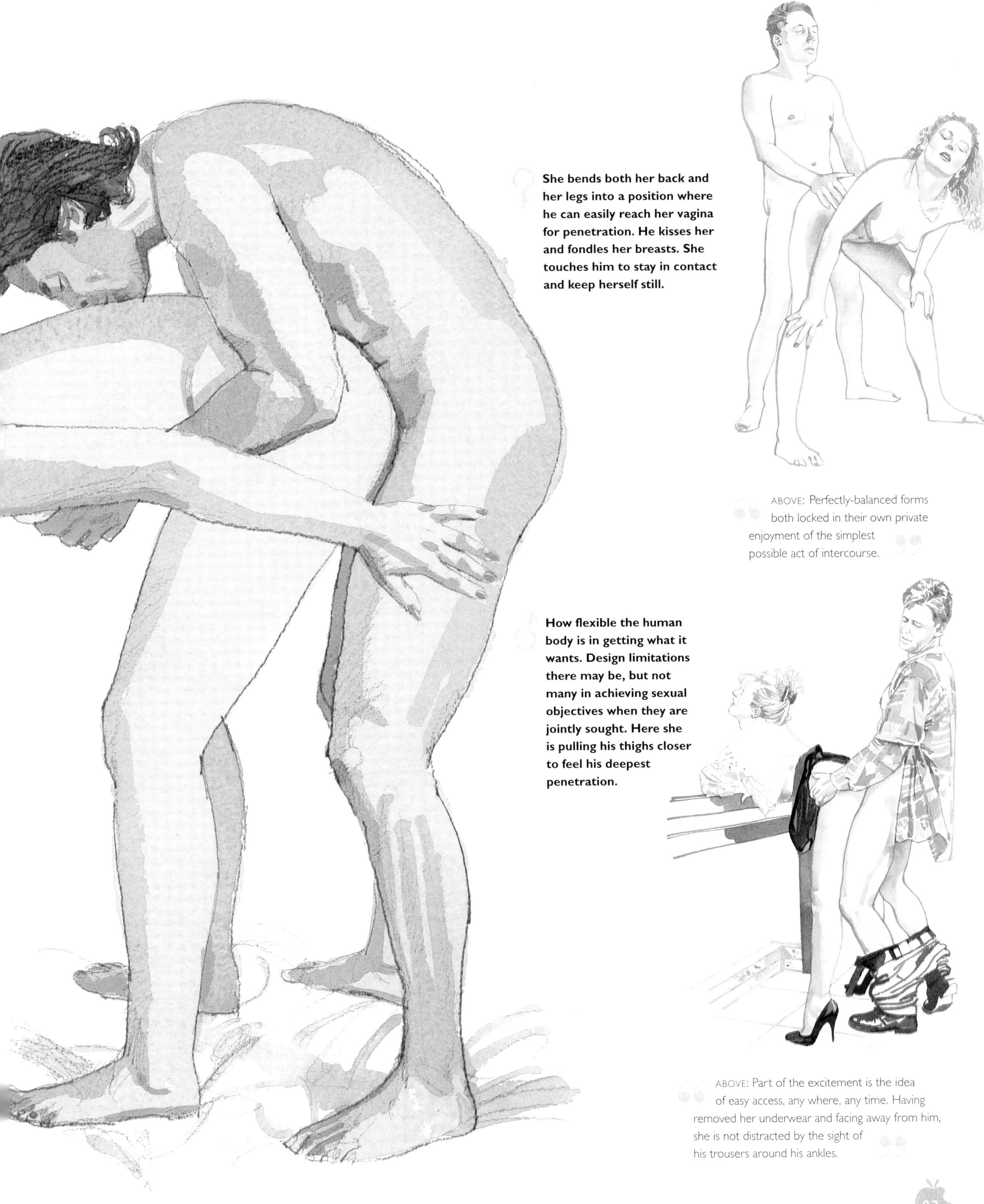

She bends both her back and her legs into a position where he can easily reach her vagina for penetration. He kisses her and fondles her breasts. She touches him to stay in contact and keep herself still.

ABOVE: Perfectly-balanced forms both locked in their own private enjoyment of the simplest possible act of intercourse.

How flexible the human body is in getting what it wants. Design limitations there may be, but not many in achieving sexual objectives when they are jointly sought. Here she is pulling his thighs closer to feel his deepest penetration.

ABOVE: Part of the excitement is the idea of easy access, any where, any time. Having removed her underwear and facing away from him, she is not distracted by the sight of his trousers around his ankles.

In The Chair

BELOW: This is serious stuff, gymnastically, and it requires a partner who is especially confident in her own muscular control. With her legs up, penetration is deeper.

A WOMAN sitting on a man's lap is part of ordinary fantasy life. The mental picture usually forms around either a powerful woman who is able to distract a man from his office work, or a powerful man who persuades a woman to come over and sit on his knee.

In its real-life form, sitting astride a man's lap takes some doing. Many chairs have arms which get in the way; knees hurt if they are squashed in too tight. Some women have legs which are too short to push up from the ground; some women weigh too much to be easily supported. He may slip out because the angle of his penis is wrong or because he is sliding down the chair – or the chair tips over.

If she is using her hands to stop herself from falling, she will not be free to stimulate her own clitoris. He can move her up and down with his hands under her buttocks, and his mouth is near her breasts to suck her nipples. Or he can put a finger in her anus. She can move up and down on his penis, or wriggle down on to its base, which creates a warm tickling feeling inside the vagina. He can feel her clitoris if she is turned outwards or is able to put her legs over his shoulders. He can pull her in towards him to touch and lick between penetrations. She can also turn over and lie across his knee, so that he can explore her buttocks and vulva. Or she can kneel in front of him to suck him.

Sitting on a man's lap might take us back to childhood memories. Smaller men like to climb up on to bigger women; smaller women like to climb up on bigger men. In our adult lives we play the role of "parent" and "child" in a variety of dependent relationships – some of them professional ones – and in our sexual relationships we play at taking those roles too.

SITTING and sex do not go easily together – these are just ways of having fun, and seeing what is possible. They tend to happen when you are both so aroused that even discomfort is fun.

The real difficulty with sitting on a penis is that the woman's weight can make its skin stretch too far, pulling at the glans. This is especially so if you are not circumcized.

She can feel the same disquiet from her point of view – that settling down on to the whole length of the shaft might penetrate her too far. If her legs are not in firm contact with the ground, then there is a fear that she will be hurt internally.

None of which will stop you trying it if you are sexually excited. These pictures offer some suggestions – probably the easier ones. Trying it backwards adds in as much complication as it is probably wise to attempt.

This story of sex in Paris at Charles de Gaulle airport is instructive. A man meeting a lovely woman running towards him out of the Customs area hugged her to him, sweeping her off her feet. She returned his embrace with equal passion.

It soon became apparent to bystanders that she was wearing nothing beneath her summer dress. She stretched her hands into the front of his jeans, and unzipped his trousers then and there, lowering herself on to his penis.

A gendarme remonstrated, and they fled to the long moving walkway which takes passengers away from the arrival lounge, pushing a trolley in front of them. At the walkway he sat on her case on the trolley, she sat astride his lap, and so they stayed the whole length of the ride, locked in one another's embrace and entirely coupled. At the end of the walkway they stood, adjusted their clothes, and left the airport with smiles of great delight upon their faces.

Perhaps the best element of sitting-down sex is in experimenting to find ways of balancing against each other and still finding sexual sensations. A man's strength can get put to the test, and a woman's agility likewise. It is another way of saying "I want you in any way possible, I want you so much."

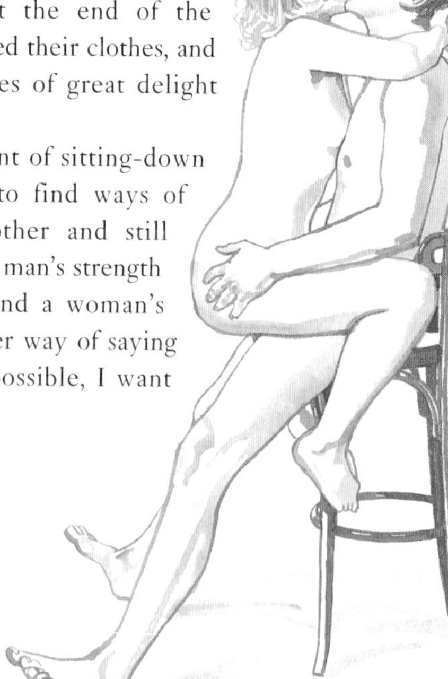

RIGHT: Whatever their differences in height, she feels equal to him up near his face in this close and gentle embrace.

First check the stability of your chair. There is no quick rescue if this one crashes to the ground, except by a very prompt withdrawal entirely under her control.

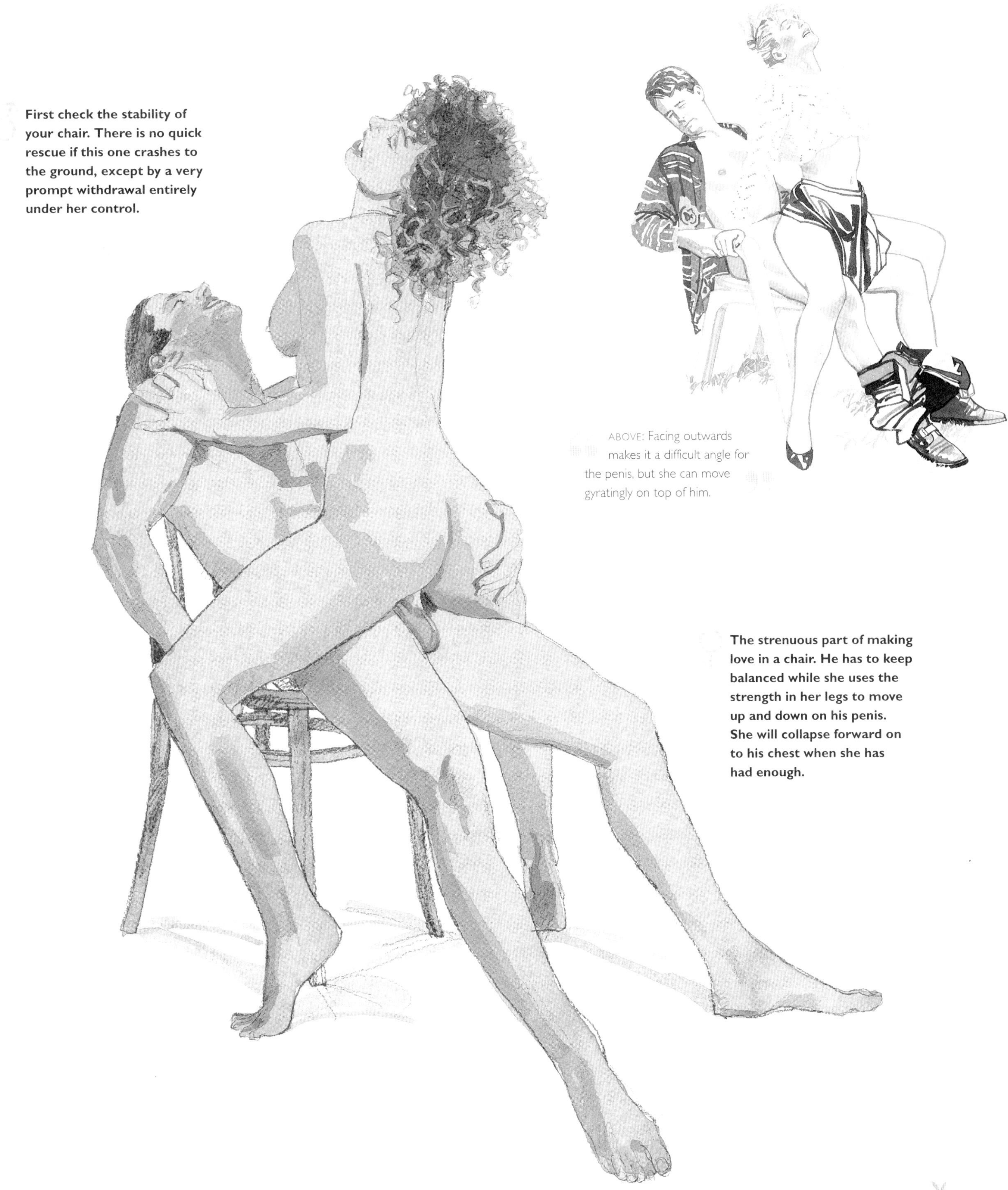

ABOVE: Facing outwards makes it a difficult angle for the penis, but she can move gyratingly on top of him.

The strenuous part of making love in a chair. He has to keep balanced while she uses the strength in her legs to move up and down on his penis. She will collapse forward on to his chest when she has had enough.

Lift Off

ALL THESE positions *are* possible, but they are more acrobatic even than the suggestions illustrated on the two previous spreads.

There are times when passion is so overwhelming there is hardly time for the niceties of making love. Sex standing up feels tremendously insistent. Nothing will do but urgent action.

Pants wrapped round ankles are a comical sight. But they also express the urgency of the couple's sex drive. Standing sex is all-action.

It is almost impossible to feel tender, having sex like this. Masculine strength, power and the forcefulness of wanting to insert, ejaculate, and feel in possession overwhelms finer feelings. Yet at the same time care and some real finesse have to be brought into play, otherwise sex standing up can be awkward and painful for your partner. Your partner knows this, of course. She yields, wants to be wanted, likes the feeling of brute passion, but also wants to be able to trust completely. That is why there has to be *some* finesse.

ABOVE: The eroticism of quick sex up against a wall: exciting but uncomfortable for the woman.

All the pictures show how important upper-arm strength is. With blood pumping round the body making an erection, it also has to be pumping hard into arm and leg muscles to supply the energy they need for such exertions. This is not a way of making love if you are not really fit – strength giving out half way through can be a real let-down!

Your partner needs to be in pretty good physical shape as well. She will be holding on hard, as well as wanting to hold on to the hardness inside of her. Standing up, or with her legs clenched around you, she has not got much control over her pelvic floor muscles. So in penetrating her, she is relying on you to make sure the angle is comfortable for her, and that you are not going to thrust too awkwardly or suddenly.

Among all the strong sensations of powerful muscles being much in use, concentrate on the very fine and precise sensations that register in the tip of the penis – your glans – in this position. It is a wonderful contrast with the muscular feedback sensations that you will be getting from the physical effort involved.

The experience is also likely to be quite quick. Standing-up sex usually produces a very quick ejaculation because of the muscular tension that is in play. It is rather like riding down a roller coaster at a carnival. The sensation is passed almost before you can settle into it, but it feels like a lot of fun while you are pretty well out of control.

THE IDEA of being lifted up and penetrated is initially thrilling and sexy, but physically unsatisfying because women are making sure that they do not fall down, and gripping their legs in a tight lock that prevents pleasure. The openness of our legs, combined with a backwards angle of the upper body, allows no contact with the clitoris and minimal contact within the vagina. The penis encounters an open space within the vagina, or maybe slight contact with the lower wall. Unless the man happens to be fit and considerably larger than she, he will manage a few quick thrusts before relinquishing her weight and placing her firmly back on the ground.

It is funny how we strive for these positions, despite their anatomical difficulty. They are a tribute to sexual ingenuity but, for women, are hardly the easiest way to genital pleasure. It is more likely that these positions meet other, less obvious, needs as we struggle, in humor or in earnest, to maintain them. A woman who is happy with her body and happy with her partner is at least as interested in returning to child-like play and comfort, as she is in being a raunchy adult woman. When did we last get to swing ourselves up around someone's waist, or feel there was someone bigger and stronger than us who could carry us?

RIGHT: Looked at from this angle, she seems to be well engaged, but it is a very difficult posture to manage.

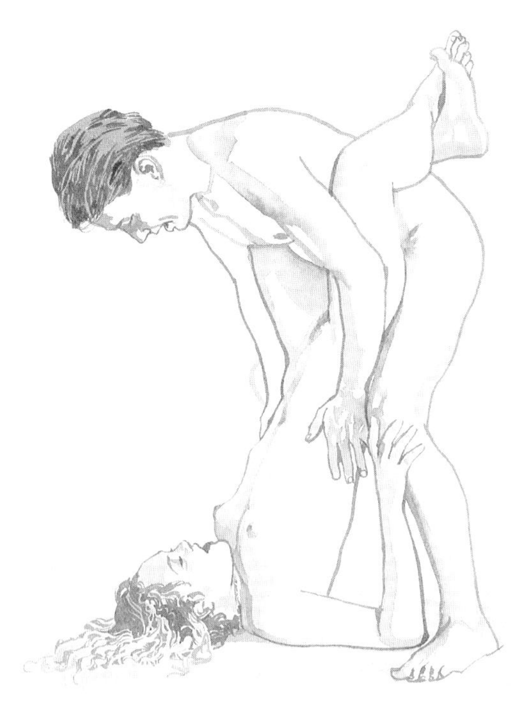

ABOVE: Not easy for either to sustain – a position we like to experiment with, for play, athleticism and conquest.

Women love to be picked up, carried and supported – physically and emotionally. Sexual excitement is more in her head than her body in this position.

This looks like the beginning of loss of control – she's slipping further away and losing penile contact, despite heroics with crossed ankle grabs. Not easy!

The exceptions are positions in which the woman is able to keep one foot on the ground, or where her back is supported. We can then use our legs and back muscles to increase pelvic tension, and angle our pelvis in such a way as to increase clitoral or vaginal friction. Standing up against a wall, with one foot off the ground, is more likely to yield good results. The woman has mobility and leverage, and she can still convey emotional warmth with her arms around his neck.

Lowered to the ground to rest on her shoulders, a woman is released from holding on, can feel more genitally, but is also made more vulnerable. Almost upside down, his weight directly over her spine, and his pelvic thrusting far from her influence, this can be a position that is frightening as well as erotic. The man's awareness of her physical fragility and psychological apprehension is important, even in the midst of his own excitement.

The best way for a woman to enjoy sexual sensations in one of these positions is to experience them in water, where her body weight is supported by the water, as well as by the man, and she can lie back and relax. The sensuality of nakedness in water and the open air help to make this an erotic and emotional, as well as playful, experience.

These days many women do actively take up sports or exercise, but many do not. Some are unfit, and starved of the ordinary physical delight of a healthy body and the sensations of close physical contact with others on a day-to-day basis. Sex is one of the ways for a woman to keep physically fit, some positions demanding strength and agility as well as joy. Leaning back with her legs around a man, she feels strength in her arms, legs and back, and shares in the delight of his fitness. When sex is playful and energizing, it satisfies a deep need for physical well-being, whatever our age or physical capacity.

Heels Over Head

THERE IS no doubt that male strength is a powerful influence during sex. One of the great pleasures of sex is to feel and delight in what makes us so unlike one another. This kind of sex does just that.

For a man, this is about his partner's surrender. She gives her body over to him for him to use. That may be not how it actually feels to the woman of course. She is involved through knowing that she *is* a person. Yet this kind of love-making can make a man realize how easy it is to see his partner simply as a body he wants for sex, and that can be quite a turn-on for both lovers.

Here, sight is the most important sense for the man in provoking desire and maintaining arousal. The man is free to take a view from as great a distance as is possible while still being inserted. He can appreciate angles, curves, lines and the smoothness of his woman in a way that sheets and clothes often hide.

There is also really good eye contact in these positions. The first contact with a person who sparks one's sexual interest almost always happens through the eyes. This position reminds us of that.

It is also true that a great deal of making love takes place at very close quarters. Slightly more separated positions like these put the entire body on view at once. It is possible for eyes to roam greedily here, exploring and absorbing and focusing.

Most of all, there is the marvel of surrender. Designed to be two halves of a world which is made complete by being sexual, these positions let one be close and distant at the same time, in positions which say "Let me have you just as I want to" from the man, and "Have me however you want me" for the woman.

SEXUAL ASSERTIVENESS is no different from any other kind of assertiveness. There is a frisson created by directness, self-confidence and deliberate awareness of the other person. Sometimes this takes the form of a verbal exchange, sometimes physical. There are times when a man wants a woman to take complete control of their sexual pleasure so he can feel what it is like to submit to her desires. At other times it is the woman who wants him to take charge – and that may involve his taking her legs in his hands, raising them or widening them, before penetrating her.

Women do not lose their strength by lying on their backs with their legs in the air. There can be an emotional excitement from being fully "taken" in this way, however awkward the contortions of the body. We also feel powerful in watching. We can see his penis and feel it gratifying us; we can see the intensity on his face. There is something about a man's complete engrossment in his penis in our vagina that separates us too.

BELOW: Penises try to belong and like to be held; vaginas like to be filled and feel engaged.

Offering ourselves to be deeply penetrated by a man who loves us reaches our hearts as well as our vaginas. Her look is one of tenderness, even in the midst of physical awkwardness.

We see his self-absorption and feel tender towards him, or wary of him, translating the strength of his desire as vulnerability. For a woman to retain her own experience in the face of such intensity, she needs to absorb herself in her own responses.

Not all women can put their legs above their heads. If we want to, it is easier to achieve with pillows placed under our back and buttocks. The further back our legs go, the more the top half of our body is restricted – making it difficult to breathe properly. With legs held apart, or over our heads, penetration can be very deep: it is important that the woman is in charge of how much, and how deep, she wants his penis inside her. We also get cramp in awkwardly held legs, locked hip-joints and aching backs. The haze of sexual passion tends to obscure painful limbs until it is all over – then we realize, as if it is a surprise, how contorted we have been.

BELOW: She brings her pelvis up to meet him because he has taken the weight of his body on his own hands.

RIGHT: Holding her legs he has control of their sexual experience – but she indicates with a hand how far to go.

The woman's genital experience is primarily of receiving a thrusting penis at different angles and depths. If she enjoys quite forceful penetration, this will be a delight. If she does not, she may become dry.

She can contribute to her own excitement by touching her breasts and clitoris. As with other positions where she is almost upside down, women experience both the alarm and the excitement of being out of control. It is important that he stops if she gets frightened.

These positions are ridiculous, of course, though useful in confined spaces like the back of the car or the bathtub. Fortunately, sexual passion creates a temporary blindness and insensitivity which helps us all deal with the crazier aspects of sexual passion.

RIGHT: Both are engrossed in giving the woman as much sensation as possible – a mixture of his pleasure in penetration and hers in being looked after.

Good sex produces the most wonderful alignment and balancing of bodies, so that one can be made out of two, as here. Connected by no more than a penile shaft held closely inside her, they are completely in contact.

Sex Out Of Doors

ABOVE: A warm entwining of limbs and genitals in the security of a sheltered garden.

THE TECHNOLOGY of book production prevents us from having music playing here, but imagine that the garden has your favorite sounds drifting across it. Imagine making love to your favorite rhythms. Or perhaps you simply want to pick up the sound of birds. Whatever your sound sense tells you, engage it here.

Then all your senses will be engaged – the smell of grass, sight of each other, touch and even taste. Try tasting your lover's body after it has been lying pressed against grass.

The special differences about sex outdoors are the sense of not being enclosed in any way; light air on your body; and the freedom that the outdoors brings.

What is happening is pretty familiar – except of course that the occasion is different. No-one should imagine that it is possible to make love in exactly the same way twice. Subtleties of mood, of context, of place and simply of skill combine to make every occasion entirely different.

Try never to make love as you have made love before, using tired routines. The miracle of the first really satisfying experience of lovemaking is still within your bodies to recapture. Remember courting is for ever.

It is courting that introduces us to the mystery of the difference of the other person. Because men are so much less attached to feelings than are women, and because so much sexual sensation lies in the tip of their penises as compared with the rest of their bodies, it is wretchedly easy for men to focus too quickly on their own gratification; and for women to believe that that is what they should allow. Protecting fragile male egos is a rotten job, and should not be off-loaded onto women. The hard wiring, though, leaves men prone to take action and women too ready to mend the hurts.

Sex out of doors is a fantasy that many people have but not many actually get round to trying out. Fear, as much as lack of opportunity, makes that so – fear of discovery and perhaps guilt about being so deliberately sexual in the first place.

Acknowledge the guilt and fear but try it anyway. Explore your personal boundaries to discover if you have to let these inhibitions spoil your enjoyment of sex. While making love is of course for most people a very private act, and real intimacy requires freedom from intrusion, fear can make us so restrict ourselves that the barriers it creates also inhibit our enjoyment.

Good, loving sex is about being uninhibited with the body of the person we love. Sex out of doors creates a setting of daring that can encourage us to be more uninhibited than most of us usually are. Try it.

IF WE ARE able to find a secluded place to pee in the countryside, we are able to find a place to make love. Much as we like to think that our own sexual acts are inspired emotional events within the privacy of our own four walls, we can also relate to the explicit urgent mating that we see between animals in a field. Sex is so multi-faceted that it can combine reproduction and play with spirituality and aestheticism. Making love in the open air gives us an opportunity to meet a myriad of needs, to overcome routine prohibitions, or sex that does not want to wait for bedtime.

Environments for sexual intimacy are as plentiful as imagination and courage permits. We make love in fields, woods and deserts; on top of mountains, haystacks, roofs; in the sea, on the beach, by a lake. Closer to home, we use our gardens, our balconies and our porches. In urban environments there are deserted parking lots, vestibules and parks. Groping under clothes against a brick wall can be just as sexy as bathing naked in a lake under the stars.

Some people are excited by the possibility of discovery; others find it worrying. Some like to watch people being sexual together. Most of us feel an innate sense of privacy about sex and want neither to see others, nor be seen. Hiding, concealment and inhibition are

RIGHT: Evening shadows, cool grass, firm earth, and blue eyes.

LEFT: Half-naked and on all-fours, she enjoys her own wildness and the sights and sounds of life around her.

Completely undressed together, she feels sun and air on naked skin. She is in a position to keep watch, and to enjoy being fully observed by him.

And so the prize is fairly won. Though he's restrained, she's just begun. We'll leave them for their private fun.

therefore likely to be features of open-air sex. What compensates is the sensuality of the experience in natural surroundings, and the urgent passion that makes even a store doorway acceptable. The experience of air on bare genitals is strange in itself. Warm sun or cold wind enlivens the naked skin. There are the smells of grass, sea, flowers and trees to inhale, and the sounds of birds and animals and rustling leaves. Apart from seeing our lover, we might also be able to see beautiful scenery. Sometimes the beauty of nature is so overwhelming that it is enough to hold hands with a lover, rather than make love.

Full intercourse usually requires one person to be on guard, and therefore not necessarily quite as able to surrender fully to the experience. The practicalities of open-air sex can be particularly difficult for a woman. She may not have access to contraception. She may be wearing clothes fit for hiking, or a tight swimming suit or a dress that wrinkles. When clothes cannot be shed, there is still the possibility of lots of touching, pelvic grinding, his hand in her bra and her hand in his pants. Taking her underwear or pants down slightly allows restricted access to the genitals and slight penetration. Where her legs are kept together by tight clothing, she can kneel on all-fours and he can penetrate her from behind. With a skirt or dress on, she can sit on top of him or lie underneath. Who minds being scratched by trees or grass, or tearing clothes in sexual excitement? And afterwards there is the closeness, the laughter, and the memory.

Pregnant Sex

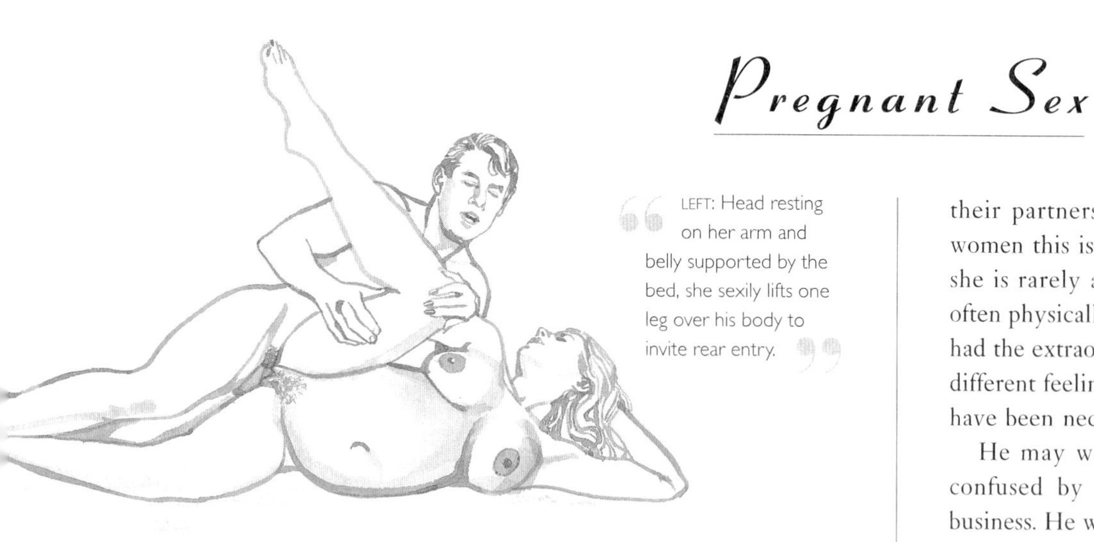

LEFT: Head resting on her arm and belly supported by the bed, she sexily lifts one leg over his body to invite rear entry.

BETWEEN LOVERS, when a pregnancy has established itself and a new life is growing inside one's partner, a man has to find out what it actually means for him. What does it mean? To whom does she belong now? Will anything be different? And what about sex? Is it alright to go on as normal?

All the evidence suggests that it is completely safe to have sex during pregnancy provided that there is no history of miscarriages. Although female orgasms create contractions of the uterus, this seems to have no effect on a developing embryo and does not dislodge a fetus.

Both women and men have different feelings about having sex during pregnancy, however, and attitudes may be more important than physiology. Some women show a marked increase in sexual interest while pregnant, especially in the middle three months. Most women are not interested in sex if they are experiencing morning sickness and other discomforts while the pregnancy establishes itself in the first three months. That is hardly surprising.

All survey evidence indicates that rates of sexual activity continue at usual levels during the first seven months of pregnancy, however, falling only in the last two months.

This, of course, is partly due to the physical awkwardness of making love with a large stomach. Despite the overall disadvantages of the missionary position for making love, most couples use that position most frequently. This is true of the first six months of pregnancy too. Then female superior and rear-entry positions become more popular.

A swelling stomach does not preclude manual and oral sex, of course. Whether you participate in these pleasures is likely to depend very much on whether they are already part of a sexual pattern before pregnancy. This is also the case with positions other than the missionary. Pregnancy is not a good time for being experimental about sex. It is a time when your partner wants to be made to feel safe, not challenged. If in doubt, cuddle.

Sex *after* pregnancy is a matter which receives too little attention. It may present more problems than sex before pregnancy.

Men tend to expect that a short time after the baby's arrival their partners will be happy to resume sex again. For many women this is a period of great conflict about sex, but a conflict she is rarely able to sort out with her partner. The couple are often physically exhausted – she more than he, probably. She has had the extraordinary experience of childbirth and may now have different feelings about her body and vaginal canal. Stitching may have been necessary.

He may well have been present at the birth, and be quite confused by the difficulty, pain and mystery of the whole business. He will also have seen his partner under medical conditions, in the hands of other people which, however clinically dispassionate, can feel like an invasion of aspects of his partner's body. Their joint intimacy, which was previously entirely reserved for them together, has been compromised.

Sex after childbirth poses problems, therefore. It requires a good deal of mutual understanding and sensitivity to each other's needs, and time to resume the normalcies of life.

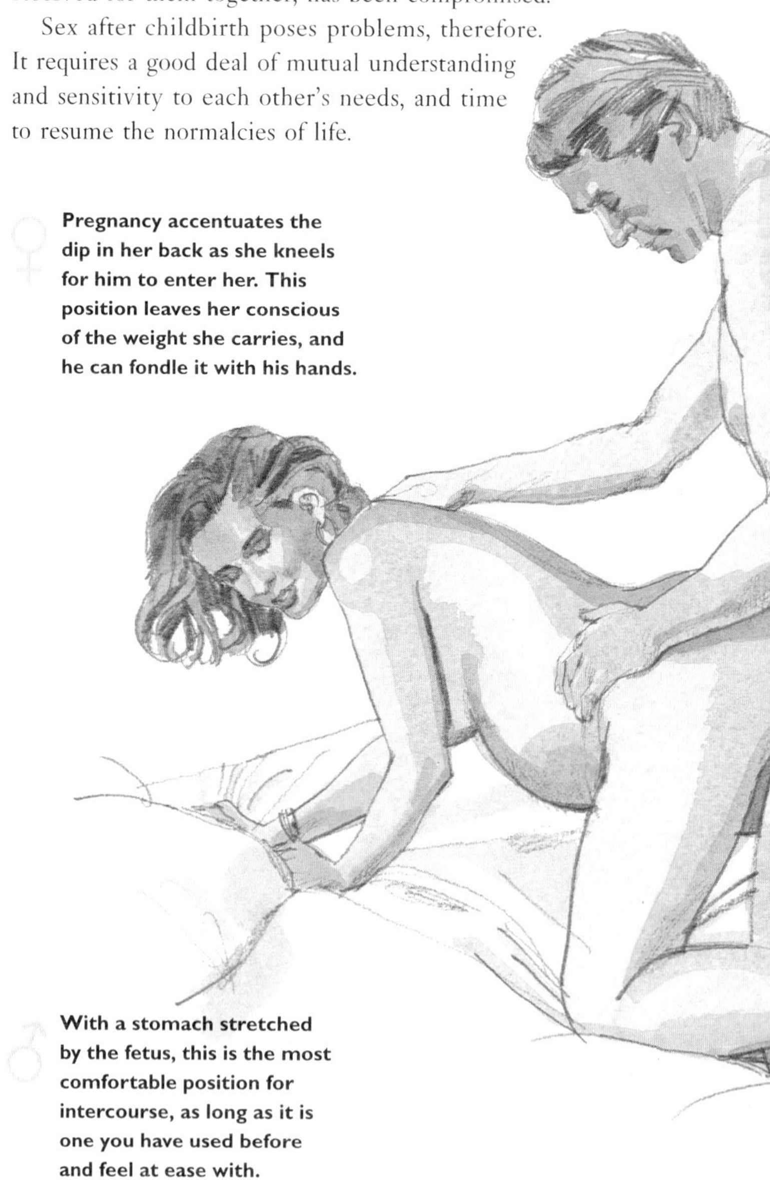

♀ **Pregnancy accentuates the dip in her back as she kneels for him to enter her. This position leaves her conscious of the weight she carries, and he can fondle it with his hands.**

♂ **With a stomach stretched by the fetus, this is the most comfortable position for intercourse, as long as it is one you have used before and feel at ease with.**

RIGHT: Not easy for her to maintain when she is very heavy. She uses her thighs to move on his penis.

ALL MEN experience a mixture of feelings towards a pregnant woman. She becomes mother, instead of girlfriend; fat instead of thin. She is a turn-on because her breasts become large and her belly swells. Some men seem to like the sense of public potency and ownership that being the mate of a pregnant woman implies. Others prefer the more private enjoyment of shared intimacy and fertility. But some men may tell us that, sorry, those pendulous breasts and thickening waistline are a real turn-off, and our obsession with the baby is rather tedious.

The peculiarity of the body changes inevitably makes women turn inwards. We want those close to us to be as mesmerized. We want acknowledgement of our changed state, but also reassurance that nothing has changed. Sex during pregnancy helps us feel normal. For women who hate contraception, freedom from anxiety and intrusive birth-control devices makes sex more relaxed and enjoyable. Women who have always wanted larger breasts feel more voluptuous. There are times when sickness or backache get in the way, but pregnancy tends to make women feel more female, earthy, beautiful, and wanting closeness.

However, pregnant women may also reject their mates. He does not understand everything she experiences. He is unsympathetic to her feelings or not helping enough. We feel too tired or too ill to be sexual. We fear, irrationally, that penetration will damage the baby or produce a miscarriage. Worse, we hate our own swollen form and refuse to believe that he could be attracted. The only good thing about pregnancy is that we can legitimately ask to be looked after.

At its best, when there is no physical or emotional rejection, sex in pregnancy is closer, more loving, than ever before. It is only in the last three months that the "tummy" gets in the way of face-to-face sex. Feeling his hands smoothing a rounded belly from behind, makes us feel proud and sensual. He can reach down and feel the vulva we can no longer see. He can play with breasts and nipples that are enlarged, and remind us that our bodies are there for sensual pleasure too, not just for producing babies and the needs of impending motherhood.

ABOVE: Spooning is a natural position when she is too swollen to lie face-to-face. She reaches out for emotional contact with his face, while he holds her breasts.

Climax

She leans forward so that her clitoris rubs against his pubic bone, or the upper vaginal edge meets his penis.

IF MEN HAVE to learn how to take things slowly and sensually, women have to learn how to achieve orgasm. It does not help that men cannot see what the problem is for women: men rarely have difficulty climaxing.

Orgasms do not happen by magic. In order to have an orgasm, a woman needs three things: to focus exclusively on herself, to hold an erotic mental image, and to have appropriate stimulation. Easy, you'd think – just as it is for men. Far from it. Making love, a woman is not focused on herself; she is focused on him. She doesn't hold an erotic mental image because she cannot think of one. She does not have the physical stimulation she needs because that would mean asking for it, or showing him, or telling him she prefers clitoral to vaginal touching, or that she wants him to bite her nipples, or any other secret desire. So we don't say anything, and we hope it will happen by itself, and we pretend it doesn't matter, and we put up with the disappointment.

An orgasm has been likened to a sneeze. There's an "itch," a build-up of sensation and a convulsive release. And, like a sneeze, we know when we have had one. The "itch" of a woman's arousal is more like a warm internal buzz which develops into surges of intense pleasure, provided we get the right kind of stimulation. Clitoral sensations become more exquisitely electric; vaginal sensations become more diffuse and throbbing.

The right kind of touch will depend on every individual woman's anatomy. In general, light friction over the clitoral area or the whole vulva, and heavier friction within the rim of the vagina, applied with fingers, penis or tongue, with enough persistence for the women to be able to relax into the sensations, will heighten her experience. Some women like a teasing touch; others, something more reliable. Gradually, if she allows herself to be completely absorbed in the feelings, she will feel her responses change from the frustration and desire of early arousal to the intense throbbing of the plateau stage. Then it takes a little more stimulation for her to tip over into orgasm and release.

At orgasm there is a simultaneous convulsion of the body and the mind. The face contorts, breathing stops briefly, major muscles become taut and rigid. It feels as though the genital and pelvic areas are exploding – sometimes powerfully, sometimes gently. There are a few seconds which can only be described as ecstasy. Physically, an orgasm can leave us feeling faint or exhausted; emotionally, it can be a time of cathartic release; spiritually, it can leave us transformed.

A man should not be blamed for a woman's lack of orgasm – that is her responsibility. But it is not helpful if he puts pressure on her to "perform," or suggests she should climax vaginally rather than clitorally. It is more helpful if he learns about her needs, and is prepared to be generous enough to spend time giving her the most sensation that he and she can create together, before he has his own climax.

RIGHT: He has brought her to orgasm by using his hand on her clitoris. She arches her back in orgasmic spasm.

AS WE POINTED out right at the beginning, sex is perfectly natural but it is not always naturally perfect. That observation has to be modified somewhat so far as orgasm is concerned.

A man has to have a climax to be reproductive. A climax and an ejaculation are, for all practical purposes, the same thing. But a woman does not have to have a climax to be reproductive. Her sexual feelings and sensations need not be involved in any way at all at the point of conception.

This causes serious complications. The man is driven to a climax, the woman has to find one. A skilful man learns that being good at helping a woman to find her climax makes sex enormously more enjoyable for him. But he may not know much about how women's bodies work; and unhappily many women do not know a great deal either.

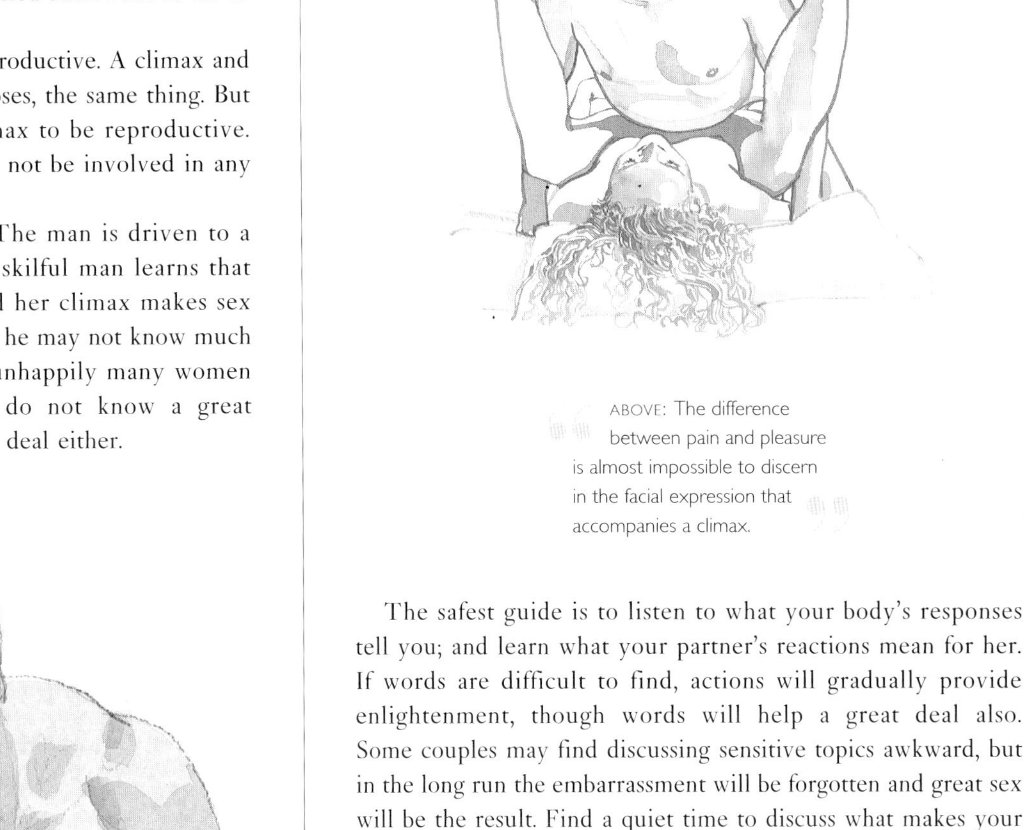

ABOVE: The difference between pain and pleasure is almost impossible to discern in the facial expression that accompanies a climax.

The safest guide is to listen to what your body's responses tell you; and learn what your partner's reactions mean for her. If words are difficult to find, actions will gradually provide enlightenment, though words will help a great deal also. Some couples may find discussing sensitive topics awkward, but in the long run the embarrassment will be forgotten and great sex will be the result. Find a quiet time to discuss what makes your partner excited – but don't do it in the bedroom after an unsatisfying episode. Have the conversation on neutral ground.

However, mixed up in this is the question of whether a man has sufficient control over his own ejaculation. If he comes every time his erection touches the entrance to the vagina, or almost as soon as he has entered, his partner will not have much fun. So part of the skill of being a good lover is to have the kind of ejaculatory control that both you and your partner can rely on. There's then a chance of achieving the orgasms that you both want.

Just plain and simple sensation is represented here, with a man who looks quite lost in his own feelings, which at the precise moment of ejaculating is almost all it can be.

Resolution

ABOVE: His climax is over but she still feels aroused and interested. A loving man knows that this is the best time to respond emotionally, even if another erection is not immediately available.

THERE IS no sensation of relaxation so total as that which follows a full climax. Immediately following ejaculation, blood that has kept the penis erect surges back into the body. Half the volume of erectile blood in the penis returns to the body within ninety seconds, and the rest gradually seeps back over the next few minutes. This is accompanied by an overall body sensation of complete muscular relaxation.

ABOVE: Words are unnecessary as they hold each other close enough to breathe the same air and smell each other's skin.

Perish the man who turns his back on his partner at this point, hugging the pillows about his curled-up body, and drops off into sleep. He will leave a woman feeling very alone, very used, and poorly cared for.

It often happens that a man's climax leaves a woman feeling woken up and alert, ready for gentle conversation and the continued evidence of loving. Some men see this just as women's perversity, and evidence of unlimited demand which they are certainly not going to give in to. A knowledgeable man, however, knows that this time is precious for cementing his relationship, no matter how long he and his partner have been together.

Take time to focus on her needs at this point. It may be that you have both had a climax, and want nothing more than to drift off to sleep in each other's arms happily exhausted. Nothing can be better than letting that happen – together. If that is not the case, find out what your lover wants and learn to respond to it. It makes for a profound sense of harmony.

Men almost always have a climax as a consequence of intercourse, so their needs tend to predominate in the post-coital phase. Women are also conditioned by all kinds of subversive signals to take care of men's needs in preference to their own. The woman who knows that the man is taking care of hers, even at a time when all he wants to do is fall asleep after his orgasm, has a man she can trust completely. There is no truer recipe for loving sex than this.

So the resolution phase is not so much about the ending of a climax. Much more importantly it is about cementing the relationship together.

ABOVE Letting the penis soften in the vagina is a lovely way to fall asleep.

PHYSICALLY exhausted and emotionally bonded, we fall into each other's bodies to rest. Arms and legs curl around warm limbs, heads lie on shoulders and nuzzle into necks. We drift peacefully and lovingly into a half-sleep, not even bothering to disconnect genitals. We speak to each other with soft words that caress, holding on to the closeness of the moment and savoring the pleasure for as long as we can.

It is strange to acknowledge that sexual bonding continues after the activity is over. It is as though we do not usually think of this – resolution – as part of sex. We separate the physical from the emotional. Yet for many of us, it is the emotional bonding that got us into bed in the first place and the emotional bonding that stays with us afterwards. Many men say that they can only talk openly and lovingly after orgasm; many women say this is the time they get the holding and intimacy they really crave. Orgasm also releases emotion, and we find ourselves tearful or frightened, angry or joyful. We lie in the security of a lover's arms trying to explain it all, crying a bit, raging or laughing. When we have been in and out of each other's bodily crevices, there is not a lot to hide, and not much that we want to hide.

However, gratitude and humor can follow sex, and the deep relaxation of bodies immersed in warm smells and warm skin. As bodies and minds return to their normal state, we reconnect with ordinary thoughts and ordinary life. We lie there talking about friends and family, events of the day, vague plans and unresolved issues. Women like this companionship and ordinariness. After the charge of sexual excitement, it is an acknowledgment of other levels of connection. We fall asleep, or get up to go to work, feeling cared for and caring as ordinary people as well as lovers.

There are interruptions to this idyll, like removing a condom or soaking up semen with tissues, or going to the bathroom, or eating because we are ravenous. Or there are children to attend to, 'phones to answer, work to be done.

Her body is softened and relaxed, breasts subsiding and face flushed. Wanting to sleep yet wanting to touch, she acknowledges his cuddling-up close to her with her hand.

She knows she's protected but free. He knows she's keeping contact with him. Both feel totally merged after making love.

There is a darker side too – the loneliness and frustration of disappointing sex. We have not climaxed, or not enough. We feel physically exhausted, but emotionally untouched. He has pulled away, or gone, or rolled over and gone to sleep. Or there is silence. Too much to say and neither person can bear to say it; or nothing to say. In such circumstances bodies remain taut, and impediments to intimacy are as huge as ever.

Fantasies

FANTASIES ARE images in the mind that have no immediate counterpart in the real world. Sexual fantasies typically contain rather more in them than *would* happen in real life. In one's mind it is easy to turn wishes into facts.

In real life it is surprisingly difficult to re-create one's fantasies. Only a medium like film, which in the hands of a skilful director can create a type of reality out of fantasy, gets close to doing it well. Yet even then we know that our eye is tricked by the magic of what we see. So fantasy seems to be a way of exploring ideas, wishes and actions which in real life are impossible or even, perhaps, too frightening to entertain. During masturbation particularly it is possible to let sexual arousal and the imagination stimulate one another.

There is a risk that if we do try to push fantasy into our real lives, it loses its interest and power to excite us. Yet sometimes we can play with thoughts that would not be so difficult to act out in practice.

Imagine the woman you love has gone to change for dinner, and then appears standing in the living room. Unexpectedly she is wearing a light overcoat, as if about to go out, and is groomed as if she were. But she slowly unbuttons the coat to show that she is wearing very little underneath, lets her coat slip to the floor, and poses with her hands lifting her hair in a way that makes it quite clear she that will be the main course.

It used to be thought that only men had fantasies and that women did not. Now it is known that both sexes indulge equally in fantasies, and that women fantasize in much more detail than men, and more easily in color, which is also true of their dreams. Women's emotional fantasies may be especially connected to feeling wanted, being held in the man's regard, or even simply being noticed. That takes us back to the importance in a relationship of paying attention, for the man who wishes to keep his partner really interested and satisfied. So many women describe feeling alone, even in marriage, largely because, when the initial phase of courtship and dating is over, they find themselves taken for granted. *Never* taking your partner for granted, and being able to rely on her absolutely because you trust her, is an ideal basis for a harmonious relationship.

Falling in love creates romance, characterized by moments of intense passion and intimacy. Long term relationships also require commitment based upon the *decision* that you love the other person and will do everything in your power to keep the relationship working through bad times as well as good. That resolution can make fantasies come true.

RIGHT: She knows what is in her lover's head, and is setting out to translate it into reality for him.

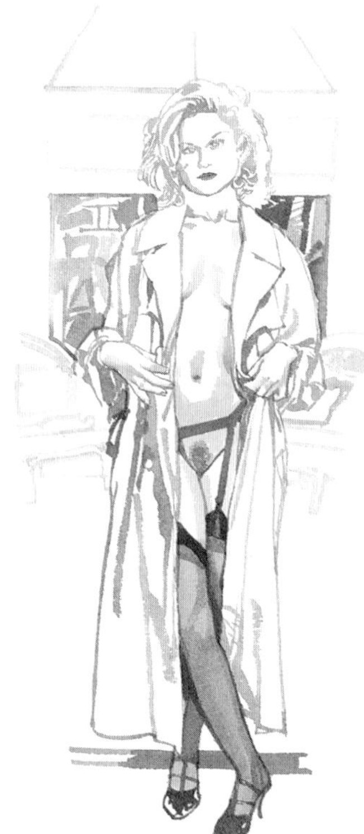

LEFT: The fantasy unravels slowly, as does the coat, so that her near-nudeness is titillating, and he is aroused watching her.

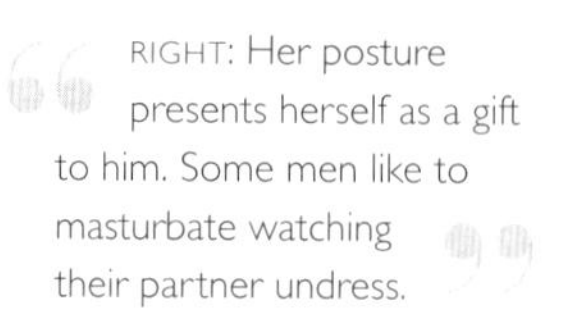

RIGHT: Her posture presents herself as a gift to him. Some men like to masturbate watching their partner undress.

RIGHT: The ultimate invitation to come and get it. How about strawberries offered from the vaginal lips too?

WOMEN KNOW quite a lot about men's sexual fantasies: they've been made public through all sorts of movies and advertising campaigns. Men know quite a lot about women's romantic fantasies: they have been made public in books and soap operas. Women know little of men's romantic fantasies, however, and men know little of women's sexual fantasies.

Women do not talk about their sexual fantasies. We are embarrassed by our own thoughts and scared of what others would make of them. Many women find their sexual fantasies disturbing, emerging as they do from the subconscious with pictures of oppressive and humiliating sex, anonymous onlookers, public sex, sex with men, women and animals. In these fantasies we are as likely to be the man or the woman, the oppressor or the victim. We know too that we would never want these fantasies translated into reality. Such fantasies are an attempt to overcome fears, and work through difficult feelings from the past. In eroticizing the very thing we fear most, we neutralize and triumph over it. In completing and enjoying something unresolved from the past, we make room for other thoughts and feelings. These fantasies become less powerful the more they are allowed into our consciousness. Like replaying a scene from a favorite video over and over again, we eventually become bored and switch off. There is then the possibility of other fantasies which are closer to our real-life relationships.

Men seem more keen to act out sexual fantasies, while women want to act out romantic ones. In a trusting partnership, we share in each other's fantasies. The convention and inhibition that prevents us from satisfying everyday sexual urges can be relinquished in the privacy and safety of the bedroom. The "doctors and nurses" games of childhood become the doctor and nurse, or waitress and customer, games of adulthood. Women tend to end up in short skirts, no panties and see-through blouses saying things like, "I've never seen one that big," and men tend to end up in bulging trousers, being strong, silent and demanding. These enactments may not be as exciting as the fantasy, but they have wonderful potential for dissolving into hilarity.

Suburban man playing woodland nymphs and shepherds might or might not look good. No matter, it is his fantasy.

The fantasy of being taken by surprise in the wild by an uninhibited stranger is one that can be acted out with a known partner in a safe place.

ABOVE: Fetishes, partialism, and a little submissiveness all combined in one experience here. It is the shoes that turn him on.

Fetishes

THE FRENCH got the word, *fétiche*, from the Portuguese, *feitiço*, which was used to describe West African gods and objects that were worshipped as having ritual magical powers. This is the word that has come into English as *fetish*. The magic comes from the power of an inanimate object to create sexual interest and arousal.

Sometimes this can be a particular aspect of the human body, on which a person has become so fixated that only that part of the body will trigger sexual responses. This is known as *partialism*.

Fetishes are usually pretty harmless, and are enjoyed in privacy. Very occasionally they can lead to a person stealing the object of their interest – taking panties off clothes-lines, for instance, or shop-lifting such items for the purpose of sexual gratification. Sometimes partialism can lead to very offensive behavior in public, when a man might try to touch a particular part of a woman's body. But for the most part, fetishes rarely come to public notice, any more than having intercourse in public is a common occurrence.

Fetishes tend to be male fixations; they are only very rarely female. Fetishes clearly show up the object-orientated side of men. It is also much in the interest of advertising and manufacturing industries to exploit this characteristic of men. Leather, rubber and plastic especially, all of which have the surface texture of skin, can be used to enhance the sexual appeal of clothes for men who are not apparently fetishistic. Women know this too, and set out to increase their attractiveness by stimulating the in-built responses of men.

Objects which have sexually arousing qualities are usually closely associated with sexual parts of the body – shoes being the main exception to this.

Most men know something about fetishism or partialism from their own experiences, without actually being specifically focused sexually on anything fetishistic, or limited in their sources of arousal to being partialistic. Both fetishes and partialisms are only harmful, in any event, when they are pursued at the expense of, or to the distress of, a real person in a relationship.

♀ **Women often comply with a man's fantasy. If she is herself turned on by high black boots and basques, she will enjoy the accentuated exposure of her buttocks, thighs and vulva.**

♂ **Enhancing aspects of the body by clothing them in natural or artificial skin-like substances is probably as old a practice as there have been hunters on earth.**

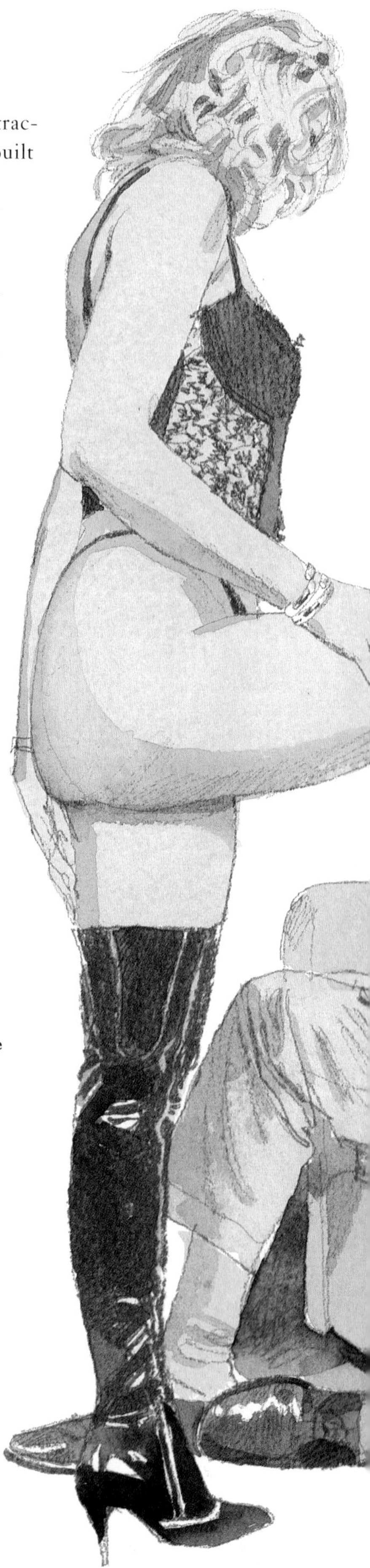

LEFT: Partial to ankles wrapped in stockings and feet encased in shoes, this man is worshipping her foot. Smell is often a very important part of fetishes, as well as touch and sight.

FETISHES SEEM to be a male thing. Women find themselves bemused by a man's obsession with feet, shoes, rubber or leather. We feel alienated, wanting to be loved for ourselves. We are affronted that our shoes are more important than our smiles.

Women are, of course, turned on by things associated with men we find attractive. We wear a partner's jumper, borrow his aftershave, drive his car. We hold on to objects which remind us of him. If advertising is anything to go by, women are interested in his well-cut suits, jeans and leather belts, fast cars and heavy gold watches. But we want the man inside the clothes too. A man with a fetish is sexually more interested in the leather trousers than the person inside them – and that is a lonely place for his partner to be, unless she shares the same obsession.

Not many women are as object-orientated as men, so a woman in love with a fetishist will normally try to change him. Or try to change herself so she can enjoy his turn-on. This may work for a while since many women love shoes with high heels, and feel sexy in leather. But inevitably we fight it too, not wanting to be in competition with an inanimate object. And a man with a fetish cannot suddenly switch his sexual desire. Some men try to keep it to themselves: a woman may notice that he is always buying her shoes or kissing her feet, but apart from feeling amusement will not necessarily be troubled by it.

A fetish is usually formed in childhood, and is often associated with the mother. It is not surprising then that the partner of a fetishist feels that she is in a competition that she cannot win. Despite women's endless capacity to adapt, eventually we go off sex or leave such a relationship.

ABOVE: Acting out a fantasy is something we all might do, but some men only become aroused when she wears the right clothes.

Sex Toys

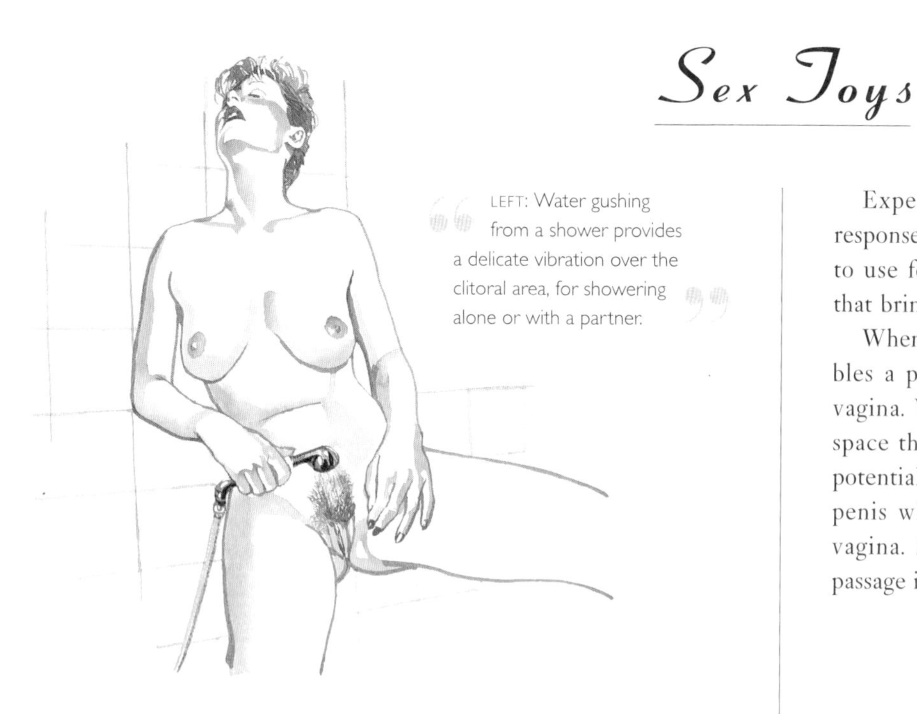

LEFT: Water gushing from a shower provides a delicate vibration over the clitoral area, for showering alone or with a partner.

ANYTHING WHICH increases sexual pleasure is a sex toy. Some, like vibrators, will be mechanical. Some, like creams or natural oils, will be an aid to lubrication and create additional smells. Some, like photographs in magazines, will be visual. Almost anything can be turned into a sex toy in the right circumstances, including lots of fruit and some vegetables.

When we are in the mood to respond to the other person more as an object than as a person, and she is in the mood for that too, then the best sex toy of all is the other person.

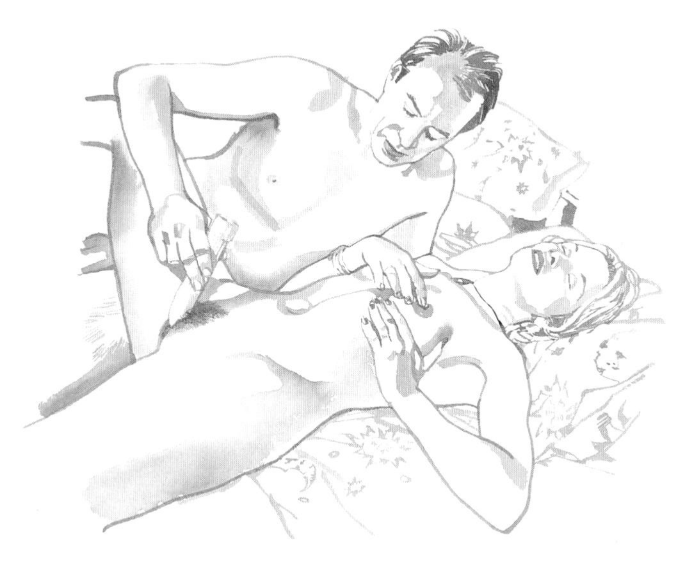

ABOVE: A generous man loves what he can give to a woman with a vibrator – multiple orgasms and her total self-absorption.

Experiment with the idea that your erection occurs in response to her. This makes your erection in effect a toy for her to use for her pleasure. As she uses it for her gratification so that brings pleasure to you too.

Whenever you are playing sexually with anything that resembles a penis, be careful about how you introduce it into her vagina. When not aroused sexually, a vagina is more potential space than actual space – just as a penis, when not excited, is potentially hard but actually limp. You cannot do with a flaccid penis what can be done with a hard one. Similarly with the vagina. Men think too readily of a vagina as simply being a passage into which a penis or other things can be inserted. Not so.

ABOVE: He uses heat-inducing cream around her clitoris, producing a rash of excitement they can both enjoy. But take care that it does not sting sensitive tissues.

It is a very dynamic and complex structure, responding to sexual stimulation by increasing its length, becoming more elastic, and opening its lips, as well as lubricating itself. If these changes do not occur naturally through a satisfactory process of sexual arousal, any session with toys will be much less interesting to your partner, and possibly actually painful.

SEX TOYS don't have to come from shops or mail-order catalogs. Women can use a warm jet of water from a shower-nozzle directly on to the vulva, or vapor rub on the clitoris to set it on fire. Video cameras and "instamatics" can be used to film each other in sexual poses – for private use only. Watching an erotic video together, provided you can find one that is mutually exciting, is part of sexual play. Then there are all the phallic-shaped fruit and vegetables. The vagina is wonderfully forgiving, provided nothing is inserted which can cause infection or minor cuts and abrasions.

Most people are turned off by the idea of sex shops and sex toys. They seem too artificial, intrusive or ludicrous. Women also resist them because we want sex to be multi-faceted, not just a physical act, and sex-toys seem pleasure-orientated to the point of dullness. However, women who have tried vibrators, and got past their artificiality, find them surprisingly freeing and almost companionable.

Vibrators are plastic, usually penis-shaped, and they buzz electrically against the skin. Some have a variety of massage heads which vibrate at different frequencies. Used against the clitoris they stimulate in a way which is impossible for the tongue, fingers or penis to do. The only trouble with them is their intrusive buzzing noise, and where to hide them if there are inquisitive children around.

Women who are comfortable with their own orgasms do not want a man to have to do all the work. The emphasis in the relationship is on desiring the very best for one another. In that sense a vibrator is easily incorporated into lovemaking where both partners can enjoy its effects, and none of the emotional closeness need be lost.

♂ **Creams and oils work both ways round. The penis has no spontaneous lubrication of its own until the later stages of arousal, and even then not very much. Lubricating the penile shaft makes it a very slippery toy indeed.**

Oils and creams make the penis or the vulva come alive more quickly. Some sex-aid creams claim to anesthetize the penis when premature ejaculation is a problem. Reciprocal stroking of bodies in the sunshine is a turn-on, with or without the oil.

Group Sex

Coupling in the presence of another couple. Some like to swap partners; others use the visual turn-on to have intercourse with their own partner.

Here couples are doing what they would normally do together, but in the presence of others. A major privacy taboo has been broken, which gives group sex its undercurrent of daring.

IN THE LONG-GONE days of the 1960s, when the world seemed remarkably innocent and fresh, and the personal benefits of contraception were high on the social agenda, sex with more than one partner seemed a very simple idea. Simple and daring all at the same time, but perfectly possible. "Wife swapping" (surprisingly, rarely "husband swapping") was not uncommon among those who liked to set the social trends in their neighborhoods, and many of these involved group sex.

Since then everything to do with the transmission of HIV and AIDS has given group sex a bad press. And, it must be admitted, it never turned out as just the simple fun it was supposed to be. Fun, often, but simple, never.

It's difficult enough to understand one other person sexually, and learn to trust them. It's even more difficult to take account of all the unwritten personal agendas that might be around in the triangles between three or four people.

If you are certain you can manage sex just for fun without damaging your core relationship, and both of you want to try group sex, and you are certain about the sexual health of anyone else who might be involved with you, then you might want to experiment. Never, though, emotionally blackmail your partner into something she really doesn't want to do. It will have bad consequences in the future.

In the past two or three decades, under the impetus of socio-sexual research, patterns of sexual activity have acquired specific names. Adultery (extra-marital sex) is no longer simple adultery. Researchers distinguish between "conventional adultery," the old-fashioned, cheating, secretive kind; and "consensual adultery," where extra-marital relationships are conducted with a partner's consent and sometimes with his or her participation.

This is what is usually meant by "swinging," or swapping partners. Hygiene and disease questions apart, there is a fundamental observation that women look to men primarily for the quality of relationship, and want sex as part of that; while men look to women for the experience of sex, and accept (or often not, as the case may be) the need for a relationship as part of that.

In these circumstances men are more likely to want to engage in heterosexual group activities than are women. Women may be willing to participate because they see it as a way into other relationships, not simply for the sex; or because they are afraid of losing their partner if they don't agree.

Group sex is largely an unexplored aspect of sex for most people. Perhaps it exists more in fantasy than in fact. To turn it into fact is, for many people, to risk damaging the balances within an existing relationship. Intellectually it seems quite possible as a course of action, but emotionally it is fraught with danger for most people – which, of course, sex being the perverse business it sometimes is, only adds to its attraction.

BELOW: Many women fantasize about being the object of more than one man's attention. Heterosexual men find the physical nearness of another man sexually strange at first.

WITH EYES closed or in a darkened room, we would have great difficulty discerning who is doing what to whom when there is more than one person present. Men who would never dream of a homosexual relationship, and women who never have a non-monogamous thought, find themselves physically responding to disembodied hands and mouths with as much arousal as if it were a long-loved partner. This is very confronting to those of us who believe that sex and love have to go together. Group sex is a lesson in the capacity of the body to operate quite independently of emotion.

It is also a chance to share a partner without the destructiveness of secrecy. Being unfaithful to a partner with their full knowledge and participation can encompass the excitement of forbidden fruit with the safety of permission. Some women like the idea of watching their partner with another person. Some of us like to be the center of attention from several people at once; some of us like the exhibitionism of making love with a partner in front of others.

The physical sensation of having many mouths and many hands over the body is the sensual equivalent of diving into a swimming pool. The whole body is brought alive in the same instant, and it is impossible to know where to focus. Intercourse might take place in couples or with many participants. Couples may want to preserve some interaction just for themselves.

What stops group sex happening more often between men and women is lack of opportunity, fear of the unknown, anxiety about infection and complicated emotions. Women tend to associate group sex with a lack of emotional attachment. However, many couples include another person or another couple once. Some make it happen by paying a prostitute; others set up something with trusted friends. Couples who swap fairly indiscriminately have a tendency to break up because there has been too little care of emotional needs.

LEFT: The excitement of a threesome. Hands and mouths connect reassuringly, demandingly, sensually. Feelings move as each body moves in and out of focus.

S & M

SADO-MASOCHISM, or S&M as it is more commonly known, involves sexual activity between consenting partners in which pain and humiliation are sources – and usually the main sources – of sexual arousal and gratification.

Elements of S&M are present in many people's sexual relationships, without them defining themselves as primarily interested in S&M gratifications. The power of a man to subdue his partner physically, and her delight in being subdued and overpowered, are normal everyday sexual experiences. However, when such sensations as these activities produce are allowed to become primary sources of pleasure themselves – such as enjoying being in bondage chains, being tied down, being whipped or doing the whipping, acting out the role of a slave, or being the mistress of that slave – then the activity falls within the sado-masochistic range.

Pain – whether it be psychological or physical – and sexual pleasure seem curious allies. Yet many people experience pleasure in small amounts of pain during love-making – being bitten or scratched being two very common sexually-connected experiences that would not be tolerated when out for a walk, for instance. The pleasure may derive from the fact that, when the body experiences pain, pain-suppressing chemicals, called endorphins, flood the body. This is what makes it possible for people to cope with the pain of injury, or childbirth, in the way that they do. It is one of the body's defense mechanisms.

Endorphins are like naturally occurring opiates, rather like morphine. If they fire off in the absence of pain, they produce feelings of considerable well-being. They are active when people fall in love, and possibly account for some of the obvious disturbances or changes in behavior which others can so readily see in people who are in love – loss of weight, over-activity, loss of concentration, shining eyes, and so on.

So it appears that there are close connections within our system between love, sex, pleasure and pain.

One special form of sado-masochistic activity is *infibulation.* This describes having holes pierced in the body so that decoration of various kinds may be threaded through the holes.

♂ **Completely captured leaves the other completely free. Surrender brings its own unfamiliar delights. Helplessness suggests also the possibility of rescue.**

♀ **Making a man captive can feel extraordinarily liberating for a woman. Love and aggression compete for dominance as she enjoys his vulnerability.**

ABOVE: Arms spread make breasts especially vulnerable. Legs bound together makes access tantalizingly difficult. Being tied up allows the "victim" to let go more fully.

Ear-piercing is a very common and socially-approved act of infibulation, but there are many others which involve piercing soft tissues that have sexual or erotic significance. Piercing the nipples in both men and women, or through the tip of the penis, or the soft labial tissues around the vagina is not unknown. Whether or not these experiences are erotic depends upon the prior history and experience of the individuals concerned. Quite clearly they would not engage in the piercing in the first place without the expectation of pleasure or pleasure-linked pain as an outcome. This presupposes something within their psychological make-up which would find such activities pleasurable.

It seems that around fifteen percent of men find the idea of S&M activities pleasurable. About three times as many men as women like to engage in S&M activities, often on a commercial basis where the women service numbers of men. Intercourse is very rare in S&M activities. The sexual gratification comes from the pain or humiliation, rather than the sexual act.

Despite the pain that might be involved, S&M activities are usually kept well within the bounds of inflicting real hurt or damage to another person. Sexual sadists, on the other hand, may do so. These are typically outside the inter-dependent relationships that S&M activities require.

LEFT: With vision blotted out, other senses come into sharper focus. Hearing, taste, touch, and smell create a world full of surprises.

WOMEN AND MEN commit themselves to each other with symbols of permanence. Some use a ring; others use tattoos. Young women symbolize their independence and non-conformity with nose-rings, multi-earrings or their own individual tattoo. Other women have nipples, navel or labia pierced with rings to express a particular form of physical courage and to explore sexual fantasies.

Women with ordinary inhibitions about sex have a hard time contemplating the allure of a whip, or the pleasures in tattooing or body-piercing. However, those same inhibitions push some people to rebel – to experience the cutting edge of sex where there is pain, punishment and intense feeling.

S + M (slave and master) is a variant of the sado-masochistic relationship in which one person is persistently bullied, humiliated and hurt by the other. S&M takes place between two consenting adults who are sexually excited by acting out scenarios in which one person is dominant and the other very submissive. We dress up deliberately – as women we are either the haughty mistress demanding things of a male slave, or the submissive servant of a male master. Rings can be pulled gently to increase sexual excitement in breasts and genitals; whips are used to "punish" before having sex, ropes can be used to tie the arms and legs of the "slave" so that they cannot resist sexual stimulation. Sometimes one person wears a collar to which a leash can be attached. These activities are all consensual, limits are agreed, and the pain is stoppable.

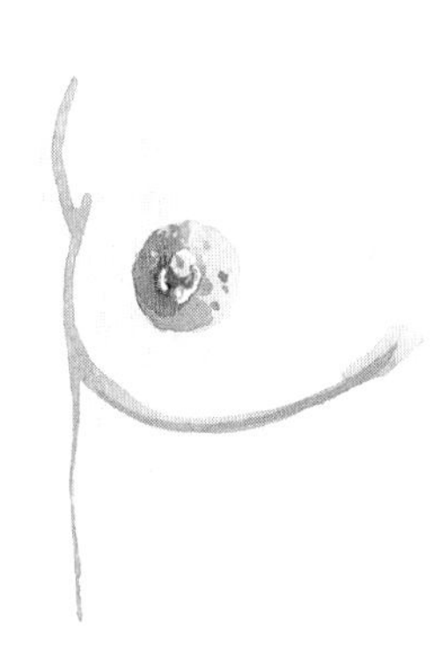

ABOVE AND BELOW: Infliction of pain on oneself can produce feelings of aliveness and heightened sensation.

It is apparent to most of us that aggression and power are part of sexual excitement, as much as love and liking, even if we do not fully comprehend why this is so. If we have never been tied down, and never felt like using a whip, we will know the pleasure of sex after a fight, the impulse to bite and scratch during lovemaking, and the deep satisfaction that comes from being with a powerful lover. We feel excited by being taken, so long as we are freely offering. We feel excited by our own conquest, so long as we know he is willingly acquiescing. In the play-acting of S&M it can be a relief to step out of a power position we adopt in other areas of our lives, and enact its reverse – a form of personal submission – in a safe, sexual context.

SECTION THREE

For Better, For Worse

There is no doubt that each one of us has to find our own way into the mysteries of being in love and being sexual. We cannot send anyone else on that journey for us and expect a postcard from the other side. Each of us brings to our adult relationships the emotional baggage of the past. We have no choice in the matter; it is all we have – except, perhaps, some in-built longings of how life and loves might be, could be, if only...

Out of experience and longing come the lives we shape. And then, of course, there is also our biological hard wiring – what has been built, on an evolutionary basis, into the design of the human system. Human beings we may all be, but male and female is how we operate. Into this also comes the social context in which we live. The later part of the twentieth century has seen a gradual move away from prizing social values into prizing individual values. In consequence personal experience is at a premium as never before.

As relationships are at the core of human experience, the spotlight has been turned on relationships as never before. The briefest reading of a newspaper makes it clear that what sells papers is a record of the minutiae of the lives of the rich and famous, who, we are often astounded to discover, also have nothing other than their own emotional baggage with which to explore their relationships.

When, in the late 16th century, marriage became an institution in which the state and church took a joint interest, and for which ceremonies and vows were devised, the idea of partners joined together faithfully for the rest of their lives became the accepted norm. In the event, death often separated people more frequently, and at much earlier ages, than divorce does now.

Significant improvements in public health and hygiene through the 19th century resulted, in this century, in a remarkable increase in life expectancy. The expected lifespan has almost doubled in a hundred years, from an average of forty-seven years at the beginning of this century to nearly eighty at its end.

In enabling such longevity, medical science has, not surprisingly, given little thought to the consequences for how people manage their lives. One such consequence, often unremarked upon, is that, when choosing a partner in our twenties, we now might expect that partnership to survive for fifty or sixty years "for better or for worse."

This is not the place to detail all the profound social changes concerning the roles of men and women in a post-industrial society; and the impossible burdens that are placed on relationships during times of rapid social change. The debates about birth control and abortion serve to remind us of the major social processes which have had a radical effect on the way people live their lives now, and how rapidly these processes have become an accepted part of our modern culture. All this makes "for better or for worse" a very difficult precept indeed. Believing in the power of change for the better as we do, there is a great tendency these days only to want the better, and not to suffer the worse.

The resolution of this problem is one that is in the hands of individuals, based upon the fact that within each individual lies enormous and largely untapped potential. It is within relationships that this potential can be most profitably explored, understood and enjoyed – though that is also the most difficult place in which to do it. We are also conscious that the experts in human relationships – counsellors and psychotherapists – may sometimes be more skillful at helping others manage their relationships, than caring for their own. Nevertheless, if the journey of an adult lifetime ends with relationships unfulfilled, it is in a sense a painful experience for which no amount of wealth can compensate. If, on the other hand, relationships have endured through the hard times and strengthened through surviving, and individuals know the power that derives from loving and being loved, then times that might seem for the worse can also turn out for the best.

In considering human relationships, we did not want to ignore the difficult parts. The next pages are about some of them. The whole of this book is about developing your potential and finding better strategies for not only coping with life but enjoying it. In this way the next section complements the fun of Section Two.

Jealousy, Anger, Hurt, Boredom

Feelings are the most important guide to what is really happening in our world. Without feelings there would be no basis for right and wrong, enjoyment, happiness, appreciation or regard; and certainly no love.

Women often think of themselves as more jealous than men, especially when they feel less powerful. Men, however, are just as jealous in similar circumstances.

Feelings are so basic to us that they are, in the end, what motivates all our actions. Despite the remarkable development of the human brain and its capacity to think logically, it is our feelings which are likely to be the truest guide to action and understanding.

There are three sources of difficulty associated with feelings, though. They can be very strong, very unpleasant, and contradict what we *wish* was happening. In consequence we can spend a great deal of energy trying to hide feelings or to deny them completely – especially when we do not want to believe what they are communicating to us, or we are afraid of revealing them to another person for fear of their reaction to them.

If our feelings prove to be uncomfortable for another person – we might be angry, but with good cause, for instance – the other person may try to deny the importance or significance of those feelings. Many faithless husbands, on first being questioned by their wives as to whether they are having an affair, launch into an attack about their wife's feelings and tell her she must be mad to suspect them. Getting trapped by her husband's assertions (and often her own inner wishes) that her feelings are not true, she can feel inwardly tortured by trying to deny what her subconscious knows to be true.

There is another characteristic of feelings which can make them very difficult to deal with. That is their ability to lie dormant within our data-banks of experience, ready to be triggered, almost like a waiting time bomb, by current events that recall them to the surface.

This is especially true in relation to painful events in our lives, especially when our self-esteem has been damaged. Unpleasant emotional experiences that happened to us as children and adolescents – when our selves were being shaped ready for the adult world – can be reanimated in later life.

Jealousy is the most powerful of all these feelings. It can establish itself with remarkable ease in childhood. The arrival of a new baby, dispossessing an only child whose feelings of rage are squashed by parents, is one ready cause. A sibling in adolescence being preferred by a father, or being excluded from a group of friends at school are also everyday experiences which, if they lie buried in the sub-conscious attached to feelings of loss and rage, can resurface as the cause of adult jealousy in both men and women.

Jealousy is the most corrosive of emotions, too, because it is usually linked to feelings of helplessness, unworthiness, and rejection. It can be so powerful that it can drive someone to kill in an attempt to expunge those feelings, and to take revenge for what may have been wrongs of many years before.

Jealousy hates the daylight. Françoise Sagan observed that nothing is more frightful than laughter to jealousy, for if jealousy is laughed at, the basic feelings of being spurned are recreated. "Thou tyrant, tyrant jealousy, Thou tyrant of the mind" said Dryden. Jealousy is very tenacious, though. "Anger and jealousy," wrote George Eliot in *The Mill on the Floss* "can no more bear to lose sight of their objects than love."

In its mild form, jealousy makes one person very suspicious of the simple actions of another. A glance at another person can be interpreted, lightning-swift, as evidence of an affair. The jealous person needs endless reassurance which, nevertheless, leaks away rapidly like water poured into a bucket with a hole in it.

Anger is a much more straightforward emotion. In its proper place, it is a healthy and necessary emotion to have too. It is the signal that the self is under attack and that it is necessary to defend one's self.

Learning to manage anger is a useful skill. Many people believe that the best way of managing it is to squash it completely – to conceal it. That is a complete error. It is a good way of precipitating a heart attack. But, like all social expressions of feeling, there are more and less effective ways of letting it show. Timing, style and verbal content are crucial.

Jealous feelings are like worms destroying something from the center. They can be immensely powerful – even lethal. Possession, ownership, and independence can be very difficult feelings to sort out.

Hurt has a thousand faces. We learn to manage the pinpricks of life as the self becomes stronger. The weaker the self, the more vulnerable to social hurts we are. The stronger the self, the more able we are to cope with minor slights. Some people are so defensive about being hurt that they lock their emotions away almost entirely, and live their lives as if under seige, never daring to let their real selves show. Eventually they have only an unexplored, defended self upon which they can rely.

Hurting someone else gives us temporary power over them. "The wish to hurt, the momentary intoxication with pain, is the loophole through which the pervert climbs into the minds of ordinary men," said Jacob Bronowski. Many men keep their women under control by little flicks of sarcasm designed to remind them who holds the whip hand. This is an impoverished style of relationship, which regrettably for many men and women seems to be the nearest they can get to affection.

The person who is secure emotionally has no need to hurt. A person who is not at risk of being hurt can dare to love. Perfect love gets rid of fear completely.

Boredom in a relationship is like water dripping into the foundations of a house. Eventually it will be found to have done a lot of damage that will need repair, but no one single drip was by itself responsible for the damage.

The Greeks recognized a terminal condition of boredom, called *accide* – the root word of "accident." It leads to cynicism and despair, and the wish to make things happen not with any overall purpose in mind, but for the sake of brief stimulation.

The modern world caters very well to the reduction of boredom through the provision of popular entertainment on a quite extraordinary scale. The more there is of it, though, the less opportunity individuals have of managing their lives based upon their own inner resources of imagination, the power of speech, and the capacity to love.

Try a brief experiment. Agree, within your household, that you will abandon television for a week: a month if you dare. The time not engaged in watching the screen will be used deliberately – in conversation with each other, perhaps, in reading, in spending more time making love as if you were dating again, or in doing anything you want to.

It will prove a fascinating experience to find out whether or not you have the resources to keep boredom out of your life without mass entertainment doing the job for you. If you cannot manage it, then some of your vital human qualities are at risk of decay. Stay healthy: do not be dependent on the media for dealing with your boredom.

Infidelity

INFIDELITY OCCURS only as a consequence of *fidelity* being expected. Dorothy Parker took her usual cynical view of the matter:

> *"By the time you say you're his*
> *Shivering and sighing*
> *And he vows his passion is*
> *Infinite, undying -*
> *Lady, make a note of this:*
> *One of you's lying."*
>
> (UNFORTUNATE COINCIDENCE)

It is in fact widely expected in our society that individuals in a sexual relationship will be faithful to one another, though estimates suggest that at least a third of men and a quarter of women in married relationships also have extramarital relationships. Some of these relationships are brief, some very long-lasting. As in divorce, the facts of what *is* happening tend to contradict the expectation of what *should* be happening.

Modern evolutionary biology is creating new insights into what makes marriage happen in the first place, and why it comes to an end. Old models that pointed to the fidelity of some animals and birds as evidence of life-long faithfulness, even in the lower orders, have been shown to be based on romantic notions of life-long pair-bonding. More recent experimental sciences show that most animals mate polygamously when and where they can, even if apparently "mated" for that season.

The more similar male and female are in size, the more likely they are to be monogamous. Humans exhibit about a fifteen percent difference in body size between men and women, which puts them within the range of animal species likely to be polygamous. Perhaps, therefore, unfaithfulness is in man's and woman's nature too.

Anthropologists have now established data on 1,154 societies of all kinds. Nearly 1,000 of these accept that a man can have more than one wife. There are a few examples of polyandry (women taking more than one husband) but they are quite rare. Moreover, further researches have shown that the more advanced the society the less likely is there to be polygamy. Thus, in evolutionary terms, human beings seem to be in the late stages of moving from natural polygamous and occasionally polyandrous societies into ones which are defined socially by monogamy.

So it may be that social evolution has outstripped physical evolution. Human beings still have within them the natural capacity to mate when and where they will – especially men – but they set out to control that impulse through the application of social mechanisms. Unfortunately these mechanisms are not

Women tend to blame themselves when an affair is exposed – whether they are the straying partner or the wronged party. Men also tend to blame the women rather than take responsibility themselves.

always very strong, and often fail to overcome the biological urges. We have not yet developed or evolved brain structures which would support complete fidelity.

What a mess! Contraceptive technology has certainly made it easier to give in to biology than was once the case. The impersonal nature of much city life, and the possibility of travel, also encourage brief liaisons. There is also a huge amount of sexual stimulation running as an undercurrent through modern society, from advertising slogans, to movies, to magazines wrapped in brown paper. This encourages males – by far the greater consumers of soft porn – to indulge in higher levels of sexual awareness than might otherwise be the case. Or perhaps, as some argue, it focuses and controls that interest.

All of which, however, leaves aside the moral question of men and women making commitments to each other, and setting out to share their lives together. As divorce becomes easier, perhaps there should be more obstacles to marriage, so that this very particular and time-honored social arrangement might be entered into with more real awareness instead of romantic fantasy.

What is certainly true is that infidelity produces some of the greatest hurts that men and women can inflict upon one another. For this reason alone, real thought is needed before a fatal step is taken – or one pursues a fatal attraction.

But if a partner is unfaithful, what happens to the relationship and what is to be done?

Reactions in the wronged partner vary tremendously. For some it creates intense shock. The bottom drops out of their world, and they suffer considerable depression, anxiety and panic. For others all those feelings get transformed into instant action. The unfaithful person is ejected from the house, and the strongest possible divorce proceedings are instituted straight away. Some people find that knowledge of their partner's unfaithfulness makes sense of subtle changes in the relationship that had been apparent for a long time, and though it is painful to know, it is also a relief.

Whatever the immediate feelings, the relationship is never the same again. An act of infidelity, once discovered, means that even if the relationship can find a new balance, it *is* a new balance, never the same as the old one.

Some people have suggested that the new order can be better than the old – that if a relationship has gone stale, the experience of infidelity may shock it into a new and better phase. Some people even use this idea to justify being unfaithful as a positive course of action.

There are better and kinder ways to revive a stale relationship than putting it at great risk by being unfaithful. Most people find that the scar which unfaithfulness leaves can too easily be turned into a real wound again.

Unfaithfulness strikes at the heart of trust in a relationship and trust is the fundamental basis of a living personal relationship, just as it is in business and between parents and children too. It is vital to think very carefully before putting that trust at risk.

For some people the possibility of discovery makes infidelity additionally exciting and dangerous – but when it happens, the fear and recriminations usually overwhelm everything else.

Female Sexual Problems

THERE ARE three stages in the sexual response cycle for both men and women – respectively they are desire, arousal and response (climax).

In everyday experience these stages typically follow one after the other – desire followed by arousal followed by orgasm. But the body has them organized as different systems within it. So although desire *usually* occurs before arousal, it does not necessarily have to. A person *can* be sexually aroused and feel no desire at all – indeed, may even feel repulsed at what is happening, and angry with themself for showing bodily reactions. Similarly it is usually the case that arousal precedes a climax. But in some instances a climax may happen without there having been any real appearance of arousal. A man may have a soft penis ejaculation, for instance, in the absence of any erection at all.

Difficulties can arise in any one of these stages, or spill over into all three. There may also be primary difficulties, in which the condition has always existed in the person since she or he became sexually mature; or secondary, in that it has arisen after a period of adequate function.

The cause of a problem may be either physical (usually hormonal), or psychological, or both. Understanding the blood chemistry of how the body functions sexually is an area of knowledge which is increasing rapidly at present. It is therefore essential in seeking help for a sexual problem to consult someone who understands both the physiology and the psychology of the processes, and how they interact; or someone who, in understanding one of these branches of knowledge, has access to resources in the other branch for appropriate investigative enquiry.

In **disorders of desire**, a woman may have either absent desire, generally low desire, or too much desire. Psychological causes might, for instance, relate to feelings of anger that she is unable to express about her man. These feelings might be either specific or general (disliking/afraid of all men, but subconsciously, and focused on a partner who triggers her reaction but is not its original cause, which comes from within her childhood/adolescent experiences). There are a variety of psychological mechanisms which can cause desire to shut down. Many current life experiences (like feeling neglected or unwanted when children have left home) may trigger earlier experiences in relationships which marriage had put into the background.

If there is no psychological or interpersonal reason for the absence of desire, then the causes are likely to be hormonal.

It is understandable, of course, that people do naturally experience very different levels of sexual desire and need, as they do with other appetites like hunger; and that there will be considerable individual variations. Often the real issue concerns the effect that a particular state has upon a current relationship. Low sexual desire in a partnership which does not enjoy much joint sexual activity within it, is unlikely to be a cause for complaint; whereas loss of sexual desire in a sexually active relationship would have quite different consequences.

Too much desire, resulting in compulsive seeking for sexual stimulation, is a very distressing condition when it (rarely) occurs. Victorian classifications of sexual problems – in an era when women were not supposed to be spontaneously sexual at all – described a condition called *nymphomania*, in which a woman was assertively sexual. This is a name which has passed into folklore, and any woman who shows a good deal of sexual interest is likely to be called a nymphomaniac. However, as there is a good deal of individual variation in

ABOVE: Wanting to be close signals the beginning of desire. Staying close and enjoying desire is sometimes more pleasurable than trying to create excitement.

LEFT: Arousal encourages contact with those parts of the body that are especially responsive to sexual touch, and so create erotic sensation. This promotes increased pulsing of blood flow which in turn enhances arousal.

sexual desire, it is probable that some women are normally much more interested than others in sex; and a few women will be very much more interested than the majority are.

High levels of sexual desire can be a problem if a man feels threatened by them. It is also the case that many women's sexual desire increases through their late thirties and into the forties, when for many men sexual desire is beginning to lessen somewhat. This can cause serious imbalances which need periods of re-adjustment.

Disorders of arousal are particularly apparent through the absence of lubrication. Lubrication in a woman is the equivalent of erection in a man. Both signal that blood, stimulated by the early stages of sexual desire, is pumping through the body and filling blood vessels which have particular sexual significance. If a woman is not lubricating, she is not aroused. It is generally a mistake to use a lubricating cream to replace missing natural lubrication as the use of the cream will mask the reason for lubrication not being present. It is not, however, a mistake to use an additional lubricant in a woman who feels thoroughly aroused but where she or her partner wants more slipperiness around her genital area and within the vagina. Nor is it a mistake to use a lubricating cream after the menopause, when lubrication might become reduced naturally, even though desire and excitement stay at previous levels or, sometimes, increase. Hormone replacement therapy will keep lubrication responsive to sexual arousal.

Disorders of orgasm are usually to do with not being able to get a climax. Many women can masturbate to a climax successfully but do not climax during intercourse. Some women have never established a climax. Some women can climax more easily by themselves than with a partner present, where they are fearful of "letting go."

Gaining a climax with a partner depends to a considerable extent on the partner's knowledge and skill; and also on the woman being able, within the relationship, to organize matters physically so that she gets the clitoral stimulation that she needs.

Most men pursue vaginal penetration as the object of their sexual activity. This is often not very stimulating physically for women, especially in the missionary position. Within the vagina the front wall is more sensitive than anywhere else. The missionary position creates hardly any contact at all with the front wall, nor with the clitoris. A woman above and astride her partner is likely to receive much more effective stimulation, from the point of view of getting a climax, than from the missionary position. This is true also for rear-entry positions, such as the one illustrated here.

Of equal importance is the man's capacity to control his ejaculation, as well as make a strong erection available. If the woman cannot count on a reliable penis, then certainly some of her pleasures in sex are going to be less than they otherwise might have been. We shall deal with those matters under Male Sexual Problems.

Difficulties with obtaining an orgasm are more often psychological than physiological; though there are hormonal disturbances which will prevent an orgasm establishing itself. A man's ignorance/boringness/impatience should never be left out of consideration, though. It is particularly hard for women

LEFT: Men can be too easily overcome by sensation from insertion. Making sure that a penis reliably produces pleasure for both partners is the key to good sex.

to deal with orgasmic difficulties when they don't know what they're missing: so here are some tips on having an orgasm:

- Set aside an uninterrupted time and lock the door.
- Find an erotic stimulus (book, movie, picture, memory, garment) and focus on it.
- Touch yourself where you feel most sensation; particularly explore your whole genital area with a moist finger.
- Use circular, brushing, vibrating movements around the clitoris, applying more pressure as excitement mounts.
- Experiment with different touches, different locations, different fantasies and images, inside and outside the vagina.
- If you lose sensation, pause and start again. Sometimes focusing too much on one place desensitizes it.
- Don't stop – even if it takes hours!

Clitoral stimulation is the easiest way to orgasm, and you can go from there to vaginal orgasm if you want to. Men tend to set higher store on vaginal orgasms because it makes them feel that they have given women an orgasm. All orgasms are self-generated, including theirs. We simply use each other as erotic stimulus. Nobody has an orgasm who does not allow it to happen themselves.

A vaginal orgasm simply means refocusing the location of excitement inside the vagina, rather than outside of it. If you are comfortable with your own way of having a clitoral orgasm, transfer your fingers periodically to the vagina while still stimulating the clitoris. Notice where you feel most sensation vaginally and don't be surprised if it feels quite anesthetized at first. Genital sensitivity increases with use and confidence. Try keeping the fingers of one hand in your vagina, while stimulating yourself to orgasm with the fingers of the other hand.

When that feels comfortable and easy, use less clitoral stimulation and more vaginal, gradually transferring the "rush" of skin excitement downwards to the vaginal opening. Use the fingers of one hand like a penis in your vagina. (It might help to keep an erotic image that includes penetration in your mind. None of this should be done without some fantasy.) As the vagina

BELOW: Learning to touch yourself sexually and knowing the specific sensations that arousal produces is part of the skill of teaching a lover what is best too.

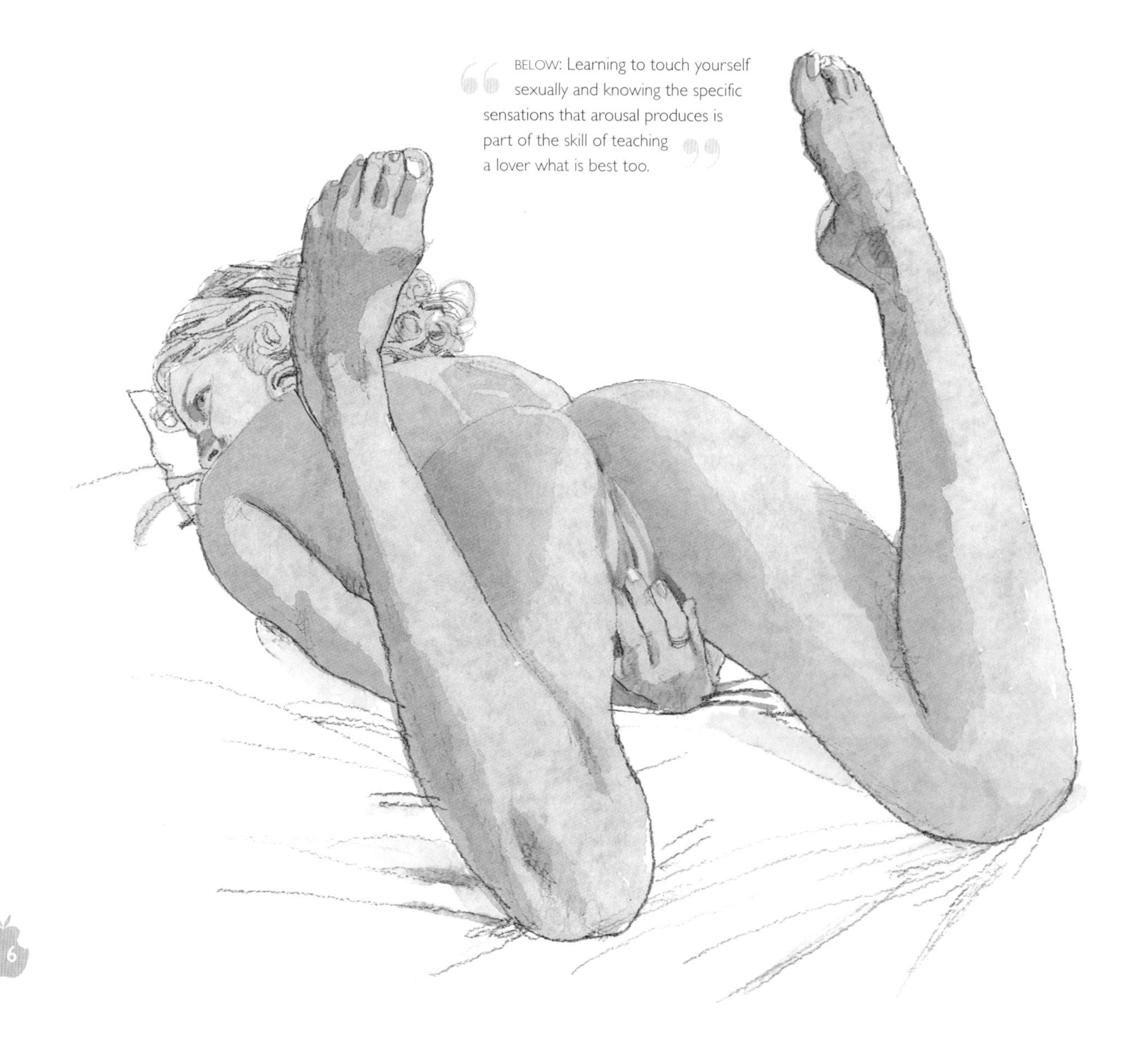

RIGHT: The G-spot is on the front wall of the vagina, about half a finger's length inside. Some women find it an especially arousing area; others not at all.

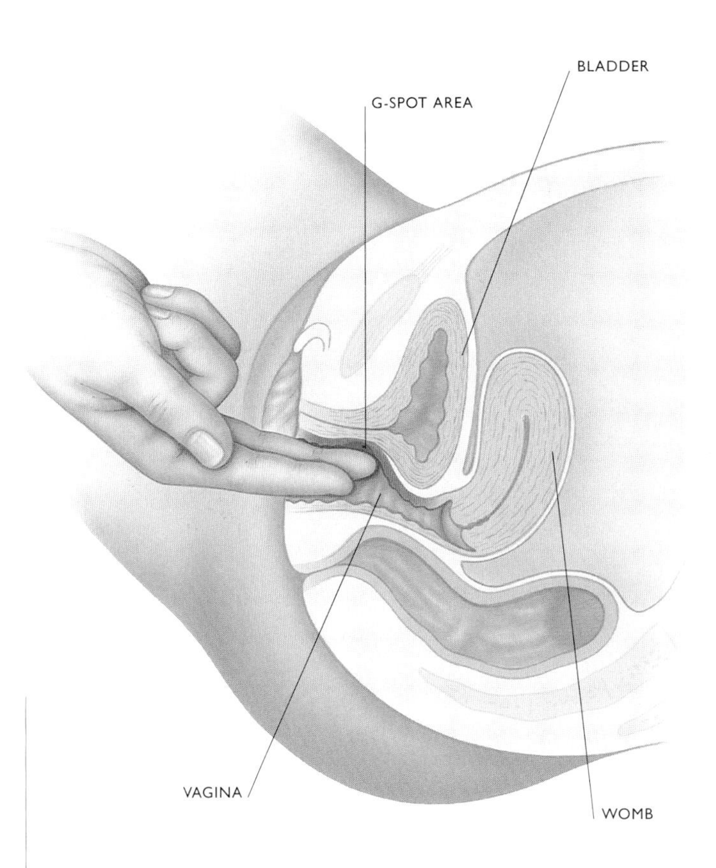

begins to feel more sensitized to your touch, apply more pressure. You might find that it is the outer rim that is most responsive, or the upper wall of the vagina, or the G-spot midway along, or a spot deep at the end of the vagina which can only be reached by deep thrusting. When orgasm takes over, it is likely to feel more pulsing and less electric than a clitoral orgasm.

Confident that your body works as well as anybody else's, you can then incorporate what you know into lovemaking so that you get the same kind of stimulus from your partner as you need on your own. You can use his penis as you used your own fingers. The more confident you feel that your body is responsive, the more you can both experiment with different ways of climaxing.

A very considerable difference between the orgasms enjoyed by men and women is that women can have repeated orgasms – what are called multiple orgasms – which seem to trigger one after the other if sexual stimulation stays right. By contrast, men typically have one ejaculatory climax, the erection goes, and then there is a period of time before the erection can be encouraged to return. The younger the man and/or the more aroused he is the shorter this period. In very sexually excited men in their late teens/early twenties, this limp period (the *refractory period*) can be as short as three or four minutes. In a man in his sixties it may be several hours. Lengthening of the refractory period is one of the consequences in men of aging.

There is one other sexual difficulty in women which is not related so much to physiology as to anatomy. This is a disorder called *vaginismus*. It comes about when the lower third of the vagina goes into spasm at an attempt at insertion. It effectively blocks the insertion of the penis, and is a psychological disorder of acceptance.

The difficulty usually occurs because a woman has been very badly treated, either by clumsy medical examination of the vagina at an early age or by painful sexual insertion. The body acquires an avoidance reflex. It is much the same as the spontaneous blink of an eyelid when a piece of dirt lands on the eyeball, and just as involuntary. It is a difficulty which can also occur as a consequence of fearing pregnancy; worrying about being hurt during intercourse; or because of actual pain upon penile thrusting. It is usually a cause of much distress to both partners, and requires very skilled and understanding help for recovery, but it has a very high recovery rate. There is an equivalent difficulty in men, which is to do with losing an erection, and which is described on the next pages too.

Male Sexual Problems

NATURE, BEING economical, uses exactly the same mechanisms for sexual arousal in men as in women, though the way they affect the anatomy is different, because the anatomy is different. In both men and women sexual desire causes blood to be pumped around the body, and from that everything else follows.

Problems can arise from physiology not functioning properly, psychological upset of recent or more historical origin, or a mix of both. Getting a problem straightened out needs skilled help from a sexual function specialist who, if not qualified both medically and psychologically, does have access to the specialty in which s/he is not qualified. This is especially important at the present time because knowledge of the way the sex hormones operate in creating sexual responses in the body is advancing quite rapidly. Even quite recently it was thought that most sexual problems had an essentially psychological basis to them. This is no longer considered to be the case. The balance is much more likely to be fifty-fifty.

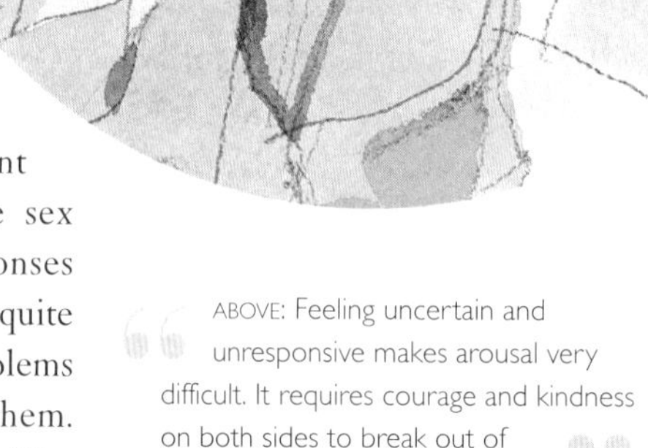

ABOVE: Feeling uncertain and unresponsive makes arousal very difficult. It requires courage and kindness on both sides to break out of sexual uncertainty.

Disorders of sexual desire in men parallel those in women. There can be absent or low desire; or too strong desire. As in women, the causes can be either psychological, or hormonal, or a combination of both.

Absent or low sexual desire comes most frequently to clinical attention because it is a cause of dissatisfaction within a relationship. A woman who finds herself in a partnership where she is apparently not desired may experience low self-esteem. A man with relatively low desire might have his desire and sexual energy raised by falling in love and courting, only to have it drop back to previous levels in the early stages of his marriage. This can create a profound sense of dissatisfaction in his partner, especially if his earlier encounters with her were in part stimulated by her higher level of sexual interest in him.

Some experimental evidence suggests that a man's sexual response is in part a reaction to the levels of estrogen in his partner – a finding that adds an extra element to the endless debate about who is responsible for what in levels of sexual interest and responsiveness between men and women.

Arousal problems show themselves very obviously in men. He fails to have an erection or it is only partial.

All sexual arousal, in both men and women, depends on there being effective physical or psychological stimulation – stimulating things happening to your body or in your mind. Unfortunately we have the power to inhibit our sexual responsiveness and/or block stimulation.

The consequence of this is that erections may not occur when and as we want them. Anxiety, depression, stress and ignorance are also effective inhibitors of sexual response. This is true for women, too. However, men's capacity to reproduce is intimately connected with having an erection. Without an erection it is very difficult to manage penetration and maintain arousal to create a climax ejaculation.

From a purely reproductive point of view, women do not have to be aroused to become pregnant, whereas men do have to be to have an erection. So a lot hangs on a man's awareness of his capacity to have and sustain an erection. Being able to have an erection means a great deal to him in establishing his identity as a man. Without it he feels powerless – hence the word impotent for the man who cannot become erect. The term "erectile insufficiency" is now generally thought to be kinder than "impotence" for this condition, but "impotence" is a word that in practice will not easily go away.

Attempts to find chemical answers to erectile problems are much at the forefront of drug research these days. There are now some drugs which, injected directly into the penile shaft, will, in some men, produce a long-lasting erection. They may have adverse side effects if used too intensively, however, and they seem best used to restore male confidence before the natural mechanisms of erection can take over again. There has also been a good deal of interest in surgical implant procedures in recent years. These leave a man with a permanent erection, but one that tends to lack substance or to look like a real erection, so that it lacks sexual aesthetic interest for his partner.

It seems probable that, within the next decade, chemical compounds will be discovered that do have a beneficial effect

on erections, at least for some men. Meanwhile, sorting out whether psychological or physical reasons, or an interaction of the two, underlie erectile difficulties is the first stage in getting effective help.

Orgasm difficulties are of two kinds – coming too quickly, and coming too slowly or not at all. The first is premature ejaculation; the second is retarded ejaculation.

Coming too quickly (or premature ejaculation) is boring for both partners. Ejaculation is controlled by a set of reflex activities which are triggered by the amount of sexual arousal the man is experiencing. The reflexes can be brought under voluntary control in much the same way that the passing of urine in small boys is brought under control.

Anxiety is one of the mechanisms that encourages quick ejaculation, so that a man who is already anxious about his control capabilities often finds himself in a vicious circle where the more he tries to get matters under control the less successful he is. This process can sap morale and seriously corrode the enjoyment of making love for both partners.

The technique for gaining control of ejaculation ideally requires the co-operation of a partner, and with sufficient application it can eliminate the problem over a few weeks of organized effort. The technique is called *Seaman's* technique, after the doctor who first used it extensively.

Both undressed, the man lies on his back. His partner kneels between his open legs, so that she can stimulate an erection by hand. Her task is to arouse him to the point at which he feels an ejaculation is beginning to develop, at which point, *and before the ejaculation becomes inevitable*, she places the thumb of her stronger hand in the position shown in the diagram overleaf on the underside of the penis, and the first two fingers around the penis, one on each side of the coronal ridge, and squeezes firmly.

This squeezing has the effect of inhibiting the ejaculation. Some of the erection may well subside too. When the feeling of ejaculation build-up has passed, she then repeats this stimulating and squeezing cycle four or five more times.

The object is for the man to have repeated experiences of being aroused followed by repeated experiences of the sensation of ejaculatory build-up being blocked.

Over a number of sessions of this kind, the man will be able to tolerate more and more stimulation without ejaculating. By this means, he begins to get the reflex of ejaculation under control. He also learns to distinguish between the feelings of ejaculation beginning to build up (ejaculatory demand) and the feeling that nothing will stop it (ejaculatory inevitability).

This squeezing exercise should be practiced every day if possible, for as many days as will make the man confident that he can work out what is happening to his ejaculatory cycle and

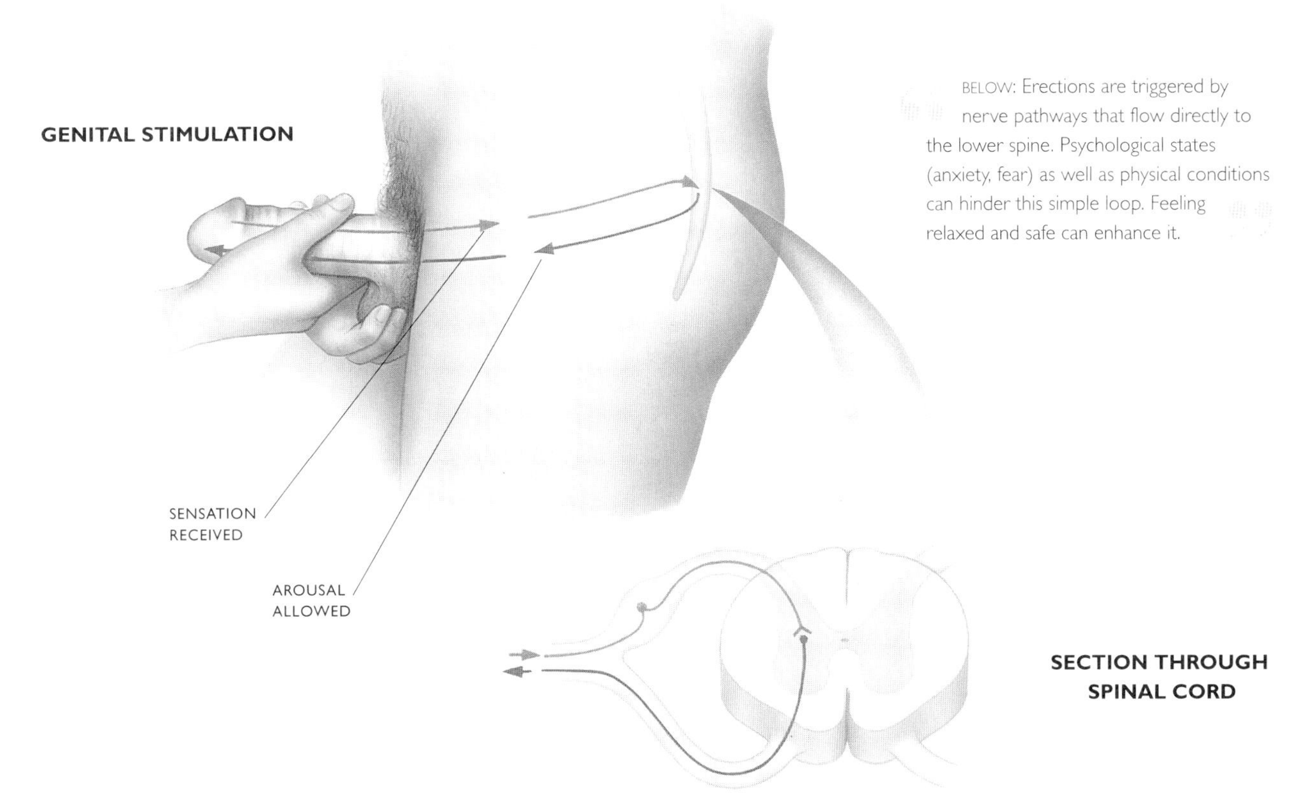

BELOW: Erections are triggered by nerve pathways that flow directly to the lower spine. Psychological states (anxiety, fear) as well as physical conditions can hinder this simple loop. Feeling relaxed and safe can enhance it.

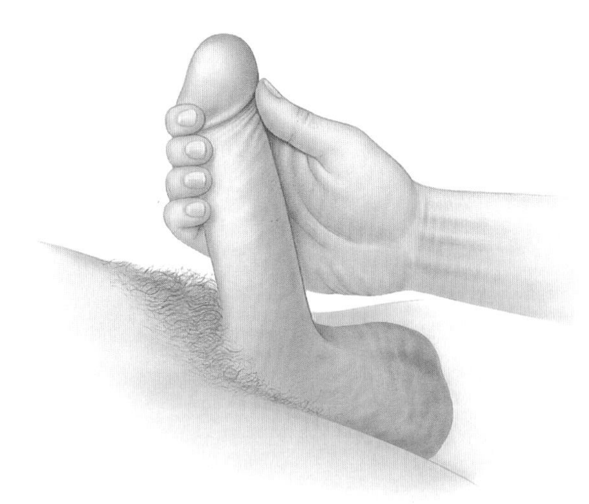

ABOVE: A strong squeeze applied by a partner's fingers like this will stop the urge to ejaculate. Practised as described, it helps build up better control of the ejaculatory reflex.

can begin to control them himself in the way that he controls the muscles by which he urinates.

When this level of certainty has been reached, then it is time to try insertion. With the woman in the superior position, try insertion and then hold the erection inside the vagina without a lot of movement. Try and increase the length of time for which this can be enjoyed without ejaculating. If the build-up feelings happen, he must let her know and she can ease herself off the erection, stretch a hand down to the penis and apply the squeeze technique again.

Gradually more and more stimulation from within the vagina can be used, with more and more arousal, until a climax happens by intention rather than by accident.

This whole process can be very frustrating for the participants, of course, as it is better not to have ejaculation by intercourse or mutual masturbation while the training technique is being used. If, as is almost certain to be the case, both of you do want a climax at some stage in the proceedings, then watch each other's masturbatory climax. For the man, let them be as slow and prolonged as possible.

There are also some drugs which have the effect of slowing down an ejaculation, and some doctors prefer this as a method of treatment. However, as with all drugs, the side effects can sometimes interfere with the process the drug is supposed to be helping. Seaman's technique gets the body's ejaculatory reflexes working to your advantage without chemical help.

Retarded ejaculation may well be caused by what is more properly described as retroverted ejaculation. In this process the seminal fluid is ejaculated back up into the bladder instead of out through the tip of the penis. This can readily be detected by examination of urine shortly after a climax has been experienced, when the urine will appear cloudy. Surgical intervention is called for here.

Otherwise, not having an ejaculation, or taking such a long time to reach a climax that a partner is discouraged from engaging in coitus, needs treatment by psychological or chemical means. There is a class of mood-altering drugs which, as a side effect, will shorten the interval to ejaculation as there are also drugs which will lengthen the interval for premature ejaculators. It is not entirely clear whether either of these drugs will have long-term beneficial effects in the absence of effective training of the ejaculatory reflex, though both can be very useful in breaking the vicious cycle of anxiety or despair that can develop around this troublesome problem.

The one other disorder of which account must be taken is the male equivalent of vaginismus in a woman. This is when a man has a sudden and catastrophic loss of erection just at the point of inserting his penis into the vagina. Like vaginismus which blocks insertion, this also effectively stops intercourse taking place.

BELOW: In the female superior position, the erection can be held quietly, moved against, or stimulated by squeezing pelvic muscles until the man signals that an ejaculation is imminent. Then the woman can slip off the penis and apply the squeeze technique.

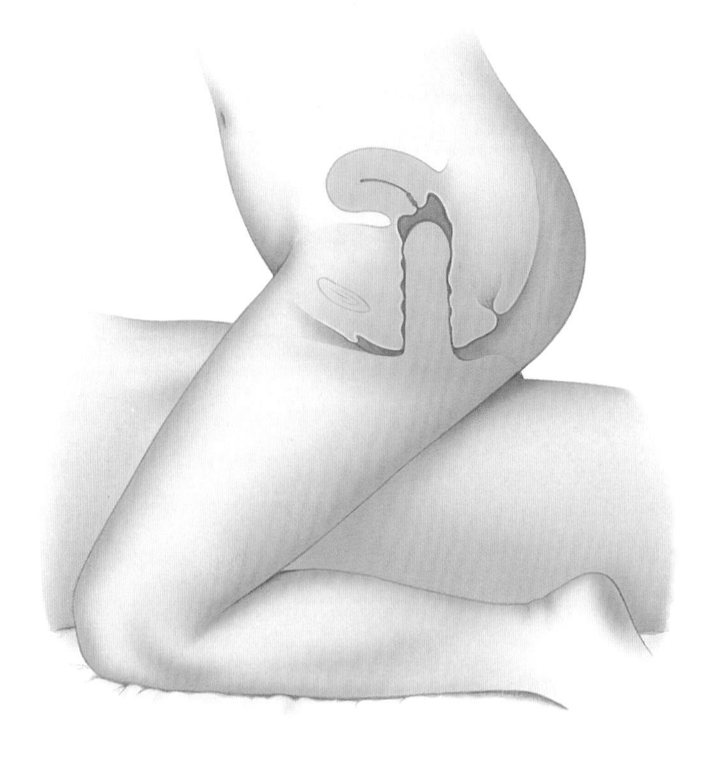

One of the causes of this is what is called *pelvic steal syndrome*. A man may have become erect in response to sexual stimulation, but when he starts moving his body around and preparing for intercourse, especially in the missionary position, the blood that was in his penile shaft gets pulled back into the muscles of his body. It is the same effect, though less dramatic, that most men would experience if, just as they were about to insert into their partner, a loud crash signalled that their front door had been suddenly broken down. The body, in emergency mode, would demand all available blood for action, not making love.

In a quieter way this is what happens in pelvic steal syndrome. By the time a man has got round to seeking help, it has usually happened often enough for him also to have developed secondary anxiety from his persistent failures, and this will also be contributing to the problem. Taking an accurate sexual history will make a diagnosis possible of what is cause and what is effect. This problem can be simply resolved by the man lying on his back while making love, and thereby using fewer muscles. As confidence returns, he can explore adopting other positions with his partner again.

If pelvic steal syndrome is not the cause of this particular loss of erection, the problem is more likely to have a psychological than a physical cause. There may be underlying fears of hurting a partner; of causing a pregnancy; or perhaps simply of not really feeling wanted. Skilled therapeutic help is clearly necessary in sorting out such matters.

BELOW: The lazy man's guide to good sex! Equally, the free woman's guide to good sex! If pelvic steal syndrome – a condition in which blood seeps away from the erect penis when a man becomes active during lovemaking – is a problem, this is the position to get things back on track again.

Aging

As with all our physical processes, the sexual system reveals its own particular signs of aging. Up until the late 1960s, it was generally thought that sexual activity should probably stop after the menopause in women and in the late fifties/early sixties in men. Now it is clear that this was unduly proscriptive and that sexual activity can go on being enjoyed into the eighties and nineties.

What is even better, it is a very healthy activity. The more sexually active that people have been throughout their lives, the longer their sex lives are likely to go on.

Sex among those over sixty is affected by physical and cultural considerations, but this is also true of sex anywhere in the world at any age. The specific changes that occur to the body with aging, however, are worth noting.

In the man an erection takes longer to appear and an orgasm takes longer to occur. Both erection and arousal to the point of climax need more direct physical stimulation than when younger. Older men are not as responsive to fantasy as they were at an earlier age. The contractions that propel the semen during ejaculation are not as strong; and the time taken for another erection to occur after an ejaculation lengthens considerably – perhaps to more than twenty-four hours.

General muscle tone is not as strong as one gets older, and movement may be inhibited by arthritis and allied conditions which make joints less mobile than they were. These sorts of debilitating and chronic disorders also affect how one feels about oneself. Feeling one is getting old encourages one to slow up and *be* old. An active sex life tends to be associated in people's minds with being young, vigorous and physically attractive, so feeling old has a negative effect: we stop doing the things that are associated with being young.

This can be a real loss. A gently active and continuing sexual relationship goes on affirming life; and there is perhaps a greater need to feel safe and secure in someone's arms and know that one is loved as age advances. It requires a good deal of courage to face old age. Nothing creates a sense of being encouraged so much as being certain that one is loved. And nothing creates that certainty so well as physical contact.

Making love is not just about intercourse. One of the reasons that it is important to build variety of expression into sexual relationships throughout life is so that these skills are well-established when they are most needed. If a man's erection is losing its strength in his seventies, and he really does not know how to give his partner a climax by finger or tongue stimulation, then her sexual life perforce has to stop too, because he is no longer physically effective. That need not happen.

A lively woman is a sexual woman, whatever her age, but social indifference can make it hard for those still loving sex to meet new partners. Some women use aging as a rationale for a sexless marriage or deeper loneliness.

Good sex comes from skills that are well practiced and enjoyed, just as good cooking does, or the routines which keep a house sparkling and welcoming.

In women the same general effects of aging occur of course. Muscle tone is lost, and a reduced intensity of muscle spasms affects the sensation of orgasm. The vagina will lubricate less after the menopause because of changes in the estrogen balance. Hormone replacement therapy can help. The vaginal walls may also become less elastic, and even quite thin in later old age, requiring care if tearing is not to take place.

In the 20th century films and advertising have made women immensely conscious of their body shapes, especially as far as breasts, waists and hips are concerned. The popularity of aerobics has pushed the socio-sexual anxieties arising from body-image to record levels. Many women are intensely anxious about losing the bodily firmness of their twenties and thirties. Feeling less and less attractive, they worry about their man's likelihood to stray. Vicious cycles of self-doubt can be set up at this stage. When, through the same media, men are also encouraged to see women as objects rather than people, the anxieties of aging for women become a real source of stress.

This is not an easy matter to change in a consumer society. Over the long term it can only be redressed by men and women valuing each other for their qualities as whole people, not stereotypes. Unfortunately these are qualities which courting, early sexual experiences together and even marrying only partially nurture. Long-term, committed relationships, therefore, are about discovering and loving the *person* with whom one is in a relationship. This is a lifetime's activity which carries us happily into old age.

Socially and culturally we are entering a period when there are infinitely more resources of all kinds available for the elderly than ever before. With rising numbers of people in the twilight of life becoming an increasing consumer force, and with relatively widespread economic security, the opportunities for continuing to explore life and its possibilities, including the sexual, into old age are greater than ever before.

The possibility of continuing personal growth is another benefit of the emancipation of the elderly. Retiring in your fifties and still having thirty active years of life ahead is now a reality for many people. Using that time to learn new subjects for your personal enjoyment and fulfilment is an excellent way of enlarging yourself as a person. Many people now find that they are more productively and enjoyably engaged in what is laughingly called "retirement" than when they were in full-time work.

Tenderness is a quality which is worth cultivating throughout the whole of life. It is the most reassuring of feelings when conveyed to another person.

Celibacy

THE GREAT thing about celibacy – unlike any other act in the sexual canon – is that it can be done anywhere, with anyone, at any time, and even in mixed company.

At least, there will be no complaints if the cultural religious background is right. It is largely Christian teaching that elevated celibacy to a higher state than marriage. Islam considers marriage and the family to be the backbone of society and disapproves of celibacy. Taoism thoroughly approves of sexuality and its expression, and accords no status to celibacy. Hindu culture produced the *Kama Sutra*, perhaps the greatest sex manual ever created, though some of it is decidedly against modern practice, like pouring hot tar on to a penis to strengthen the erection.

In its strict form, celibacy means refraining from all sexual activity, including fantasy and masturbation. It presupposes that sexual activity is a sin; that if it has to be engaged in at all (because the higher state of celibacy cannot be maintained) it is better done so in marriage, where at least it can be used for organized procreation; and that being without sin (i.e. non-sexual) will lead to heavenly benefits.

This view of the sexual world was promulgated by St. Augustine in the 4th century A.D. It did not stop the Crusaders bringing back syphilis from the Middle East, an unhappy legacy of their attempts to gain control of the Holy City.

In modern society people pursue celibacy for a variety of reasons – bearing in mind that it is an eminently reversible state. There are those, of course, for whom it is connected to a religious vocation, and so has meaning within a deeply-held value context. Some find it one way of making a positive statement about not getting involved sexually with others, for whatever reason. Others consider sexual activity outside marriage sinful, and so are celibate until such time as they marry. Yet others find work demands so much of their life that celibacy arrives as a state almost by default.

♂ **Positive choices about not expressing sex physically can enrich a life enormously – though they also create their own special pressures.**

♀ **Celibacy can be a chosen state of independence for women – whether within a religious order or simply in ordinary life.**

However, some celibate people still want children. The idea that there is not time for sex, or that it is messy, or that celibacy is to be preferred, has produced a rationale in recent times for artificial insemination.

While artificial insemination has brought tremendous joy to many couples who would not otherwise have been fertile, there are consequences of separating sex and procreation. In some ways it is quite logical. If we can have sex but, through contraception, can stop having babies, by implication then if someone does not want sex, but does want a baby, non-sexual means of creating children are the logical course of action. The more successful such means become, the more likely is the argument to be accepted.

Yet this kind of logic ignores entirely the fact that the fullness of being human is only possible through being in a relationship. An infant, newly-born, is completely dependent upon a relationship for its survival. For life to start without a relationship seems a contradiction in terms.

When the sexual act and procreation were completely bound up together, and there were no methods of artificial insemination, being celibate meant being without children (unless they were adopted). But being celibate in the late part of the 20th century does not prevent either men or women from being involved in creating life. No one yet knows what this means for the future of relationships, but it is certainly a long way from anything that St. Augustine was imagining.

The strict definition of celibacy requires that a person foregoes all sexual activity of any kind – no masturbation, heavy petting, mutual masturbation, or even erotic kissing. Sexual arousal in any form is off-limits.

Given that the body has evolved with the capacity for erotic sensation, and that consciousness allows us to imagine, explore and perhaps understand our experiences, then celibacy seems to be a way of limiting our experience of life. It only makes sense if it serves a purpose.

In the Christian tradition it obviously serves the purpose of denying bodily pleasures in the belief that that will help a person attain a higher spiritual state. Deliberate poverty falls into the same category. From this perspective, celibacy is not so much to do with sex, as the denial of sex being a way of mortifying the flesh and enlarging the spirit.

In other circumstances a person may choose celibacy in order to gain strength from the experience, or to avoid something too painful in intimate relationships.

Unwelcome celibacy is a state which requires some adjusting to. It occurs at the loss of a partner through separation or death or, for some people, by patterns of work or forced separations such as imprisonment. Under these conditions the body has a remarkable capacity to adapt its rhythms to what the person is experiencing psychologically. The capacity for change, even if stressful, is also a quality inherent in our bodily systems. This reminds us that sex is something that requires a context. In the wrong context, or when that context is severely disrupted, celibacy may be a quite natural response.

Friendship of a very deep kind, and a complete regard for the other person's physical boundaries, are both ways of acknowledging love without sex.

Many people in long-term relationships are celibate for a while. Companionship can feel more important than sex.

SECTION FOUR

With Reference To Sex

There are not many places that one can easily get reliable information about sex, other than from books and women's magazines. For almost any other subject of such great interest to adults there are countless evening classes, television programs, and videos readily available.

Videos about how our bodies work sexually and some aspects of adult sexual behavior are beginning to appear, though with a variable balance between entertainment, soft porn, information/education, and therapy. Television programs are usually inclined to entertainment, and do not devote much time to real information because of the way that programming functions.

What a pity, some of us thought, that, in the shadow of AIDS, sex could only go public under the threat of this disease. How much better it would be, long term, if sex were seen as central to the skill of managing relationships well; and that loving sex was celebrated as a great attribute of the human race.

There is of course a difficult boundary between the essentially private nature of sexual activity and public knowledge. It could be argued that government should have nothing to do with sex in any way at all. Public health concerns have long blurred that boundary. Trying to get hapless sufferers of venereal infections to clinics, euphemistically called "special clinics," was long the preserve of terrifyingly official posters in public lavatories.

Our view is that there should not be any limitation on the publishing of information designed to make people more knowledgeable about sex, as long as it does not involve the portrayal of other people as objects. That to us is pornography.

There is now a good deal of understanding about what constitute healthy and unhealthy relationships; and what the lifelong consequences are for one kind and the other. Involved daily as we ourselves are in clinical and counseling settings with the sexual difficulties that afflict people, it seems to us that whatever can be done to offer people an informed and open view about sex, based upon current knowledge effectively and clearly portrayed, is to the benefit of people's well-being now and in the future.

In order to complete this book, therefore, we have included a reference section on how the body works sexually. The pages which follow set that out as best as diagrams will allow, difficult though they sometimes are to relate to our actual three-dimensional bodies. We start with diagrams of the body, which remind us of how complex the human structure is and what a small space is occupied by our sexual

sexual and reproductive organs. Yet how much depends on them. Used wisely and for pleasure, they create loving sex and allow us to love sex. Abused, they can traumatize and effectively destroy another's life.

Making sex better comes from having knowledge, the right kind of experience, and sometimes through skilled help.

If there is any one guide to making sure that you enjoy loving sex, let your feelings guide your actions.

This is easier said than done, but it is extremely important. You may be frightened of your feelings; you may be worried that they will not be acceptable to your partner; or that your feelings may not be very well developed, and therefore not a reliable guide to action.

If fear is a problem, try to distinguish whether the feeling you are having involves the kind of fear which says you should not be doing what you are doing – a sort of conscience feeling – or whether it is fear of the intensity of the feelings that you are experiencing.

If it is the second of these, then it might be worth exploring these feelings further to see what happens. This is especially true if the feelings are new to you. Fear and excitement can be mixed up together, and your feelings may beneficially be moved away from fear and towards excitement.

If, on the other hand, you realize that the fear is simply the dominant feeling in your system, believe it and get out of the situation in which you find yourself. Then, more calmly, you can reflect on what was happening and analyze whether the feeling was true and relevant (you were in danger and it was a proper defense mechanism), or whether it was a fear that, looked at calmly, was part of an underdeveloped sense of knowing how to manage powerful feelings. In that case, you might want to risk re-visiting that emotion.

Sexual feelings are very powerful. They can make apparently wise men act foolishly, and wise women regret their actions later. But this is the shadow side of the fact that sexual feelings are also powerfully good. There are none stronger in human experience. Not surprisingly they can have powerful negative effects, as well as intensely powerful positive ones too.

This section is a guide to the anatomy and physiology – the structures and the workings – of what underlies those feelings. It is through our anatomy and physiology that we humans explore our experiences.

Male Sexual Anatomy and Physiology

Anatomy describes the structure of the body. Physiology tells us how it works. Sexual anatomy consists of the *internal* and *external* sexual organs. These pictures show in diagrammatic form what they look like, and where they are located in the body. Brain structures secreting blood chemistry as sex hormones are also important, and that takes us into physiology.

The physiology story goes like this.

Something triggers interest or desire. That "something" can come from outside – such as seeing the person we love, or a complete stranger we are attracted to, or a film that is sexually stimulating – or from imagination inside us.

That trigger of sexual desire sets blood flowing round the body. It flows into the spongy tissues of the penis. Erection starts to happen, which signals a shift from desire into arousal. The sensation of arousal itself becomes part of a physical feedback loop which creates further arousal.

If arousal continues, there will be an increasing urge to satisfy it by having a climax – either through intercourse, masturbation, or sometimes even spontaneously if the stimulation is very strong indeed.

Then, after a climax, the body returns to a quiet state of non-arousal. Another erection and ejaculation will usually not be possible for several minutes in a young, highly aroused man; a good many more minutes, up to several hours, in a middle-aged man; and perhaps a day or more in someone over sixty. This delay before another climax can take place is called the *refractory period.* Women do not have it. They have the capacity to be orgasmic several times in succession if the stimulation is right.

A great writer on sex, Eric Berne, described a woman's sexual organs as being like a downy chamber approached through a carefully-guarded pathway; while men's sexual organs, especially when aroused, were like a hamburger stand with neon lights all over it. Men advertise what they've got – even if many don't know much about it, how it works, and how to use it responsibly. For women their sexual aspects and selves have to be discovered – not only by men, but also by themselves.

Operating behind the obvious aspects of men's sexual anatomy and physiology are the processes which go on working away to create sperm and the seminal fluid that is ejaculated at a climax. Indeed, one way of thinking about the male sexual apparatus is as a manufacturing, storage and delivery system.

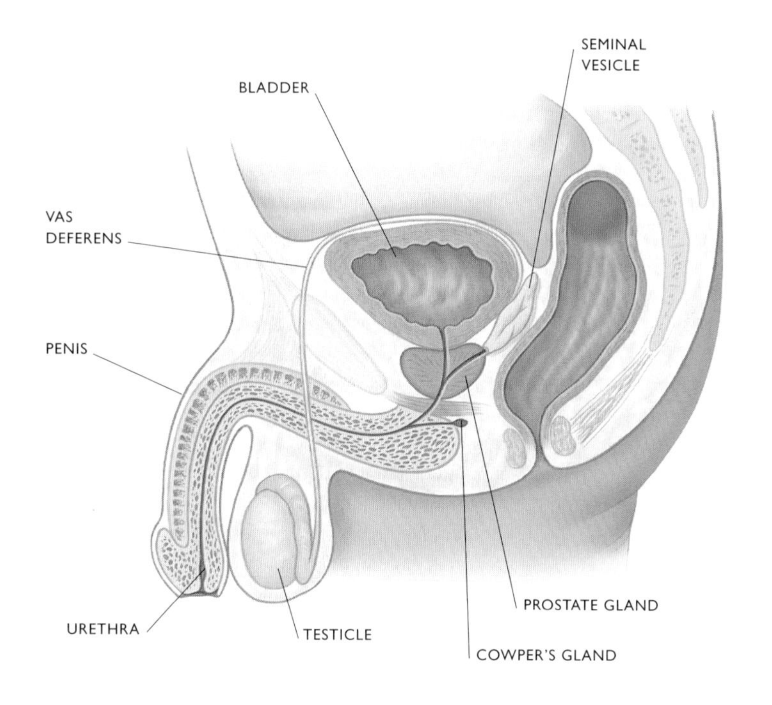

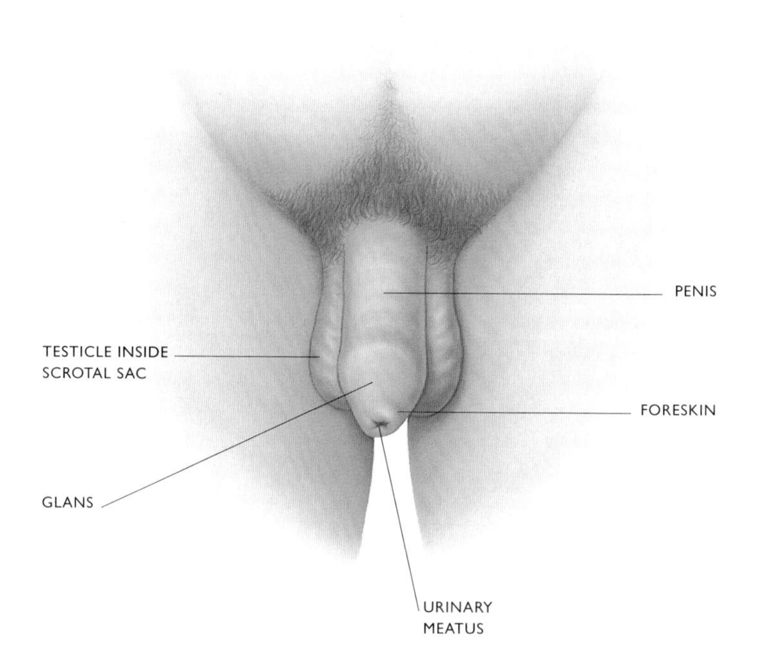

ABOVE: The penis is filled with spongy tissues inside a skin sheath. Without arousal, its function is to get rid of urine. When aroused and erect, it becomes a highly efficient fertilization delivery system – or just a source of erotic pleasure.

The testicles hanging in the scrotal sac have an immense length of fine tubing, the epididymis, coiled around them. These tubes store the hundreds of millions of sperm that the testicles create. During arousal sperm make their way up ducts called the vas deferens from the tubes around the testicles. The prostate gland, vas deferens and seminal vesicles contract and concentrate seminal fluid for ejaculation in a little bulb near the root of the penis. Ejaculation will occur when special muscles contract rhythmically and force seminal fluid in pulses along the urethral tube and out through the tip of the penis.

About a teaspoonful of fluid carrying hundreds of millions of sperm will be ejaculated during one climax. The urethral tube will have been lubricated before a climax by secretions from Cowper's gland. This colorless fluid can often be seen oozing from the tip of the penis in the later stages of arousal. It probably also acts as a nutrient for the sperm in the dash to create life as they swim up through the vagina, seeking an egg in one of the fallopian tubes.

That is what happens physiologically during a climax. The *experience* is something quite other. The physiology is pretty much the same in every male. The experience will be different for everyone.

A MAN'S SEXUAL RESPONSE CYCLE

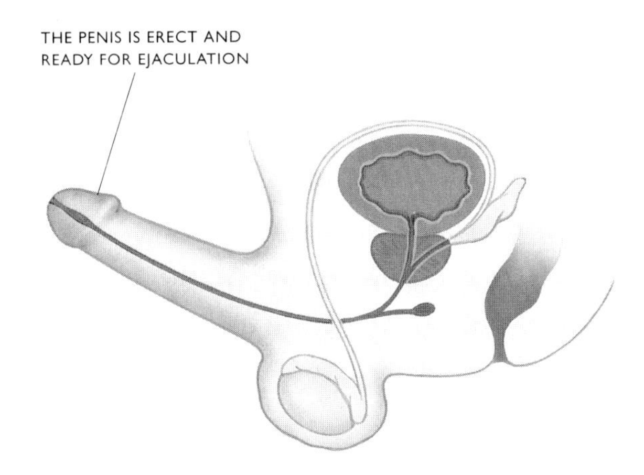

ABOVE: Fully erect, but without any of the sexual fluids ready to emerge. The penis can stay in this state for a very long time, and is dependent on the levels of stimulation – physical and psychological – that it is receiving.

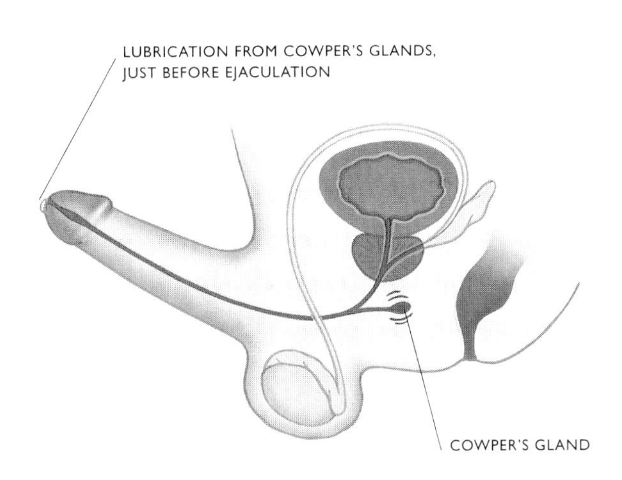

ABOVE: The precise function of the Cowper's glands and the colorless fluid that comes from them along the urethra to the tip of the penis is not entirely known. It certainly lubricates the tip of the penis to help penetration; and perhaps gives nourishment to sperm swimming into the vagina.

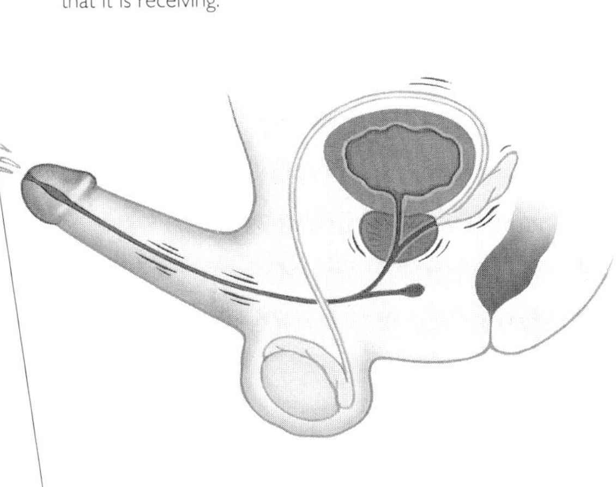

LEFT: Ejaculation is triggered by there being sufficient stimulation. Muscles surrounding the base of the penis, just inside the pelvis, create spasm contractions to make the seminal fluid spurt out.

Female Sexual Anatomy and Physiology

These diagrams show the sexual structures of the woman's body, and how they work. They are much more complex and subtle than the man's. Being designed from an evolutionary standpoint first of all for child-bearing and rearing, and then for achieving sexual pleasure, there is something of a separation between the structures that link to sex and those that link to reproduction, as well as a great deal of sensation passing between them.

The clitoris is unique in the sexual system of both male and female, in that its only purpose is as a receiver of sexual stimulation. All other external sexual organs in both men and women have at least two functions. Sexual sensitivity is connected to reproduction or waste disposal or both. But the clitoris, hiding in the upper folds of the lips surrounding the vagina, is a source of pleasure alone.

As with the shape and size of men's penises, the external appearance of women's sexual organs is very variable, which is true of all other human anatomical characteristics like noses, eyes and chins.

Women's sexual arousal occurs in exactly the same way as men's. Interest, whether from physical or psychological stimulation, starts blood coursing round the body and locking itself into sexually significant tissues. Instead of erection, however, a woman starts lubricating as the first sign of arousal. Tissues in the wall of the vagina become filled with blood, and the pressure in the blood vessels creates a very particular reaction through the walls of the vagina to create lubrication. Men do not experience anything similar to lubrication.

Shortly after lubrication has started, other tissues begin to fill with sexually-stimulated blood flow. The inner and outer lips of the vulva begin to fold back under the influence of increased pressure in the tissues and may change color from light pink to a much stronger pinky red. The vagina increases in circumference and length; the clitoris hardens and its shaft lengthens; and as blood pumps around the body, breasts become firmer and the nipples become erect as arousal increases.

As with the man, all these reactions fade after a climax, which in women is not an ejaculation of any kind but an intense, rhythmic contraction of pelvic muscles creating, at its best, intense pleasure. A woman may continue with a series of orgasms after the first if the stimulation she is getting is right for her, though not all women want to. After the peak of climax, the body gradually returns to its resting state.

Female sexual desire is affected by mood, relationship, medication, stress, environment – to name but a few of the factors which can propel her from intense desire to lack of interest, and

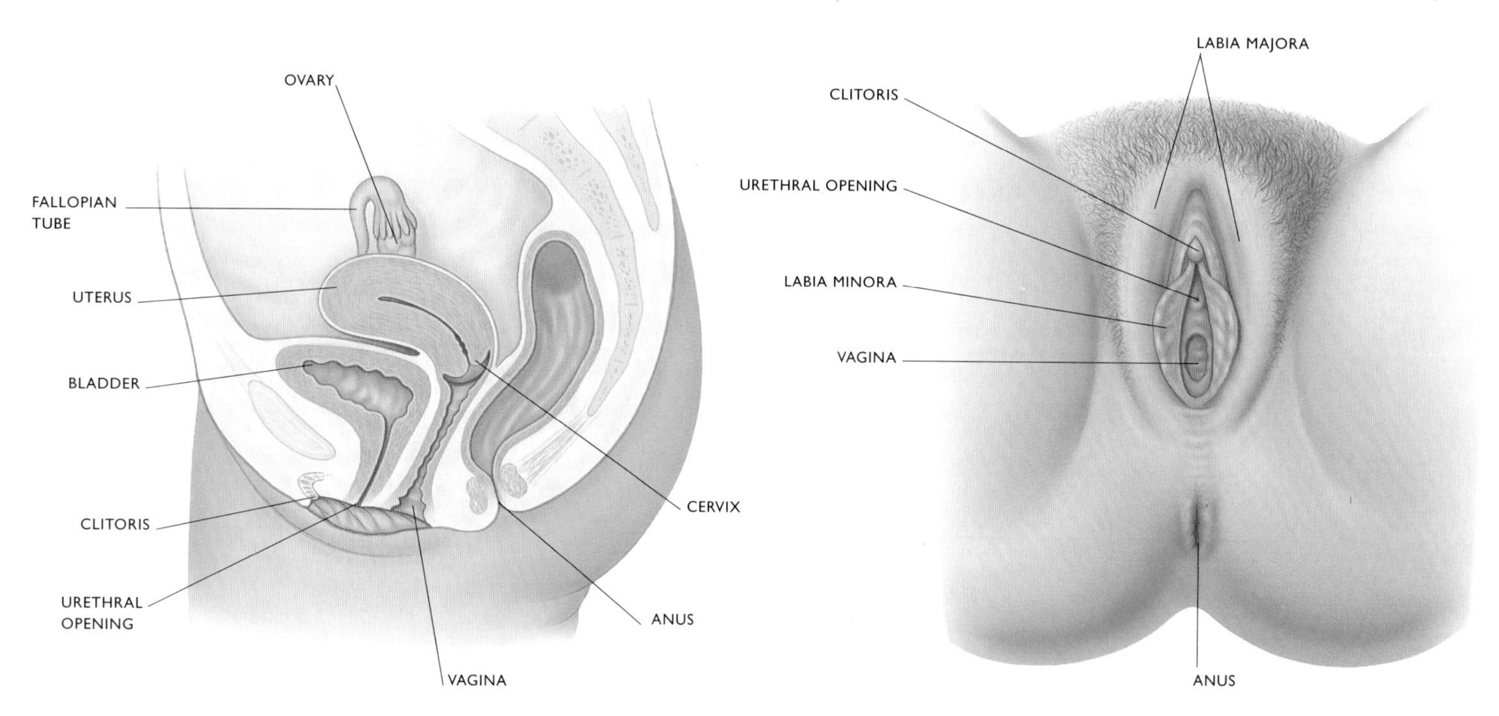

ABOVE: All a woman's sexual organs are tucked away. They are cradled by the bony structures that girdle her pelvis, protecting them and a possible fetus against harm. They are much more complex than a man's.

vice versa. In an effort to understand more about how women function, studies have been carried out to examine whether there is a link between the rise and fall of hormone levels during the menstrual cycle and her level of sexual arousal. It was expected that female desire would be at its highest when estrogen levels peak at ovulation, and at their lowest when menstruating, to coincide with sex and reproduction capacity. However, the findings are equivocal.

While some studies support this finding, others have found that women variously reported higher sexual desire pre-menstrually, during menstruation and post-menstrually (see Kaplan, *The New Sex Therapy*, for further reading). Recent studies, again looking at sexuality from an evolutionary viewpoint, have found evidence that women display themselves more around ovulation time.

Many women experience pre-menstrual symptoms, with depression, irritability and tearfulness being noticeable. Some women have physical symptoms such as over-sensitive nipples and swollen abdomen. However, women respond differently to these phenomena – some repudiating any physical contact at all, and others craving the comfort of sex. Perhaps the only certainty, as with female sexuality as a whole, is that it is responsive to a myriad of tiny influences, any one of which may make the difference.

A WOMAN'S SEXUAL RESPONSE CYCLE

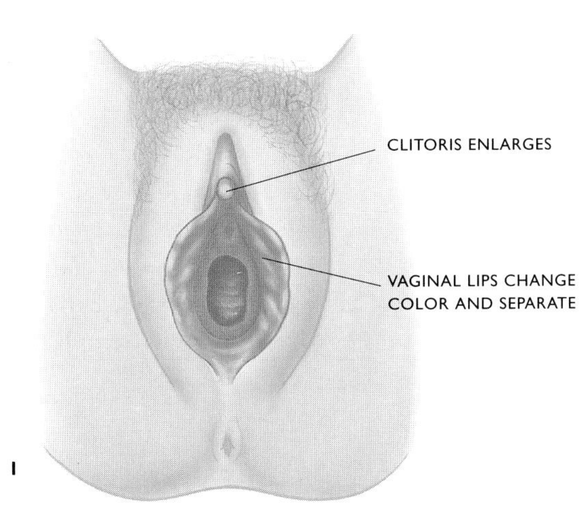

ABOVE: As blood begins to fill the soft tissues of the outer vaginal lips, they become firmer, change color from pink to a deeper hue, and separate. The vaginal opening reveals itself, and lubrication inside the vagina – the first sign of sexual arousal – will occur. The clitoris also enlarges, and feels firm to touch.

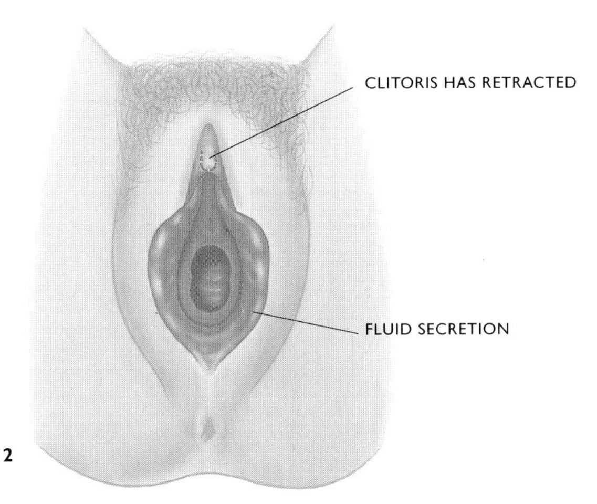

ABOVE: As arousal continues, the clitoris pulls back beneath the fleshy hood that covers it; the lower part of the vagina nearest the entrance swells so that it grips the penis more tightly; the vagina itself stretches in length and widens at the top. A mucus-like fluid is secreted by glands just inside the inner vaginal lips.

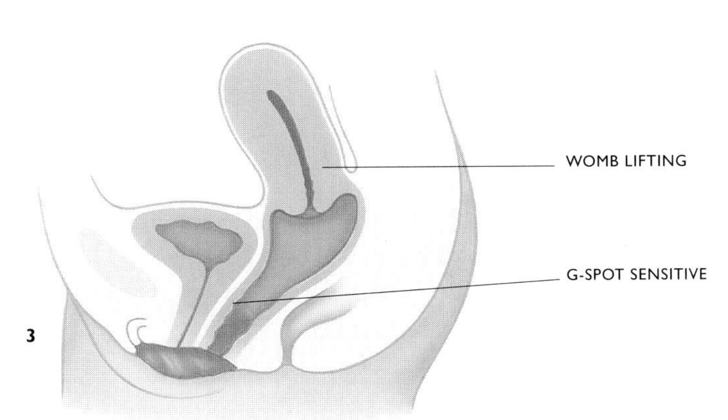

ABOVE: In the late stages of arousal the area of the G-spot becomes especially sensitive; all the vaginal tissues and the vaginal lips are filled with the blood that excitement has been pumping through the body; and the womb begins to lift and the neck of the womb extends.

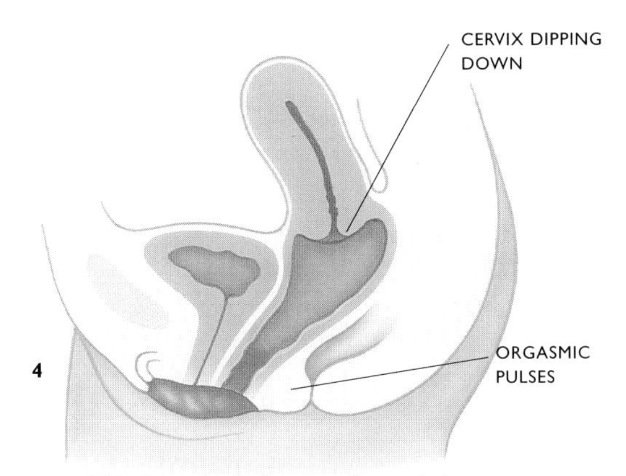

ABOVE: This shows the final stages of arousal at orgasm. Strong contractions that start in the womb are felt pulsing in the vagina; the womb has lifted to its full extent and the cervix dips down to help any sperm at the top of the vaginal canal find their way to the fallopian tubes.

Contraception

THE HISTORY of contraception is as old as civilization, though it is not until very recent times that reliable contraception has been widely available.

There are three main methods of contraception.

The first is to stop the man's ejaculation entering the vagina at all. Wearing a condom is the obvious answer to this, as long as the condom is reliable and will contain the ejaculated fluid without allowing any to escape. A female condom is also available which can be inserted into the vagina as an internal sheath.

Over the centuries all kinds of natural and artificial products have been used to try and make an effective condom. In Roman times sheep's gut was used as a condom, and continued so until the invention of rubber in the early 19th century. Contraceptive sheaths then became generally known as "rubbers," though with the widespread use of artificial and very thin membranes now for condoms, the word "rubber" for this purpose has almost disappeared.

The second method is to prevent seminal fluid getting past the opening of the cervix and so up through the womb into the fallopian tubes, where conception might take place. All sorts of substances have been used for blocking the top end of the vagina where the cervix joins it, ranging from crocodile dung in ancient Egyptian times to a sponge soaked in oil and vinegar in classical and quite recent times.

A Dr. Grafenberg invented a silver ring in the 1930s which was placed round the neck of the cervix to try to restrict its entrance. Perhaps the most widely-used form of blocking device is the diaphragm – a rubber hollow disk with a sprung steel band embedded around its edge which, if properly measured and placed in position, blocks the top of the vagina and keeps sperm from entering the cervix. Its disadvantages are that it is not easy to put in; can sometimes be even more difficult to get out; and may be taken out before all the sperm left after making love have stopped moving, so that a tricky one might still make the journey to successful fertilization.

A much more widely used device over the past thirty years has been the intra-uterine device (IUD). This is a small coil made of plastic or copper which is placed inside the womb. Its job is to slightly irritate the walls of the womb. In consequence, the womb tries to expel it and, though unsuccessful because the coil stays in position, the womb does expel any egg that happens to have been fertilized and which would otherwise become implanted in the wall of the womb.

The third reliable method of contraception is to control the hormonal processes of the menstrual cycle through the taking of a contraceptive pill, so that the lining of the womb appears as a monthly menstrual flow, thereby preventing any fertilized egg from implanting itself into the wall of the womb and starting

USING A CONDOM

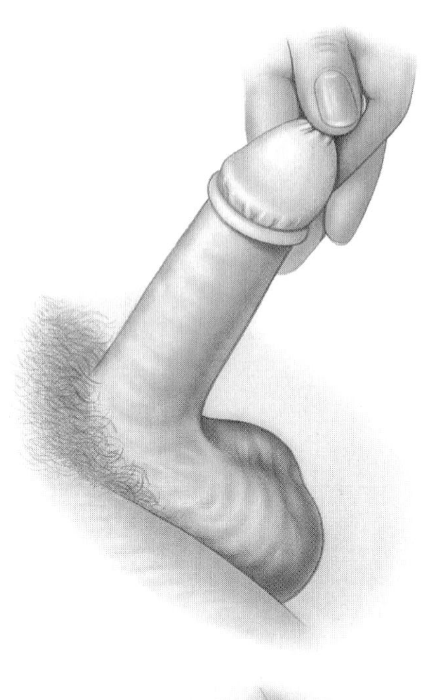

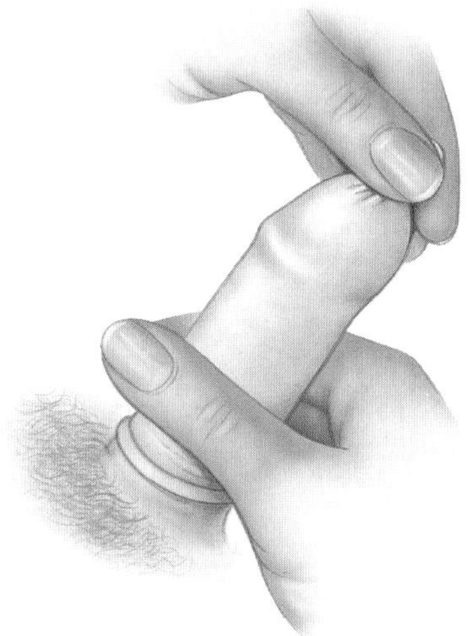

ABOVE: Putting on a condom can be fun or a troublesome interruption. Either way, develop the skill of pinching the teat to make sure that there is room for your ejaculate, that all the air is excluded from around the sheath as it is slipped on, and that it is rolled right to the base of the penis.

to become a viable embryo. This is the most successful form of contraception, though not without some risks to the health of some women in the event of long-term usage. Research is also under way to try to find a pill that can be used by men to render sperm inactive before they are ejaculated; it is probable that such a pill will be available in the near future.

There are other unsafe methods of contraception. One most widely used is for the man to withdraw his penis from the vagina just before he ejaculates. This is highly unreliable as a form of contraception, not only because the man may mistake his withdrawal, but also because sperm may be leaked from the tip of the penis before ejaculation takes place and a pregnancy caused that way. Similarly, relying entirely on identifying "safe" days in a woman's menstrual cycle on which to have intercourse by such means as taking the vaginal temperature or making calculations with a calendar is notoriously unreliable. Ovulation is not always predictable to the day, sperm can survive much longer than we might think, and not all of us are good at arithmetic. Those people who use it as their main method of contraception are those who are good at sticking to timetables.

Abortion is widely used in some countries as a form of contraception. In Communist Russia statistics reveal that the average woman has up to eight abortions during her sexually active years. Abortion is not really a form of contraception at all, but a way of removing the beginnings of life after a fertilized egg has attached itself to the lining of the womb.

Similar to abortion, though less drastic, is what is called "the morning after" pill. This is a hormonal mix which stimulates the womb to create a menstrual flow, whatever the time of the woman's monthly cycle, so preventing a fertilized egg establishing itself as a pregnancy.

These then are the main forms of contraception. Since the highly reliable contraceptive pill was introduced in the early 1960s, a separation has gradually grown up in people's minds between sex and creating new life. It is now possible to engage sexually without fear of pregnancy – an enormous blessing.

INSERTING A DIAPHRAGM

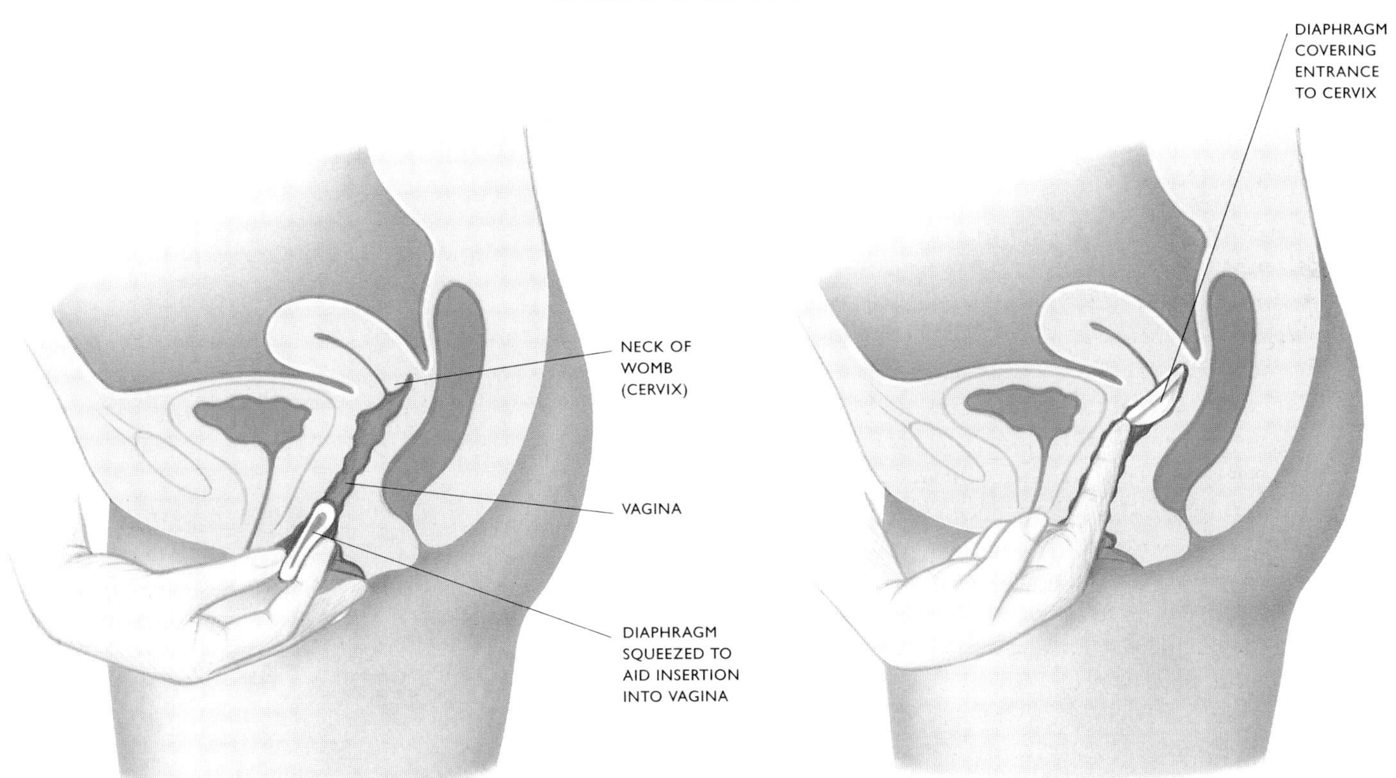

ABOVE: The diaphragm or cap is designed to stop sperm getting through the neck of the womb and up into the fallopian tubes where one might fertilize an egg by blocking off the entrance to the cervix. As a mechanical barrier, used with a spermicidal cream, it is effective, but some people find it not very easy to use and it needs forethought and planning.

Safe Sex

ABOVE: It can be a special delight to be close and enjoy physical contact without having to be actively sexual as a consequence.

The one form of contraception that we did not include in the last spread is the safest one of all: abstaining from sexual intercourse altogether.

It happens, however, that under the influence of the powerful emotions to which sex gives rise, very few people can regularly resist sex.

But abstaining has come to have more significance with the worldwide epidemic of AIDS (Acquired Immune Deficiency Syndrome) – the illness that commonly (though not always) occurs as a result of acquiring the Human Immunodeficiency Virus, or HIV.

HIV is very readily transmitted through sexual activity when HIV-infected bodily secretions come into contact with the blood of an uninfected person. This can easily happen through small scratches on the skin, or through bodily fluids like semen being absorbed.

Although originally identified as a disease of homosexual men, HIV is now widespread in the heterosexual population. It is especially common in cultures in which there are high levels of sex with more than one partner, and in sub-cultures where drug abuse, especially by injection, is common.

AIDS is a tragedy of modern times whose significance and destructive power we do not yet entirely understand. Until we do, and until the mechanisms of the disease are better understood and can be fought more successfully, the only course of responsible action is to engage in safe sex.

The best means of doing this is to be sexually faithful to one person whom you know to be free of the infection. If, as is currently believed, HIV does not transmit itself through ordinary social contact of any kind, the risk of acquiring it is effectively lessened under these conditions.

If sex does take place with people whose infective status is unknown, then it makes sense to make it safer than would be the case if unprotected intercourse were to take place. Unprotected vaginal and anal intercourse are high risk situations. Using condoms is the single most effective course of action that can be taken in making sex safer, especially if the condom contains a spermicide like nonoxynol-9.

This is, in fact, good advice generally in safeguarding against the transmission of many sexually transmitted diseases and infections.

Safer sex can also be enjoyed by *not* having intercourse at all, but creating sexual arousal through means which do not involve penetration, such as mutual stimulation by fingers. This has been referred to as outercourse, to distinguish it from intercourse.

Unfortunately the alternatives to intercourse are rarely as fulfilling as intercourse itself, which accounts for the general failure of public-awareness programs designed to get people to change their sexual behaviors. Even when the likelihood of acquiring HIV is very high indeed, people still are prepared to take the risk rather than not to have the sex at all. Given the intelligence with which humans are endowed, this is some kind of perverse tribute to the power of the sexual forces by which we are also driven.

So we end this book with a serious note of caution. None of us would be here at all if it were not for sex. Loving sex means loving another person fully. In its turn, that means having respect for the other and delight in both giving and taking. Loving sex means taking care of the other, and being taken care of too.

BELOW: Between lovers all aspects of the body take on new meanings. Intimacy is a special gift of each to the other. Sexual arousal without penetration is also a safer form of sex.

Further Reading

HUMAN SEXUAL RESPONSE
William Masters and Virginia Johnson
Little, Brown & Co., 1967
A ground-breaking book which, for the first time in scientific medicine, reported the results of many hundreds of laboratory investigations into sexual arousal and response. It initiated a proper understanding of the way the body works sexually.

HUMAN SEXUAL INADEQUACY
William Masters and Virginia Johnson
Little, Brown & Co., 1969
Following on from their laboratory findings, Masters and Johnson published this first account of the systematic treatment of sexual difficulties which they had developed from their laboratory work. Although some of the details of their method of treatment have changed over the years, the basic understanding that they developed is still the essence of sexual function therapy – even if the title was one of the worst ever for a book on sex.

HUMAN SEXUALITY IN A WORLD OF DIVERSITY
Jeffrey Nevid, Lois Fichner-Rathus and Spencer Rathus
Allyn and Bacon, 2nd edition, 1995
The widest-ranging and most comprehensive book of knowledge on sex that we know. Very highly recommended both for its scholarship and the quality of its presentation.

HUMAN SEXUALITY AND ITS PROBLEMS
John H.J. Bancroft
Churchill Livingstone, 2nd edition, 1989
John Bancroft was one of the key sexual function researchers in the UK before becoming Director of the Kinsey Foundation in the USA. Like Kaplan's book, this is a wide-ranging text deeply grounded in a great wealth of clinical and research experience. It is the main clinical text on sexual problems to have been published in the UK.

MAKING OUT
Zoe Schramm-Evans
Pandora, 1995
A guide to sex for lesbian women.

MY SECRET GARDEN
Nancy Friday
Pocket Books, 1974
This is the book that enlarged everyone's thinking about women's sexual fantasies.

MEN IN LOVE
Nancy Friday
Hutchinson, 1980
This told us more than was commonly known about men's sexual fantasies too.

SAFER SEX
Peter Tatchell
Freedom Editions, 1994
A guide to safer sex for gay men.

THE FEMALE EUNUCH
Germaine Greer
MacGibbon & Kee, 1970
A ground-breaking book concerned with women's sexual and emotional liberation – of great importance in the history of feminism and in terms of re-defining men's and women's understanding of one another.

THE NEW JOY OF SEX
Alex Comfort
Mitchell Beazley, 1991
Sexual positions viewed as food for thought. *The Joy of Sex* was the first big information and picture book on sex for pleasure after the changes in public attitudes and knowledge brought about by Masters' and Johnson's work in the USA. A worldwide success, *The New Joy of Sex* is its natural successor.

THE NEW SEX THERAPY
Helen Singer Kaplan
Penguin, 1974
A sex therapist's guide to male and female sexuality. Helen Singer Kaplan took Masters' and Johnson's findings and put them in the context of general clinical practice. This is the book that most of all taught therapists what they needed to know.

TREAT YOURSELF TO SEX
Paul Brown and Carolyn Faulder
Penguin, 2nd edition, 1989
If you are having difficulty, this is the best-seller self-help manual that has been in print for twenty years.

Index

Bold numbers indicate a section devoted to the subject specified, with text and illustration(s). Numbers in *italics* indicate an illustration and/or caption.